THE HIGHER

CHRISTIAN EDUCATION.

BY

BENJAMIN W. DWIGHT,

AUTHOR OF "MODERN PHILOLOGY, ITS HISTORY, DISCOVERIES AND RESULTS."

FOURTH EDITION.

A. S. BARNES AND COMPANY,
NEW YORK AND CHICAGO.
1874.

GENERAL TABLE OF CONTENTS.

ANALYTICAL TABLE OF CONTENTS.

I

III

V

INTRODUCTION.

THE Author feels that he has essayed indeed a great theme. But having in his life, as a Teacher for nearly twenty years, sought to realize in practice the ideas here expressed in words, the joy of the greater labor has emboldened him to undertake the less. However much the statement of the subject may justify itself, on its very announcement ; and however familiar the combination of ideas contained in it ought to be ; it is still, strange to say, not only new to the public ear, but the class of truths denoted by it remains yet practically undeveloped, as a whole, in the world, in any of their larger proportions and relations. No interests, however, need more earnest and immediate treatment, than those pertaining to the Higher Christian Education of the youth of this age and country. If the author shall succeed in awakening new and adequate attention, in any direction, to the momentous work of rightly developing the mind and character of the rising generation, deep will be the satisfaction that his labor has not only been lovingly, but also efficiently, expended. The school, rightly conducted, is one of the greatest of all moving forces, by which the advancement of each new age beyond the preceding one is to be accomplished. How great the pleasure of doing any thing to deepen and widen this conviction in the community!

Each of these connected treatises was intended to be a distinct, independent treatment of the topic contained in it, by itself; and yet the topics were chosen in reference to their mutual fitness to be gathered together into one group. Some of the subordinate parts accordingly, come into view again, from time to time, but always in a different relation, and for another use, like different sides of the same sphere revolving before the eye; each running, as a part of one harmonious whole, into and out of the others in immediate connection with it. Whenever, therefore, the same face or angle of the whole subject comes partially into view again, as in the similar discussion of correlated doctrines in theology or philosophy, if it has before received a full treatment it is only glanced at, anew, and presented rather for its bearings on connected parts, than for what it is by itself. And so, if there is at any time a similarity of outline, it will be found that there is a variety of details ; or if there should occur in some places a general correspondence of details, they will be so differently grouped, and placed in such a different light, as to make quite another scene, and to answer entirely other ends. It is hoped that all will be deemed to constitute one harmonious whole with no part lacking, and none aggravated beyond its proper dimensions.

While abuses of all sorts, dead or alive, have been freely attacked, if demanded by a determination to be just and true in spirit to so great a theme, no wanton wish or willingness has been consciously indulged, to denounce or satirize any class of men. And yet if indifferentism, which is so prevalent in this world towards all the great things of Heaven and earth, be one of the worst of the many forms of human guilt, can any one who sympathizes with God and His plans, fail to feel, that it is nowhere more misplaced in itself, and more terrific in its results, than in the cause of the Higher Christian Education. May God speed this divine cause, and if the feeble attempt here made can, with His blessing, be brought to subserve its advancement, may He give it, so far, favor and power and true influence, to His praise!

DWIGHT'S RURAL HIGH SCHOOL, CLINTON,
ONEIDA CO., N. Y., *August* 1, 1859.

I.

THE TRUE WORK OF THE HIGHER CHRISTIAN EDUCATION.

I.

THE TRUE WORK OF THE HIGHER CHRISTIAN EDUCATION.

THE highest result of any form of civilization, and therefore the brightest and topmost flower of Christianity, ought to be found in its system of Education: in the perfection of beauty visible in its mode of training each successive generation for the great work of life. Here, if anywhere, its loftiest tendencies should be sure to culminate: here its ripest fruits should hang glittering in the very light of Heaven. But were the Christianity of this age subjected to such a test, applied unsparingly to the aims, ideals, processes, appliances and issues of our present style of education, what material might not the infidel find for his false and foolish boast, that by the very tenor of its achievements its spirit was proved to be feeble and its power small, ascribing, as he would with wicked logic, to this great divine system of truths and influences the infirmities predicable only of those that undertake to manage its machinery.

Our subject demands a twofold treatment:

I. Of the nobility of the Christian teacher's vocation.

II. Of some of its normal guiding principles.

I. Its Nobility.—The bearings of the work of Education upon the progress of religion; the relations of the school to the great scheme of redemption; the divinity of its office, work and power; these are themes which, although old in Heaven, are verily still quite new in this world. Trade, politics, fashion, the constant changes of the times, and all the petty swell and fall of each day's small excitements, suffice to occupy fully the thoughts and hearts and tongues of men. But, in respect to the uplift of the rising generation to a true comprehension of its duties, interests and labors, to whom all earth's history, literature, art, commerce, enterprise and religion are so soon to be committed; and who are to have, and to use, according to their will, all that this world contains of good, after so long a procession of great influences upon it: whose heart seems to be anywhere ablaze with high and strong thoughts concerning so divine an undertaking? In the City Above, all their accumulated interest during centuries of hope deferred for man, and yet of ever-brooding love over him, centres in the work that is to be done, well or poorly, for God or against Him, to those who are to receive, from this generation, the mighty trust of the world's fate and fortunes. And, as all the vitality and vigor of a plant, when in its perfect bloom, are spent in preparing the way for the life of its successor, so the proper function of each generation of men, when at the height of its development, as of each man in it: not only their highest service, but also their appointed work, the true divine use of their time and faculties and resources: consists in laboring to prepare the next generation to fill worthily the place which they are to vacate for them, and to do worthily the work which they are to drop into their hands. Looking thus, from an earthward stand-point, upon the true sphere and scope of the work of education, how vast do we find its dimensions! and how tremendous the pressure of its wants upon a heart of true sensibility towards God or man! And how would the highest possible earthly estimate of its claims be aggrandized, could we but look at it ourselves from a Heavenward point of observation! Could we but get some true gauge of the vast inward dignity of the human soul, as immortal and divine, and could we feel the power of the world to come upon our hearts, in all its magnificence of wonder and fruition, the employment of training one little child to act well its part, here and hereafter, would appear at once to be grand and godlike. Can the blight of sin upon the tenderest sympathies and warmest impulses of the human heart, be anywhere found more plain and terrible than in the cold, neglectful indifference of men, at large, to the highest and best interests of the young? And when we remember how great is the furniture of latent capabilities in every one, and how much more each man has in his nature than either circumstances or his own highest industry have ever made visible, and how many more might have been evoked, by grand crises or great impelling motives exciting them to action, into a gigantic demonstration of themselves on every varied field of human effort, what an array of splendid possibilities presents itself before the true Christian teacher in his work!

And, yet, no profession stands in less honor with the ignoble mass of minds, proved ignoble by so low an estimate of so high a calling, than that involving the labor and the art and the joy of fashioning the inward man to all nobleness, according to the patterns of things in the skies. A painter, who but copies a likeness of the mere face of flesh, which is so soon to crumble back to dust; a sculptor, who only carves, in cold and silent marble, an image of our form of clay; or, a poet, who merely describes a man when performing some great action, or enjoying the repose to which it entitles him, in order to prepare himself for a greater: these are, each of them, honored as artists, and even worshipped for their genius. But what of him who, with multiform toil and skill, slowly but surely shapes the mind, the immortal mind itself, into every possible form of strength and grace, and who adorns it with all those intellectual and moral excellences of which physical beauty, wherever found or introduced, is but a faint shadow in mere material forms and aspects? What of him who makes the very man what he is, whom others seek to find fixed somewhere, in his life, in an engaging attitude for their pencil, pen or graver? He is thought by the majority of observers to have marked out for himself a very insignificant course of life, which no one could possibly pursue who was not forced to it, by lack of means or want of success, in some other sphere of action. The conception that there is in his high calling any thing, or rather every thing, fitted to inspire genius, to set on fire the whole soul with divine enthusiasm, and to summon forth a giant heart upon a pathway of ever-abounding activity and joy in its service, would seem strange, if not ridiculous, to multitudes. Some can understand how one might find, perchance, in a president's or professor's chair, a little pleasure, or, at least, excitement, in the work of teaching ; for there is honor in the name. What a bauble ! Honor is not a thing of circumstance, but of character ; not of titles, but of actions. But how, the wonder is, how can any one find aught to captivate and stir his soul in the dull, prosaic life of a schoolmaster ? In many communities, indeed, this honorable designation stands in very much the same repute, for dignity, as the names tinker, cobbler, peddler, and the like. And, to make the marvel perpetual, that any should ever admire the employment of a practical teacher, society pertinaciously closes, and keeps closed with iron-handed obstinacy, every door to genius in this divine occupation, but that which, by the help of God, it forces open for itself: offering ordinarily but a pittance for one's support, and withholding the praise which it bestows on the same amount of talent in every other field of demonstration ; while, to complete its all but positive interdict, practically, upon a calling so noble in itself, and so necessary to its own continued life and power, it stands and gazes agape, in stupid wonder, at such as can hear, amid the Babel voices of this world, any loud call without, or feel any warm impulse stirring within, to enter into its delightful labors. Men have an eye for vaulting, momentary heroism ; but, for that of ever-repeated, earnest, glowing, unselfish toil for others, whether itself seen or unseen and whether admired or even despised, embanked and embowered, like a strong stream running through deep channels, in the truths and the promises of God, it has no appreciation.

The cause of God is thus not only everywhere cheapened in this world ; but even the very mode and style of His perpetual joyous employment of His own infinite powers and resources. The grand, ever-active life of God Himself is that of a great, wise, infinitely tender and watchful educator of all His children. He made the physical universe, in order to people it with happy, intelligent beings, fashioned in his own image, to enjoy his high company forever. And, when having made the theatre for their action, and themselves to occupy it, what remains to be done but to develop and perfect them for his own blissful communion ! Thus the very end of creation itself is Education ; and the glory of God, as a Creator, terminates in his glory as an Educator. Surely what engages his great attributes and resources, at all times, in full exercise, may well employ ours ; and what suffices to fill his boundless nature with joy, will suffice certainly to fill our own. In nothing does He admit us into such grand intimacy with himself, as in the work of fashioning character, and of opening and directing forever the latent capabilities and possible destinies of the immortal mind. Such, yes! such is the vocation that even Christian men consider, among the commonest in the world, appropriate, in its very aims and terms, for men of phlegmatic mould, who have not energy enough for traffic or political contention, or any such talents as would make them shine in some sphere of ostentatious self-exhibition; while, all the time, no calling requires such a breadth of preparation in order to meet its real demands; none such a variety of all high characteristics in combination; and none so much energy bodily, intellectual and spiritual, for its right execution. Shame on such base thoughts as, consciously or unconsciously, put open dishonor on man's nature and on God's; as well as on all the deep spiritual mystery of this life and the splendors of the life to come, opening, in full view, before the soul that is truly trained to receive and enjoy them. All Nature waits on man, to light him on his way to Heaven: the mountains stand in their quiet strength around him, as if the very sentinels of God, to see that he has time and space for his work of high self-advancement. For this the stars watch over him in their courses; and for this, like ministering angels, the seasons come and go in the revolving circle of the year. Nothing on earth is great but man: man, made to be within the outward temple of nature erected for his worship, himself the soul-temple of Him who, while he dwelleth not in temples made with hands, does dwell with him who is of an humble and a contrite heart. "Lord! what is man!" how grand are the proportions of his being! "that thou shouldest be mindful of him, and the Son of man, that thou shouldest visit him!" For six thousand years has God brooded lovingly over our race, in the outward world of sight and sound, so full of change; and in all the inward consciousness of ever wakeful thought, in order to attract us, one and all, in our affections, to himself. Hail therefore to the men that enter, unattended by the crowd, into the deep sympathies of His great nature, the very Holy of Holies in his heart; and that earnestly employ their time and strength in the same sublime sphere of interest and action in which he occupies his whole being. This was the business of which the Great Teacher spoke, when he said to the mass of indifferent and unemployed listeners around him, dull-eyed to all true conceptions of either God's nature or their own, "Wist ye not that I must be about my Father's business!" and this was the work to which he alluded, at another time, when he said, "My Father worketh hitherto, and I work."

Like what "a crackling therefore of thorns under a pot," full of noise without sense, does it seem to one, whose ear is open to such voices, to hear a parent say, as so many do virtually, and some even openly, to a son: "Choose any calling but that of a schoolmaster or a clergyman," as if there were any offices so high, to be filled or found out of Heaven, "for nowhere will you find such toil, and nowhere such poor pay." What pettiness is this! How do such forget that man does not live by bread alone! There was a peculiar significance in the appointment of the great temptation of bread to the Saviour, as his first trial in entering on public life, as it is under the pressure of this temptation that men everywhere so readily succumb. Bread! bread! the body! time! mammon! these are the watchwords of the Evil One in all ages. But a man's life consisteth not in the abundance of the things that he possesseth. There is an inner life of the heart, a life full of deep, glad thoughts, affections and impulses, following each other in a broad and constant outflow and overflow, of which such earthly minds know nothing: the life of a magnanimous nature, ever waiting, like God himself, to be gracious unto all, and to communicate, without let or hindrance, the riches of its goodness unto the whole world of men around.

In the many appeals made to the young, in either brief occasional addresses from our most thoughtful earnest men, or in those more formally prepared, with a full circumspection of life and its high demands, for our selectest college assemblies, who has ever witnessed an effort to stir their spirit of patriotism, or of general philanthropy, or of large Christian usefulness, by the claims and the charms of the work of education ? Where is the professed teacher even who is known to publicly magnify his office as unsurpassed, if not unequalled, by any other in beauty, honor, power and joy ? And, even in respect to the chances of emolument, which so many covet as the chief recommendation of any employment ; although those having such thoughts, only or chiefly, are interdicted, by their very lust for gold, from entering truly into a vocation that demands the utmost purity of sentiment and purpose, in reference to both its objects and its subjects : what might not be said, in behalf of a profession, where so many openings for enterprise abound, as well as so many opportunities for introducing higher standards and ideals of achievement ; and where noble aims and efforts will be sure to place their happy possessor, in such glorious contrast with a vast crowd of laborers in the same field?

We hear the three learned professions often alluded to, law, theology and medicine ; as if there were not three times three ; as, those of education also and of editorship, practical chemistry, civil engineering, architectural and mechanical drafting and public lecturing. Could any greater traditionary absurdity be perpetrated than that of leaving out from among the learned professions the one, on which they all depend for their very existence; especially, when the title itself, Doctor or Teacher, given to him who excels in them, is one denoting the fact, that now its honored recipient is deemed capable of instructing novices, in the elements of his vocation! And what a double dishonor is done to the work of education, in not only taking away its name, as a profession, but also in transferring the very title of those engaged in it to others.

Let no one enter upon the sublime work of the Educator, whose own high appreciation of its value does not impel, or, at least, attract him to its delightful labors. Mean thoughts will infallibly break forth, from beneath the surface of whatever enterprise we undertake with them. Let only such come into this sacred employment as have heard, in the depths of a consciousness illuminated with God's felt presence, His voice summoning them imperatively hither. All true hearts have a call from him, to do what he appoints; and no one is asked of God to teach, whose heart is not aglow with love to him and to man, as his child, and who does not feel that nothing on earth has charms to his soul like the joy of training his own heart, and the hearts of others, to all manliness and godliness. Call it enthusiasm, who will; still the fact remains, that no man ever undertakes to imbed his own character and life, deeply and permanently, in his age, whose heart is not on fire with the thought that he is working for God. Under the power of instincts, bruised and broken it is true, but yet divine, the ancients felt the near approach of their imaginary gods in every thing, and introduced them into all their philosophy, poetry, history and art; and, in their dramas, they actually brought them down from above, by formal machinery, upon the stage. A present deity was the necessary seasoning to a Greek's mind, of every thing seen or done in life. Here was the power of divination, of augury, of the priesthood and of those oracles, which, heard everywhere as the voice of God, could, at any time, set the whole world in motion, or bring it to a sudden solemn pause. Thus Homer's heroes were all, to the mass around them, Jove-born. So, Numa had nightly interviews with the goddess Egeria; and Socrates was guided by an attending genius. And, so, the most wonderful of all human lives, for aim and scope and energy and issue, the Apostle Paul's, became what it was, under the inspiration of that great Master, who made it His own meat and drink to do his Father's will, by the purpose to know nothing among his fellow-men but Jesus Christ, the Crucified. The star of destiny, of which Napoleon so often spoke, was, in Luther's mouth, the word and the will of God. So is it always : no man is really great whose eye is not ever fixed on what is beyond and above. The moral hero is such, because he seems to himself to stand, at all times, under a vast overshadowing future, as under the brow of some high mount of solemn vision. God seems over him and around him and within him. His life holds its place, as the full moon to the sun, directly over against a divine object, and is, in all its light and strength, but the manifestation of his conceptions of its attractions and demands. "Cast ye down her battlements ; for they are not the Lord's"—is a sentence written by the angel of death, not only on the walls of ancient Jerusalem, but also on all other human walls and human plans, that are built in a state of separation from God.

Let no one therefore venture, heedlessly or complainingly, into this greatest of all human callings ; for he goes with such a spirit into the very work and presence of God, as a horse into the battle, not knowing that it is for his life. My brethren, saith the Divine word, "be not many" of you "masters" or Teachers ; "knowing that thereby," that is, if unfaithful, "ye shall receive the greater condemnation." But let not him, who finds a soldier's zeal stirring in his veins to do battle in so large a field, tremble or pause, because of the greatness of the undertaking. God will aid him ; and, if man thinks lightly of his toils, Heaven does not. To such an one, if to any upon earth, God is ever beckoning to mount upwards, with ever new gladness of spirit, into His own blissful company and communion forever.

In many things, the work of true Christian education is above that of the ministry ; if not in its aims, yet in the variety, adaptation and power of its appliances, and in the immediateness, determinateness and perpetually renewed productiveness of the results gained by their use. The minister teaches indeed, but he does not train. He teaches at intervals, while the Educator does his work of love from day to day. The preacher points to the right path, but he cannot make his hearers walk in it ; he cannot constrain the will and bind it firmly to its duty ; nor can he use the power of personal authority and discipline, or bring his own entire individuality, with all its freight of knowledge, principle and power, to bear upon his people, as can the teacher upon his pupils. He devotes his efforts also to those whose habits have become thoroughly indurated by length of time, and who have long since lost their fresh and natural sensibility to the truth. The very hearts, all full of the fire and flow of youth, which he neglects, the hope of the world and of the church, are those on whom the Teacher exerts all his energy, plastic under the gentlest touches of his hand, and tenderly responsive to all his ideas and feelings.

To be a true Teacher, of the highest dimensions of power and qualification, requires a breadth of resources and qualities natural and acquired, a depth and fulness of means, tact in impressing one's self on others amounting almost to a species of personal magnetism, skill in government, talent in exposition, power in analysis, fulness of knowledge, readiness of illustration, a sense of the beautiful in nature, art and language, a simplicity of character, a singleness of aim, a patience of spirit, a steadiness of purpose, an acquaintance with human nature and a development of religious feeling and principle, as well as an energy of will, a fire of thought and an amount of physical vigor; which, assembled together, make this field of human endeavor altogether paramount to every other in its demands upon the whole man, his whole time, his whole heart, and his whole strength within and without, at all times, in all things. No marvel is it that there are so many poor teachers! for in no other style of man is such a height and breadth of manhood necessary.

II. Some of the great normal principles, of the true mode of conducting the Higher Christian Education.

1st. Its great, all-informing life and spirit must be true, earnest, practical Christianity.

"The truth as it is in Jesus!" what a volume of meaning is there in these few bright words of Revelation! All truth flows out from Him upon the universe, and, dispensing its blessings everywhere, circles round again, with its results, through all the vast circumference of things, to the same grand reservoir in his heart from which it started. He is the way, the truth and the life. Science, history, nature, providence, experience, all point to Him as the centre of every thing great and good: the All in all, the same yesterday, to-day and forever. No motor-power can be applied to the intellect and heart of teacher or scholar, like love to him. Every other influence is finite, in its scope and duration. No stimulus to effort is worthy of man's nature, of his high powers, of his possible attainments and pleasures, and of that unending, gorgeous future, of which his life here is but the vestibule, except that of Christ's love to him and his love to Christ. Under the power of steady, burning affection for him, all tendencies to waste of talent or of time, all aimless, objectless habits of thought will disappear as tow before the fire. In right relations to him, perpetual joy will be ever coursing through the heart, turning what others deem life's burdens into its greatest pleasures;

since, carried for him, they become labors of love, offerings of friendship of a sweet odor, not only to him but also to the heart that bears them into his presence. With what full concentration of energy and delight can a Teacher, under the power of complete devotion to Jesus Christ, address himself to his cherished work : cherished in itself, as having great dimensions of its own, cherished in its relations to all his personal aptitudes of thought, feeling and action, and cherished, above all, in its relations of service to him who made man, and made him to be his own glorious temple forever. How can such an one be literally anxious for nothing, except to please him who hath called him to enter, with Himself, into His own high labor of love.

There has been so little good education in the world, as there has been also so little good government in it, because what toil has been expended has not been expended for him. This is the reason why the march of the ages has been so slow, and that each generation in succession advances so little, and with such an agony of effort, beyond the one preceding. It is the perpetuation of poor, imperfect education at home and at school that keeps up such a perpetuation of sin and sorrow in the world. When every one teaches for him and studies for him, with no stinted outlay of time and money and effort, summoning with gladness every moment, every thought and every faculty and appliance, to the work of glorifying him in all things, what an irrepressible outburst of all manliness and heroism, and earnest intellectual activity, and of high literature, and of philosophy and poetry, and all human greatness and goodness, will be exhibited over the whole face of human society! What an argument therefore does the present sad state of our world thunder in our ears, for a radical and universal reform in the work of education! This earth made with such variety and fulness of preparation, to be the outer court of the world above, has become but the purlieus of perdition. Practical heathenism everywhere prevails. The world is in a heath-state: deserts abound, where the lily of the valley, the rose of Sharon and the cedars of Lebanon, the Lord's cedars for the Lord's house, should be found in abundance.

To the ancients the highest stimulus to action, was the desire of fame. To many a man in Christendom, a higher impulse has come, although not the highest, from a sort of general ethical sense of duty, which has been but a merely intensified expression for private honor or public expectation. Thus Bonaparte used to say that he hated the English, because they were always talking so much about duty; and so Lord Nelson said at Trafalgar, "England expects every man to do his duty." But how different in its power to stir the conscience and to sway the life in any field of effort, is the sense of duty, as a mere philosophical or poetical abstraction, a misty phantom of the half awakened moral nature, compared with the vision of duty as an angel full of heavenly beauty from on high, and as but another name for the obligation to love and serve Jesus Christ in all things, who is the bright and morning-star of time and the glory of eternity. Whether for action or endurance, whether for height of aim, or breadth of movement or depth of purpose, whether for energy of mind or health of body, whether for greatness of results to others or of enjoyment to one's self, there is nothing in the universe, that can be for a moment substituted for direct, earnest, practical love to the Saviour; and there is nothing, which, brought into comparison with it, is not infinitely disparaged by the contrast.

2dly. The higher Christian education must be conducted on the principle that the body is made for the mind, rather than the mind for the body.

Simple as this statement is, its just inferences will be found to be quite antagonistic to many of the prevailing ideas and modes of education. The power of matter over mind is very great, and far more determinative of individual and social development than most imagine; and bodily organization and temperament have much more to do with the varieties of intellectual manifestation and moral character, than is generally allowed; but greater by far is the influence of the mind over the body, over its health, its energy and its beauty. There is no stimulus to the circulatory, nervous or even muscular system, equal for real inward vitality to that of an ever-active, eager, joyous mind, perpetually travelling on high courses of thought and feeling, towards great commanding objects. Heroes are always hale: their very thoughts give vigor to their nerves; and men, in the full tide of activity and prosperity in business, are usually men of abounding health. Success is on this principle a great minister to the welfare of the body. In this lies the benefit of travel: it stimulates the mind, which in turn excites to favorable action, by the impulse of its cheerful sprightly moods of feeling, all the forces of the material organism, with which it is so strangely and delicately interlinked. The true hygiene of the body is mental and moral hygiene. Grief wastes, care deadens, and anxiety corrodes all the inward subtle vitalities of our being. Hence the physiological, as well as spiritual, beauty of the rule appointed for us by our great Maker: rejoice in the Lord always, and again I say rejoice! Joy is ever the deep abiding possession of God's heart; and as our hearts are fashioned to be like

His, although in such diminutive proportions of height and scope, such is the state ordained for us, to the inspiring vitalizing influence of which the working of all our faculties is adjusted. Hence the wicked, who are like the troubled sea casting up mire and dirt, are not to live out half their days; while the righteous shall flourish like the green bay-tree; and hence also the command to children to obey their parents, that they may live long in the land.

The great determining laws, therefore, of our compound nature are the laws of the mind. The body is made for the mind, as its tabernacle and its movable apparatus of mechanical powers, and is adapted skilfully to it in all its relations, susceptibilities and uses, as an engine to the force which is to diffuse its energy through all its springs and wheels. The conditions therefore of vigor, enlargement and conscious pleasure, perpetually, to the mind, are the conditions by which the time, aims and enterprise of the whole man should be gauged.

And what are these conditions? They are two-fold. The first of them is ceaseless activity in gaining knowledge; so as to come, both receptively and potentially, into full relationship, with the spirit and the understanding, to the surrounding universe, with which it has already so fixed and formal a connection; and the second is a constant earnest outlay of power, as a cause, adequate to work effects of its own: ever asserting its appointed superiority over all obstacles in its way: taking the helm, by the divine right of its immortal nature, over all the forces and circumstances of life; and, when acting according to its noblest capabilities, lavishly bestowing its acquisitions and energies upon others, for their profit and their joy. For ceaseless action work and progress, the mind is made. Without opportunity for them, it stagnates at once within itself. Ennui, the only other element necessary to be added in full strength to a deep damning sense of guilt, to make a hell on earth within the soul itself, extinguishes in its dark abyss every treasure and pleasure given to us from above. No wonder that men of vacant heads and hearts desire, and laugh wildly when uttering the wish, "to kill Time," himself indeed their best friend, but made by their own misconduct their worst enemy; and that they call their boisterous mirth, in attempting to do it, pastime.

But have not many, even good men, intellectual men and professional educators too, views which are, practically at least, quite at variance with these? What multitudes on earth spoil nature, truth, religion, life and art, by their own false theories, for themselves and others. The mass of men are indeed but mere tinkers with themselves and with every thing on which they lay their hands. Commend us to the man who receives every thing naturally into the depths of his being from without, and goes forth naturally with his whole soul to every outward object from within. Who knows where such men are to be found? Not so pertinaciously absurd are the Flathead Indians, in trying to alter the appointed shape of the head, or the Chinese, that of the foot, or a Parisian belle, that of the waist, as are vast numbers of even intelligent men, in imposing on their hearts and on their minds the unnatural restraints often called fashionable or politic, which they have invented, to the full free outburst and force of their inner life: thus setting aside with their follies, whether self-originated or traditionary, the very ordinances of God.

How many parents, students and teachers, of every grade of talent and knowledge, suppose that there is something very exhausting and even dangerous in protracted earnest study; and that one must treat both his body and mind, in respect to mental toil, as if broken vases, that need the most careful handling, in order to keep them from falling asunder under the pressure of life's burdens. One would think that there was enough stolidity in this world, without having any of the leaders of society stultify themselves, to any degree, by theory.

When a scholar's health fails, it is the common, as it is certainly a very easy, solution of the enigma, and one which the mass are always ready to accept at once, to say, that he has killed himself by too much mental labor. Other men die of all sorts of diseases, endemic and epidemic; but scholars of only one, too much study. With what a show of wisdom, that costs nothing but goes far, does many a doctor after measuring a youth's pulse that habitually eats too much, or studies and sleeps in a close room, or indulges in vicious habits, say to his parents, while raising his spectacles and looking gravely around, in order to prepare the way for some wonderful announcement, "Your son delves too deeply into his books; his brain is large, as might of course be expected in the noble scion of such a noble stock; let him relinquish all study at once and have free scope out of doors"! The doctor is pleased with his own wisdom, and the dispensation which it gives him from any farther thought, as well as with the fee secured by so little effort: the parents are pleased with the distinguished capacities of their son, and are willing to abide the needful time, for their best development; while the child himself is delighted to escape the laws and restraints of earnest mental and moral culture, and will trample, with as much devotion to theory, as any of the parties in the premises, all the treasures that he had begun to gather as an intellectual and immortal being under his feet. The love of labor, the desire for knowledge, the sense of his own higher nature, the training of his mind to right aims, efforts, habits and achievements, all these are thrown by system, as if doing God himself service, like chaff into the fire. The edifice of his future character and destiny which a teacher's loving hands had been, carefully and prayerfully, constructing with all science and skill, is, from the fatal hour described, not only to be neglected and to fall into decay; but is even to be zealously pulled down to its very foundations. How many has every teacher of wide experience thus seen spoiled, forever spoiled, that is robbed, for this is the meaning of the word, robbed for life of what they might have been. Not a greater crisis is it to a tree, to be dug up or blown over by the roots when in its full summer-bloom. Thoughts, desires, impulses and habits, that before were vigorous, are ever afterwards paralyzed. The idea has taken possession, as if with a demon's spite, of the before glowing soul, panting for every excellence, that there is a ban in its own feeble nature upon every thing but mediocrity and irregularity of effort; and that therefore it must content itself, with being what it can, rather than what it would. With what gladness does he who loves to ruin men, read that universal epitaph of all students who die early: "Here rests a poor soul who killed himself by hard study." The final analysis indeed of the causes of disease and death, among professional men generally, is thus stated in all directions; and the form of the statement we have copied literally from a recent daily paper: "He broke down at last, from the reaction upon the system of an overtasked brain." How different the idea thus insinuated, about the dangerousness of thorough mental industry, from that involved in such commands of God, as "not to be slothful in business," "to do what our hands find to do with our might" and to remember that "herein is our Heavenly Father glorified, that we bear much fruit." Well does Satan know that if earnest mental toil can be kept at a discount in this world, a perpetual extinguisher will be thereby put upon any large or desirable growth of religion in society. Who ever thinks of ascribing a scholar's poor health to the selfishness of his aims: a fact which if true, as in so many cases it is, would alone rob him of all the stimulus to action and enjoyment, without which the Divine Mind itself, with all its other vast resources, would be no longer divine or happy, the stimulus of love, as well as the power of the greatest of all objective summons, in the supreme claims of God upon the soul, to the high and broad action of all his faculties. Who refers his maladies, at any time, to the indulgence of constant cares and anxieties, which eat away inevitably the root of every lofty sentiment and hope that they attack. Without joy, it is as impossible for either body or mind to put on beauty or strength, or even to keep them when acquired, as for the lungs or heart to maintain their normal action, in air full of corruption, or for steam to be generated in abundance with insufficient water or fuel. Who ascribes the failure of a student's health to constant improprieties in food and clothing ? Who, to that almost universal plague of all our houses and public buildings, carbonic acid gas, with which almost all students, by thoughtless or even wanton indifference to the subject, allow themselves to be surrounded and poisoned, both by day and night ? No wonder that such need frequent vacations, and that both teachers and scholars, of such a sort, are ready to volunteer their testimony to the exhaustive effects of real study. Many even imagine themselves half ready to go mad, at times ; they are such amazing thinkers ! and then how many stories are there, of brain-cracked geniuses, as of heart-broken lovers ; and what an argument against being a genius, or ever indulging in love ! But a really great student is, in this country at least, a rare specimen of our race. It has never been the author's lot, although associated with scholars all his days, to come in contact with a man, who could justly be described as hurting himself by hard study. The nearest apparent approximation to such a fact, to be found within the bounds of his experience, occurred in the case of that distinguished oriental scholar, Nordheimer, who died so soon after coming to this country; but, on inquiry of him it proved, that the cause of the injury done to his health was not too vigorous action of the mind as such, but too little sleep; since, for years he had allowed himself, when in Germany, but three hours repose at night, and that on three chairs, in full dress, under the call of an alarm-clock. Such systematic self-abuse would have killed any one, but an enthusiastic, happy student, long before it did that devoted and spirited linguist.

Nothing, next to worship and direct beneficence to others, so fills the heart with such sweet all-pervasive satisfaction, as active and energetic habits of thought, perpetually busy in exploring the outer universe which God has made, and the inward relations of science, doctrine, providence or secondary agency, by which its wondrous harmonies are fashioned and established. Let earnest vigorous study abound, not only for its own sake but also as one of the surest means of bodily health; but always let it be with a brain supplied, as freely in doors with air, *vital* air, as if out of doors. There is nothing that this age, from whatever point we survey its wants, needs more, physically, intellectually and morally, than thorough ventilation.

And yet a voice has been recently raised, a professional voice from one of our large cities, and multiplied with many echoes through the public press, as if place and form and repetition might give it some importance, warning our Boards of Education to reduce at once the term of daily study in the Public Schools to three hours, as a matter of simple duty to the next generation. Quite as good advice would it be, for the physical profit of the coming age, to propose a general public administration daily of opium to the whole community of youngsters, in order to make them keep their limbs still long enough to accumulate a little more fat. The bane of this world now is too little thought, too little study, too little growth and grasp of mind, too little occupation with the objects of reason, science, truth and faith.

The fountain of perpetual youth in the heart has often been said to be Poetry ; it should rather be called Thought : thought in whatever high earnest form, but especially in those forms which are most full of activity without, and gladness within. Merchants, farmers, mechanics and others, if arriving at extreme old age, often if not generally pass away from earth through the cloud of second childhood. But thinkers, scholars, philosophers, poets have, in great numbers, like Samuel Johnson dying when 76 years old ; Leibnitz when 70 ; Sir William Herschel when 84 ; Goethe when 83 ; our own Emmons* when 95 ; or Alexander Humboldt, who has just deceased at 90 and over ; and Jacob Grimm now abounding in many and great labors, at the age of more than 70 ; been hale and healthy, with the fire of their youth undimmed in their eye, and the natural strength of their heart unabated, to the end.

When one points to the Germans, as a hardy long-lived happy nation of severe students, the reply is often made : " Oh yes ! but the climate of Germany is very different from this : there is some undefinable element, unfortunately, quite peculiar to our North American atmosphere, that forbids here such close, mental application." How strange that no one has ever discovered the influence of this marvellous fact upon our bodily characteristics and enjoyments ! But no ! that would not be a profit-

* In " The Reflections of a Visitor, in Ide's Memoir of Emmons " (Vol. 1, p. 169 of Introduction) occurs the following passage, of special interest in this connection : "The clergy of New England tasked themselves, as if they were of antediluvian mould. We read of the two Edwardses, Hopkins, Smalley, Stiles, Chauncey and Dwight as at their books thirteen, fourteen, fifteen and sometimes eighteen hours of the day. Dr. Emmons, in this respect equalled any of them."

able part of the plan of "the mystery of iniquity," in the world. It is only the mind, and that only in its higher uses and attainments, that is endangered in our too oxygenated, or changeable, or otherwise faulty, atmosphere. We are indeed a nation of dyspeptics, but not because the air given to us to breathe is not as good as that of any other nation under heaven; but because all our arrangements are adapted to exclude it, and to substitute in its place the most deadly gas on earth: necessary indeed to all vegetation, and so indirectly necessary to us: a part of all the beauty of nature, and of the very sustenance of life, but yet itself directly fatal to our lungs and nerves. We read almost daily of persons suffocated in vats and subterranean caves and old wells; and yet, shutting our doors and windows with great care, as we retire to sleep, as if purposely to shut out the presence of our best friend, we prepare for ourselves systematically a bath of the same poison in our chambers and rise out of it in the morning, as from our seats also in churches, lecture-rooms, concert-halls and railroad cars, sick and ready to say, like the youth in Scripture returning from the field to die, and for the same reason, because the hand of death is resting, for the time, upon our shoulders: "my head! oh my head!" And how do multitudes continue the same course of constant self-poisoning day after day, sick and discouraged, and wonder why God did dash our cup of earthly sweets with so many daily ills, and long for their spiritual body, as one, that, in a better sphere, shall be ever free from all the trials of their mortal life. Our common form of salutation, in meeting each other, however casually, is one that implies that every man expects to find his neighbor ailing in some way. The only ventilation to which most have yet attained, whose eyes are at all open to its necessity, amounts simply to great care to ventilate one's rooms, after they have left them ; as if out of respect to the general cleanliness of the house itself, instead of ventilating them, when present themselves to enjoy the benefit of such ever-changing, pure, refreshing air, as God himself always carefully gives to those who take the air as he furnishes it for them, in the outer temple of His works. How strange that the first prescription given by the physician to a valetudinarian, "to take the air," every day, and more and more according to his strength, should never be thought of afterwards by him as a rule of health when well ; or that any one should suppose, that it is any the less healthy, when taken pure in doors, than when taken out of doors. There never was a nation that closeted itself, on theory, in confined apartments, like our own : not the Greeks or Romans, whose life was literally an out-of-door life ; nor the

Germans French or English, who are all much more addicted to the air, than are we. And what a terrible compensation do we receive for such utter neglect of the essential conditions of health, in our two great national diseases, dyspepsia and consumption !

In what weak and even dishonorable ways, do good men, so called, often speak of God ! A youth, for example, violates all the rules of health and the conditions of protracted life, and ere long by an accumulation of many transgressions, each small and unnoticed at the time, brings on a crisis which he alone has prepared ; and parents and friends stand gazing and wondering at the scene, and exclaim, "what a pity ! what a mysterious providence ! that such a charming youth should fall so suddenly and so early, in the field."

Many, if not most, of our colleges and boarding schools are quite entitled to be called, slaughter-houses : so great is the sacrifice in them of health and strength. College classes, often, and it is believed generally, contain at their graduation but half of the whole number that have belonged to them throughout their course. Half have fallen by the way, during four years ; and this of boys from the best families of the land : all of course, as most people please the devil in thinking and saying, by hard study. The necessity of an actual and constant change of the air to be breathed, by day and night, whether taking it as prepared by the Maker of it and us, or preparing it for ourselves, is a fact yea a law not yet known, or, if known, recognized by teachers in our colleges and seminaries ; who sit themselves in close rooms all day long, and hear their recitations in narrow apartments, breathing with thirty or forty pupils, for two and three hours daily, air that is made unfit for respiration in a few minutes : not only not insisting on a perpetual renovation of the air themselves, but laughing heartily or at least secretly at those who do, as being crotchety and angular enough in their views : not seeing meanwhile, as those around them do, in their own pale faces and slow gait and languid manner, that they are steadily and surely drinking every day for themselves a draught of the cup of death.

3dly. Another of the great guiding principles in the work of the higher Christian education, one fundamental to its right prosecution is this : that true education is, in each individual case, a development of what is within, instead of an accretion from without.

On this cardinal idea hinge many subordinate ones of importance. The teacher who has such a conception of his work will regard the stimulation of his pupil's mind to great wakefulness and energy of action, as one of his own perpetual duties and pleasures. The art of successfully stimulating another's mind to ever higher thoughts and nobler aims, is, whether for subjective intellectuality or objective usefulness, one of the highest of all arts. He will accordingly address himself, as does an enthusiastic gardener to the work of cherishing and perfecting a favorite plant, to the grand inspiring enterprise of educating, that is, as the word signifies in its component elements, constantly educing or drawing out, all the hidden riches of his scholar's whole inward self, as prepared by his Maker with all wisdom and love for the very purpose of such education. The stimulation that a loving Christian teacher will be ever bringing to bear, with the greatest possible intensity of force and constancy of application, upon a younger mind which God in his providence has given to him to train for him, while it will have within it all the constraints and pressure and goading impulse of authority and law, will yet be charged to fulness, like God's own style of government and influence over his intelligent creatures, with all winning, inviting, beckoning elements of thought and feeling and manner. Such a teacher will be ever in the van of his work, and of his pupils, bearing the banner before them of the highest possible progress in it. How different such treatment of a scholar, in its influence upon him, compared with that of indulging him in his own ideas and ways, for which he may often ask and indeed stand waiting, as a privilege, only to despise him who ought to refuse it, if, on the contrary, he weakly grants its bestowal. In the one case, the pupil's real good is seen and felt to be the starting point and inspiration of every movement; in the other, he is his own guide; and the teacher is rightly viewed, as both intellectually and morally, incompetent for the post of leadership.

On the doctrine, that true education is a development, and not an accretion, hangs also the farther idea, that its great object is thorough mental discipline, and not a mere accumulation of knowledge. The mind is to be trained to do each part of its appointed work in life, in the most perfect manner possible, whether in the form of endurance or of action. Drill makes the scholar, as it makes the soldier: steady, sturdy drill. Difficulties must be set before him, and when in his ignorance or sluggishness he draws back from the effort necessary to conquer them, he must be held persistently to the task. This is God's mode of developing talent, enterprise and piety in His kingdom: to set over against men the trials and necessities of life, in such a way for number and size, that, if they do not arise and crush them, they must be inevitably crushed by them. By making however the efforts adequate to a triumph, the soul is lifted up into the atmosphere of a new consciousness of itself and of a new vision of its privileges. Not only is it more blessed to give than to receive, but the active pleasures of our being, generally, are higher than the passive. God has therefore placed the prizes of earth and of heaven so near us, as to invite our desires by their size and their beauty, and yet so much above us, that we must climb hard and high, in order to obtain them. So must we purposely cast the pupil upon his own resources, and discipline him, not only to rely upon himself and do his own work, but also, when he does it, to do it with all his might, that neither he nor his Maker may be robbed, at any time, of the proper results of his agency.

The idea that all real education is a development, instead of an accretion, will make its possessor, if himself educated, an artist in his work. A true teacher is the greatest of artists. Every part of his work is carefully designed. He studies the mind itself, that he may comprehend fully what are its necessities, and what are its capabilities, as well as what are its germinal elements, and also their inward processes of growth. He studies the universe of matter and mind, without, that he may rightly understand the scope and field and forms of human activity. He studies life itself, its many phases, wants and issues. Thus armed, he lays out every energy, with study and prayer and ingenuity and watchful observation, to educe and exalt all the fundamental capacities of his pupil's whole nature into full harmony with themselves, and into full correspondence with the many duties and opportunities of the world around him. Had ever any other artist so wide a field, or so high a work, or so splendid a train of results attending him? For the better appreciation of him and of his work, consider what are the achievements of a true education.

§ 1. He who has obtained it has obtained the full use and possession of himself. The acts and states of his mind are under his own control, in respect to their direction, continuance and force. He has passed out of his state of intellectual childhood, when he had eyes but could not see, and ears but could not hear, all the glorious things around him and above him. He is, under the King of kings and Lord of lords, himself the lord of the world within, not in feeling as inflated with pride, but in fact, as the conscious owner and manager of its great and complicated forces.

§ 2. He is in a state not only of natural, but also of skilfully developed, responsiveness to all influences and summons from without. The great argument of universal nature to every attentive observer is beauty, perpetual divine beauty by day and night, in the heavens above and the earth beneath and the waters that are under the earth. That beauty he sees, he feels, everywhere ; and his heart looks out upon it, from a throne of gladness, rejoicing in it and in Him who made it for the pleasure of his earthly children.

The argument of humanity, as he gazes upon its dark waters, foaming out their own sin and shame, is pity. From every quarter he seems to himself to be implored for help and he hails the universal summons. He would do service to his fellows. True manliness seems to him to be essentially demonstrative of itself and perpetually communicative of its treasures unto all men.

And, as to the sweet influences from above distilling forever upon him from his Father's heart on high, they give him all the flavor of life. Hence comes the light, hence fall the showers, by which every grace and virtue in his heart are nourished. To smile with joy in the beams of His presence, to be covered with the adornments of his spirit, to minister to his glory and pleasure, is the very summit of his desires and endeavors. His whole aim in life is to make, on the one hand, the greatest possible use, as the steward of God, of all privileges bestowed upon him, and, on the other, the greatest possible outlay of every faculty and resource, as his loving friend, in the promotion of his kingdom.

§ 3. He is in a state of perpetual normal growth, in susceptibility, power, usefulness and enjoyment. The main result of education, as a developing process, is "to draw out" the inner life of the man, in right proportions and into right directions. How often do we hear of a finished education! The word is a misnomer: the conception is an impossibility. Not more deficient in finalities is eternity itself, than the mind of man. The scope of a true education is unlimited and illimitable. The intellect possessing the greatest dimensions of power or of attainment on earth, stands but at the first beginnings of a series of endless progressions. But, to start rightly, to go forth towards the true objects of our being in a true manner: this is the problem; and the high divine work of the educator is, to initiate those forms and habits of thought and feeling, of aim and action, out of whose full-flowing influence may be realized to their possessor, by the very necessity of cause and effect, in ever unfolding manifestation, the highest, broadest, richest future, of which the soul is capable.

What a work of art, therefore, of sublime and altogether unappreciated art, do the achievements of a real education show a true teacher's labor of life to be!

4thly. Another of the great normal guiding principles, in the work of the higher Christian education, is this: that its ultimate end to the individual is character.

As the scale of life's activities and pleasures is three-fold, bodily, intellectual and spiritual, and in the spiritual the others find their culmination and fulfilment; so is it with the developments of our nature itself. The moral is the pinnacle of our whole being. The starting-point, as the terminus, of all virtue or vice and of all good or evil, experienced or performed, are there. All the wondrous attributes of God draw their light and heat, their worth and beauty, from the central, all-controlling attribute of his love. It is God's character alone that makes him God, or that makes this universe properly His universe. But for his capacity for character, man would have no powers to be desired: none, that would not deserve to be dreaded, as powers fitted only to lash and torment and destroy each other, in an uproar of never-ending contradictions. Whatever therefore is done in the work of education in a true way, must not only be done with design and skill; but there must be also an ever-present, ever-constraining reference to the question of its influence upon the character of the pupil, the final issue of all the labor bestowed upon him there.

Character is commonly of a wild hap-hazard growth, in this world. The very phrase Subjective Art, and much more the statement, that this is the highest of all arts on earth or in Heaven would seem to many who suppose themselves to be educated Christian thinkers, a singular novelty. And yet there is nothing that mortals can do, which interests God in them personally, except the work of adorning themselves with those ornaments of the heart, which are in his sight of great price. True education makes the man himself, and not some mere outside addition to him, however beautiful or imposing. Every thing else is but a means to this great end : the building up of the inner temple of the soul, or the transfusion of as many divine elements of thought and feeling, as possible, into the whole inner framework of one's being, as its permanent characteristics and its great ruling forces. Without such ideas and aims in his work, the teacher walks in a low and narrow path indeed ; but with them he walks on the very Highway of holiness, on which prophets and apostles and God's great army of heroes have ever gone up into the skies.

All true mental and moral growth is self-growth : progress made for one's self by continued effort in a right direction, under the perpetual stimulus of a right will. Not the few who without many advantages yet distinguish themselves, but all, with advantages or without them, are self-made: some, indeed with greater facilities, purer models and more inspiring influences than others; but all, self-made. A splendid character is but the splendid accumulation, of a vast number of right choices and right deeds: the soul's own pile of all its past ideas and hopes: itself, in every thing that it has done and desired to do, throughout its entire history.

As every thing in the universe has its uses out of itself, in a grand harmony of connections, dependences, influences and results; and every thing material was made for something moral; and things bodily and intellectual always culminate in things spiritual: so, to display character on God's part, and to form it on the part of His creatures, these are the ends, for which the whole universe was made. Time, space, creation, providence, redemption, all, have their common end and function here. The High Priest of this holy work on earth is the teacher. And what is to be his ideal of his calling, and of its true results? The elements of it are to be found in all the actual and all the possible of greatness and goodness, in all time and eternity and in all Heaven and earth. As the true conceptional model of any species of plant or animal, cannot be found in any one individual of the species in fact, but must be an aggregate of the excellences of all individuals combined, so, the true ideal of human development must be composed of an assemblage of all the most bright and beautiful attainments of intellect, wisdom, science and skill, and of all the most lovely traits and noble dispositions conceivable of the soul. Unlike other artists, the Christian educator is not left to form that ideal for himself; for it stands before his eye, in a beauty and magnificence all its own, in the person, life and spirit of Jesus Christ; who came on earth not simply to die for us, but also, although forgotten by so many, to live for us, and to teach us in such a way, how to live for each other: telling us that except we have His spirit we are none of His.

The whole end therefore of all true education is, on the one hand, to make the pupil like Christ in his character and in the style and sphere of his outward activity, and, on the other, to qualify him most thoroughly to fill out, at all times, the complete dimensions of his being with the greatest possible use of his time and strength and opportunities for him. "Look to Jesus"! is to be therefore the one bright radiant guiding motto of the school-room, as of the church and the household.

5thly. It is also a normal, guiding principle in the work of all true education: that the highest influence that can be brought to bear upon it by the teacher, is that of his own personality.

The greatest influence exerted by any man is that which is insensible. Occasional influence is but the influence of occasions ; which have, from their very infrequency and temporary duration, but little effect upon the great current of human affairs. But the influence of ourselves, our own real char acter, example and spirit : this is a light that shines for good or evil everywhere around us, and that makes us an epistle, known and read of all men. As great as is the sublimity of his vocation, and the wide and lasting reach of its results, so great is the pressure of obligation upon the teacher, to be magnanimous himself in his aims and efforts, and to be a true man before God. The nearest merely human model of the true style of spirit, which an educator should possess, is furnished in the laborious untiring joyous life of that wonderful worker for God and man, the Apostle Paul. Had he, instead of being a preacher to the Gentiles, undertaken to serve Christ with the same heroic earnestness and faith and prayerfulness, in the work of educating the young for him, he would have best exemplified, thus far in the world's history, what wonderful elements of power belong to this sublime vocation. He gave himself wholly to the work of inspiring others with true views of life and of the glory of the world to come : all his plans were grand and all his ideas heroic.

No influence can be exerted in this world so great, next after God's, as that of one man directly upon another. We dwell indeed, so far as any inward personal inspection of ourselves is concerned, but that of the All-searching eye above, in a closed castle, each one shut up within himself in the temple of his own body; but in our occupations, aims and habits, in our desires and hopes and pleasures, in our features, gestures, footsteps, tones and in all that we leave undone and unregarded, we are perpetually and unconsciously revealing what we are, and inworking the very substance of our hidden selves into the characters and destinies of others. Individual, personal influence is the greatest earthly force in kind, that resides in any human organization or movement. One great reason, accordingly, why good results are so few and so temporary in the working of the vast social machinery cf life, whether in the Church or in the world without, is because of the general low estimate of the largeness of individual obligations and individual privileges.

Where, then, shall a student, whose heart is on fire with high thoughts of his own nature made in the image of God, of the great work of life to be done for Him, and of the splendors of an eternal future to be spent in his presence: where, shall such an one, eager to make the largest possible preparation, in intellect and character, for running the race of life like a hero, find a company of teachers whose eyes and hearts burn with the same zeal for his good, men full of all great strong loving thoughts and showing it, in every kind of genial, generous, kindling look and word and way? Alas! routine takes, almost everywhere, the place of daily, hearty, skilful effort to stimulate and develop, in every way, his whole nature. Mechanism is the main reliance, and not ever wakeful personal love, so earnest that it will not brook the denial of the object at which it aims, the pupil's greatest and best advancement in all things. How sere and stale is the experience of many teachers, after persisting a few years in such terrific trifling with the amazing capabilities and issues of their divine calling! Quite as many sear their consciences, as with a hot iron, by a series of awful negligences, as others do by a series of overt crimes. There are also those who undertake not only to account for dull mechanical habits of teaching, but even to justify them by the plea, that the teacher has too many under his care to cultivate a special interest in each and every particular pupil. How unlike God is such an one, in the tone of his heart, who feels ever restrained by the want of more recipients of His love; so that however gracious he is at any time he is always waiting to be more so. Love grows by indulgence.

The very fact of numbers and of their continual succession, and so of the ever renewed calls for fresh toil and skill which their wants present in constant repetition, is a perpetual reiteration of pleasure to the teacher who loves his work. But that there should be such constant sameness in the style of his labors, is, in the eyes of most, the greatest drawback upon their pleasurableness. All such, as do not feed on great ideas, but live only on novelties and changes, would soon tire of the long labors of a true teacher's life, although so grand in their results. But novelty is neither needed nor felt as a spur to effort by a noble soul. The Infinite Mind finds perpetual joy in perpetual work, with no novelty whatever. And since God, from the very infiniteness of his knowledge and pleasure, can have at no time any new idea or experience, he satisfies the wants of His vast nature, in leading his creatures into ever new knowledge and ever new gladness of spirit ; and surely to the finite mind also the communication of new wisdom and new goodness to other minds is greater joy than the reception of them, in whatever surprising forms of novelty to one's self.

But what dull views of life must he have, who can complain of a teacher's duties, as monotonous. And, pray, tell us where is the monotony? Certainly not in the objects of his zeal who are always coming and going upon the stage : not, in the degree of their natural capacities or personal acquirements, nor, in sameness of results under the most skilful and laborious culture. In the healing art which captivates so many, there are but two great secrets for the practitioner to solve : to diagnose well, so as really to find the actual disease, as it is ; and the other, to be equally wise in discovering the one exact remedy. And yet, what material for constant excitement and pleasure, does the devotee to this noble profession find, in traversing each of these fields of research ! And can any one think, that, in the school-room, there can be any less opportunity or necessity for thoroughly studying human nature generally, or personal idiosyncracies in particular, than for studying the secret hidings of disease in the sick chamber ; or any less exhilaration, in carrying points of order, instruction, discipline and personal influence, with tact and effect, in the character, than in sending away some brief pain or sorrow from the tabernacle of the flesh. No man has the spirit of a true teacher, who does not, each day, enter into the toils of his work, as a strong bold swimmer leaps joyously into the moving tide, as the element in which he must be in order to be happy. If there is any employment upon earth, that to be rightly executed enlists and demands every faculty, energy and resource of a man's whole complex being, however armed with intellect or character, natural or acquired, it is surely this one; and he, who can make it seem dull and monotonous, infallibly stamps himself thereby to his own consciousness, as a man both of feeble ideas and also of a very low range of moral feeling.

Much is said of the ingratitude of youth, as a great offset to any high sentimentalism about the pleasure of devoting one's self to their education. Those who encounter their ingratitude, usually deserve it. Children are never more quick, than in finding their true friends. The logic of their instincts is swift and unerring. It requires real nobility of soul, rightly to manage and mould childhood. Few possess true benevolence enough, to put on the patience necessary for the right conduct of any large plans for their good. Few are divine enough in the temper of their souls, to make it desirable, for the church or the world, to commit to them the formation of the rising generation. If engineers for public improvements, and those who guide the affairs of State, need to be men of mark for their wisdom and efficiency, what should be the high qualifications of those who form the very men, for whom all civil and even material things exist, as those who are to be educated by them and among them, for an entrance ere long into grander scenes and nobler society, and a life of ever bright and joyous experience on high.

6thly. Another guiding principle, in the work of the Higher Christian Education, pertaining to it as a whole, is one of intellectual and moral economics: so to manage it, as to bring it to the greatest actual productiveness possible.

A real issue in the best attainable results, or a natural full tendency to such an issue, is the gauge by which we measure the moral quality of any action or combination of actions. The results of the present educational system of this country, as indeed also of this age, are not satisfactory. They are right, in neither quality nor quantity. Who, that is engaged with all his might of intellect and heart in the profession, does not feel what heights of excellence there are in it, yet untrodden? And who that has obtained an education, of the best type yet afforded, does not often say to himself: "What awful mistakes were made, in my education! Had my teachers but seen things in their true relations: had they been deeply freighted, themselves, with knowledge and thought and love, and moved forward in their work with all the energy of their whole united nature: had they but known my weaknesses and my wants, my hidden energies and my blind indeed but active impulses, ever to be and to do something greater and better,

I knew not what: had they but really loved me and given themselves, heart to heart, to me: what! oh what might I not have become! I am and I must ever be, from their fault, but the shadow of my own real self, as God made me to be and to stand up in his presence on the earth."

The economical working of the educational forces of the age demands that as little waste, as possible, should be allowed in the result. It is not, by any means, a matter of indifference who advances and who does not under the instruction given. To fall back stolidly on a sense of one's own dignity, which alas! in such a case is utterly wanting: to comfort one's self, without any earnest self-inquisition or vigorous effort to amend the difficulty, in respect to the poor progress of a pupil, by his supposed dulness of nature, a dulness which is commonly indeed only supposed and not real: to habituate one's self to the idea of moving on contentedly, with the mere use of means and appliances, without reference to their effect: is not this to be a driveller in one's ideas, a spendthrift of one's resources and to be a man utterly deficient, not only in all true conceptions of art in fashioning character and destiny, but also of mere industry and even of honor, decency or duty, before either God or man? But are there none such, in this sacred calling? Yea! rather are there not many, in every department of it, low-browed men, indifferent in their walk and speech, who consider not only their own employment, unsurpassed as it is in value and dignity by any other upon earth, but also life itself a drudgery. Such are the men that teach, because they do not know what else to do; that never give new ideas to their pupils, because they have none themselves; and, provided that they keep their hours and stick to their book and continue some how to look and act, as if they knew a good deal more than they do, believe that they surely quite equal the mechanical demands of their mechanical work. And these men, leaving to fate or chance the results of their agency or rather want of agency, look with as unmoved hearts upon an utter destitution of all good effects or even an abundance of evil effects around them, as could so many wooden men themselves. They are but mere apologies for teachers. Out of many institutions not more than half, and out of most not so many, come forth with any real preparation for the work of life or any earnestness of spirit to undertake it. The amount of waste, in nearly every case, is indeed terrific.

The aim should be, on the contrary, more eagerly and persistently kept, to achieve the greatest possible results, of which either the true system of Christian education itself is capable, or those, on whom it is brought to bear, have capacity in themselves for development, than, in the world of business, the merchant or manufacturer maintains in conducting his affairs. His will works steadily and effectively towards its proper goal, like the most finished enginery under the power of steam.

Heaven and earth call loudly, for earnest, working, joyous laborers in great numbers, in the sublime work of educating the rising generation, for the honors, duties and enjoyments of true manhood.

II.

THE TRUE STYLE AND MEASURE OF THE HIGHER CHRISTIAN EDUCATION.

II.

THE TRUE STYLE AND MEASURE OF THE HIGHER CHRISTIAN EDUCATION.

He who should carefully measure the dimensions of man's whole complex being, and conceive of him as in a state of full preparation, in respect to all his powers, for the issues of both time and eternity, would be best able to appreciate and determine the true style of his education. And yet how far would be the thoughts of such an one, if of earth, from filling the entire horizon of the subject!

As it is our design, in this essay, to furnish but a general map of what belongs to the full-orbed idea of real education, it will be impossible to dwell at length upon any one part of it. The following view, it is believed, will furnish an outline, at least, of what ought to be included in the idea of a complete education.

First. In reference to the body.

Our physical system is certainly the basis, while we are in this world, for the manifestation of all the rest of our nature, whether to our own consciousness or to the eyes of others. Our intellectual and moral faculties abide in it as their tabernacle, and work through it, as their instrument, upon the surrounding universe. While fastened to the body, therefore, and compelled to receive all our impressions and enact all our deeds through it, it is a matter of great moment what its best condition and development demand.

God, himself, always places the physical first, in both individual and national advancement. And how, in preparing the way for his church, so dear to him that her name has been always graven upon the palms of his hands, did he deal with her, as we do with children, in her earlier years: educating her by appeals to the senses, at the first, in impressive forms, ordinances, ceremonials, and symbols. First, that which is natural, saith Paul, and then that which is spiritual.

Men are now, indeed, beginning to realize the vast importance of a right physical education. The ancients were far wiser in this particular than we. Not only their literature and history, but also their very houses, as still standing disentombed in Pompeii and Herculaneum, show that their life was one passed out of doors. Their active games, so many, so varied, and so exciting ;* their military movements, in which all engaged, statesmen and scholars as well as others ; and all the preparatory training which these necessitated and inspired ; their frequent bathing ; the vitality and social hilarity of their daily activities and experiences ; and the constant summons everywhere made upon them for quickness and power of action, gave them an arm, and a breast, and a pulse of far greater strength than men nowadays possess. Such a busy, bustling style of life accounts for the high estimate in which they held action in oratory : so that Demosthenes once, in stating that three things were necessary to oratory, declared them emphatically to be "action ! action ! action ! !" And, for the same reason, we do not find landscapes among the paintings of the ancients as in modern art, but only men, or gods, and their agents : not still life, but demonstrations of energy in some form ; and so likewise their imaginations animated and impersonated every thing around them.

And yet the bodily development of the ancients was but a moiety of what ours might become, from

* The education of a Greek youth at school consisted of but three parts : grammar, music, and gymnastics ; the latter of which occupied, up to his sixteenth year, as much time as the other two combined, and, from that age up to eighteen, excluded them altogether.

their utter want of those high, moral, and religious stimulations to all the secret springs of health which we have, as well as from the positive injurious influence upon them, of their frequent and various heathenish excesses.

A wonderful diversity of ends can be gained by special bodily training, in the different directions of strength, endurance, agility or skill, in deeds of muscular force, personal bravery, mechanical contrivance, or elaborate workmanship in forms graphic, pictorial, surgical, musical, gymnastic, or artistic An absolutely special education, by itself, is not yet much in vogue among us, where so many departments of successful labor are open, on every side, to those who possess a more general style of qualifications for honorable toil.

I. What, then, it is our first question, are the ends to be gained, in the body, as a matter of general attainment, applicable to each individual, in the course of the higher Christian education ?

1st. Soundness or health.

With the fact of health, as with the very word itself, what a variety of things is closely connected ! Health, heal, hale, whole, and holy are all, etymologically, derived from one common root. The same man, with health, is as different, certainly, from what he would or could be without it, as almost any two men can be from each other.

(1.) Health is a duty. It is not indeed wholly, but it is surely to a great degree, in our own power, and, so far as it is, God holds us responsible, not only for its safe keeping, but also for its improvement. Good health is one of the greatest endowments that a man can receive at his birth, and one of the greatest treasures that he can obtain, at any time afterwards, whether by accident or design. When every man is taught to feel, that there are definite laws of bodily health, and that he wrongs himself and his Maker in violating them, as truly as in taking up arms against reason and conscience in any other direction ; human life and human labor will receive, at once, a great enlargement.

(2.) Health is also a power. Vigor of muscle, nerve, and pulse, is a wonderful preparation for strong thinking, feeling, and action. Success ministers to health, and health to success ; mutually helpful to each other, as thoughts to words and words to thoughts, or as effort to attainment and attainment to ever new effort. By far the great majority of those, who have impressed their ideas and plans upon the world, have been men of abounding health.

(3.) Health is a joy. Mere animal health, where no power of thought is connected with it, to give quickness or sweetness to the flow of daily consciousness, is itself a constant source of pleasure

The air, earth, and sea, are each alive with happy creatures, gamboling, under the inspirations of health, in constant ravishment with their brief lease of life.

(4.) Health is also beauty. God hath made every thing beautiful in its time. Things inanimate abide usually as he has made them, or, if they change, change into forms and by processes of his direct contrivance. Throughout the whole domain of organic life, the same general principles prevail, except so far as man, by his abuses or neglects, perverts their original constitution or appointed uses and relations. He it is, that has turned the world upside down, and subjected the same ; so that, through him, the whole creation groaneth and travaileth in pain together until now. But for man, God would now see in looking down upon the work of his hands, as at the creation, that "it was all very good." Any uninjured animal organism that has health, is whole ; and is therefore in the state in which God made it to be ; and that state is beauty. He can make nothing wrong. All his works praise him. Wrong means wrung,* twisted, out of shape. All his works are done in truth. He can make nothing ugly, in reference to the place

* Compare French word tort (twisted): the word right (from rectus), being the exact opposite, in the form of the figure, ruled or straight, to that for wrong, or crooked.

which it is to occupy, or the ends which it is to accomplish. All the great intuitions and the instinctive decisions of his infinite nature would interdict it. He is not a God of confusion, but of order. He cannot be tempted with evil, in any department of his sublime being. Beauty is the very brightness of his image, and is therefore distributed as universally over all his works, as the beams of his presence.

No cosmetics, no arts of dress, no studied adjustment of light and shade, can adorn the human face or form, like health. The perfection of all colors on earth is flesh-color, which blends them all in one, in the mortal face of an immortal ; and the perfection of that is seen, only in the rosy tint of health. The glory of all forms on earth is the human form, in which the delicacy, dignity, grace, might, and majesty of all other animate forms, are nicely balanced and harmonized together ; and the glory of the human form can be maintained in the strength and finish of its members and their functions, only by the ever-quickening impulses of health. The ancients, for this reason, had far more beauty of form than we, and were much more alive to its charms. Formosus, excelling in form, is the Latin word for beautiful, referring, like the kindred word speciosus, making a fine show, and præstans, literally standing up before, to the whole outward contour of the man. On heathen ground the human face never has been, and never can be, that thing of beauty, which, in the light of Christianity, when all aglow with divine ideas and great heroic aims and impulses, it becomes. The heart has no such training there, as qualifies it to interpret or appreciate or even to receive into itself a demonstration of moral beauty, in either the works of God or the aspects of men. The very word face (facies from facio) implies, indeed, that this it is which *makes* the individual appearance of any one man what it really is : as the very making of the face itself is also expressed in the word feature (Italian fattura, Latin factura) from facio. Here are presented the high signals of his own distinct personality. And yet it is not the grouping of the mere lineaments of the human visage, however fine, which constitutes its special glory ; but the moral expression, breathed into them and filling them with its deep, inward illumination. The divine light of this higher beauty can be caught and kept in the features, only under the power of the cross, and from the very reflection upon it of the heart of Christ, dying and triumphing while he dies.

2d. Large positive acquisitions of strength.

The duties of life are arduous. Health will answer the demands of a man's own nature upon itself. But there are burdens to be carried, enterprises to be undertaken, and hazards to be encountered, by a true man, in behalf of a world whose social, civil, governmental, religious, and educational ideas and influences are, so many of them, false in their aims and mischievous in their results. Does an ordinary laborer need much strength, in order to vex from the bountiful earth an abundant harvest ; or an artisan, to work the metals into new forms which are yet so willing to be melted, pounded, drawn, and tortured at his will ; or a soldier, to go successfully through the field of battle, where the chances of an hour may, at any moment, disappoint the highest plans and the greatest efforts ? Then, what an estate of bodily vigor must he lay by with care, who is to be a fellow-laborer with God, in striving to erect everywhere, as each man is made and called of him to do, among the desolations of ruined humanity, as many temples of immortality as possible to his praise forever !

Many shrink back from labors and rewards, which greater preparations of strength would enable them to assume with gladness. One may sometimes serve God in the most acceptable of all ways, in getting ready to endure hardness, by and by, as a good soldier of Jesus Christ. Not only do " they serve who wait," but they especially, who prepare themselves carefully to serve.

Positive vigor of nerve and muscle is one of the

greatest necessities and duties of good men, at all times, and in these days peculiarly, when, to say the least, health and strength are rare commodities among scholars. An energetic will needs an energetic body, with which to execute its purposes. And, when girding itself to endure, with calmness, any of earth's many dark or sorrowful experiences, the mind, however heroic in its bearing, needs to find in planting its foot firmly for the shock, a sure foundation in the amount of its bodily vigor on which to stand. In running after the prizes of this life, and much more after those of our high calling in Christ Jesus, the corruptible crowns of this world, or the crown immortal on high, a degree of diligence is required, sufficient to cover the greatest possible outlay of energy and of time ; and, in meeting trials in the service of God, or struggling manfully against the changes, disappointments and losses of this world, the heavenly-minded and the earthly alike need all the aids that they can procure, from the highest and best condition of the body.

3d. Grace of mien and manner.

The bodily powers are capable of very high culture, in a wide, comprehensive variety of details, which aggregated make a wonderful contrast in the result to what would have occurred in their absence. Health and strength, in one of true intellectual and moral elevation and refinement, will almost irresistibly produce grace in his looks, attitudes, gestures, tones, and motions. As certain thoughts, moods, and habits of the mind are expressed clearly in the all-revealing features of the face ; and so painting can show us, in the well-drawn outer man, the inner spirit that possesses him : so men, when sitting, standing, walking, speaking, and acting, at once disclose in their very postures and motions, and in the quality of their voices and manners, to the eye of every intelligent beholder, the hidden history of their ideas of themselves and of others, and the style of their impulses, intentions and tastes. All personal culture brings a rich harvest of pleasure to its possessor. The finished gentleman, indeed, as he bears about with him perpetually the consciousness of his own refined sensibilities and gentle feelings and generous sentiments and cheerful loving looks, tastes himself, all the time, the gratification occasioned to others by such characteristics, of which they quaff only single draughts at long intervals in his presence. And yet the number of those who know any one of us, in merely the most incidental and general manner, and who, therefore, obtain from us only the benefit to be gained in the most occasional way, is so much the great mass of those who know us at all ; and here, for the same reason, lies so much of our whole field of action and influence in this life; that it becomes every one, who would be either manly or godly, to take heed that the multitude before whom he moves in so infrequent and momentary a way, still see in him, at all times, everything to admire and love, to desire and imitate. The leading grace, in the bearing of the outward man, is declared by the world at large in the very designation of the word gentleman, to be gentleness. Gentle and genteel are in origin the same, and denote facts quite as much connected with each other, as the words used to describe them. No single word could so well epitomize all that belongs to real exterior refinement. Gentleness contains among its elements, self-possession, self-restraint, the power of thought, regard for others, ideas of taste and subjective art, and habits of high self-culture. Gentleness was one of the highest manifestations that Christ made of his divinity, when on earth; or that God makes perpetually of himself in his universal providence. On gentleness as its stock, any and every grace, internal and external, may be easily grafted; while without it all other personal refinements, of whatever sort, would soon become but withered flowers upon a broken stem.

II. What, now, we ask briefly, are the means of gaining these ends described?

1st. Conformity to the laws and conditions, appointed for the body as such.

Not more truly are the planetary worlds under the power of exact mathematical law, or the mechanical and chemical forces and elements of nature in their action, than the muscular, nervous, circulatory, respiratory, and vital energies, both severally and in combination, of the animal organism. The higher, indeed, the sphere of its applications, the more certain and absolute is the reign of law throughout the works of God. The conditions of bodily welfare pertain, variously, to the subjects of light, air, heat, water, diet, clothing, exercise, climate, occupation, and all the mental and moral habitudes of the mind. Health is the nice and even balance of many delicate and subtle elements and agencies, at work in every part of the complicated framework of our entire being. Some, in seeking to regain their health, attach quite too much importance to mere muscular exercise, which alone, as many well know, will do but little towards the thorough renovation of the physical system. Here, as in other things, "bodily exercise profiteth little;" little, if not mixed largely with other and better things. A wide circle of many influences must be concentrated, as in the balancings of the upper spheres, on the point desired; and, above all, within the wheels of even animal life must be for its living spirits, giving them all their motion, faith, hope, and charity: the only abiding elements of power and progress, of health and beauty, in the human bosom. Alas! how little of religion is there or even of science, in the mode in which most men treat their bodies! How are its strings, which are skilfully attuned to the wants of three-score years and ten by its Maker, so broken over all the earth, that the average life of the race does not amount to even half that brief term of life! Those who grasp most eagerly after the mere pleasures of the body, most abuse it in the act of doing so, and take the directest course possible to lose even the petty prize for which they seek. Whatever laws God hath seen fit to make for us, we must see fit to keep. Christianity alone dignifies the body, as it makes this fleshy tabernacle the temple of the immortal soul; yea, rather of God its Maker. Your bodies, saith Paul, are the temples of the Holy Ghost; and him that defileth the temple of God, shall God destroy.

2d. Thorough mental industry, especially about great commanding objects.

The body, like a flute or viol, is all the more improved perpetually, as the music of sweet and stirring thoughts is breathed through it. The greatest impressions made on the vital forces of the body are made from within, and not from without.

The currents of life in our veins are chiefly, for the fulness and strength of their tide, what the mind itself makes them. There is no one law more fully enthroned in all the inner chambers of the soul, in respect to its own conscious pleasure, or the greatness of the results of its action to others, than that of the necessity of constant, earnest employment. Not more truly must one lay out all his powers to climb a lofty precipice, than we must toil with continual though delighted energy, to make any just approaches to that sphere of neighborhood to God in our aims and efforts, for which we were made. For such a life of ever renewed lofty labor our minds were constituted; as was the body to sustain and serve just such natures, in their highest courses of action. Thorough, successful mental labor; and to be successful it must be thorough and unremitted: is one of the greatest of all stimulants to health, and of all safeguards of it. The higher the object of pursuit, and the more perpetual the felt inspiration of its claims, the deeper and richer will be the satisfaction of strong and steady toil to obtain it. The face of a vigorously industrious man has a light in it, that other faces have not. A man's wisdom, saith Solomon, maketh his face to shine; and the impudence of his countenance is taken away. His step has a force and quickness in it, his form an erectness, and his whole bearing an air that publishes to every one the arrival of a true man, wherever he goes.

3. Habitual cheerfulness.

There is everything in God and nature, and in the work of life and its results, to fill the heart with joy in running its earthly career. We are capable, also, of possessing such a style and assemblage of Christian graces; and there are so many inducements, invitations, summons and helps to us to obtain and exercise them; that it is wholly our own fault, if a single drop of bitterness remains in the cup of sweets, which our Father in heaven presents to us here below. Whose heart was not made to be, and therefore cannot and ought not at all times to be, full of gratitude, love, faith, hope, zeal, and holy peace? Such exercises ever spreading their light and heat over the soul, and through the soul over the various functions of the body, will stimulate all their energies into a full growth. Earnest self-improvement, constant happy service unto others and full devotion to God: what will not these do, when combined, to quicken and strengthen the innermost elements of life in the organism of the body?

But careful, full conformity to the physical laws of our being, thorough mental industry and habitual cheerfulness, are not surely haphazard qualities, of which a youth can become possessed, he knows not how. His guides to manly greatness must zealously lead him to seek and to obtain these permanent resources of health, honor, and happiness.

Secondly. In reference to the intellect.

It is in this part of our nature, that we differ most from the other orders of beings around us. Here is the throne of our manhood. The very word man, coming from the same root as the Latin mens, mind ; memini and reminiscor, to remember ; moneo, to admonish ; and Minerva, the goddess of wisdom ; and as also the Greek μένος, courage ; μῆνις, wrath, μνάομαι, to remember ; and μηνύειν, to reveal ;* as well as the German mann and mensch, a man ; and meinen, to guess or intend ; means a thinker : so that he belies his very designation as a man, who neglects to use and improve his mind, as the very crown and summit of his whole being.

What now is the complement of things to be gained, in this part of our nature, by a true, full education ?

I. Intelligence.

Wonderful, indeed, are the mind's powers of receptivity : opening outwards to all parts of the

* Compare also μαίνομαι, μαντις and μαντεύω and German minne, love ; the Danish minne, remembrance ; and the Slavonic minyeti. to mean.

universe, and capable of taking them all in and expanding also in its dimensions, at each new outlay of its strength. The uses and pleasures of knowledge are the very highest of our being. The kinds of knowledge that must be gained, in a course entitled to be called that of the higher education, are various.

1st. Acquaintance with man.

Into what a proverb of universally acknowledged authority has that pithy saying of Pope's passed, "The proper study of mankind is man." It certainly is one of our proper studies. In ourselves, individually, as in a synopsis or diagram, we are to find all the elements of our science of man; since in each of us are the contents of our whole race. It is always he, who best paints, sings, or preaches his own thoughts and feelings as they are, that most evokes the sympathy and admiration of all around him. The chord of mutual fellowship is, at once, struck deeply in their hearts. The different kinds of acquaintance with man to be gained are such, as,

(1.) The knowledge of human nature.

Our whole life is, from first to last, one of constant relations to others. The social harmonies of our being are the highest part of its frame-work. But how can we gain from others, or give to them what we should, without an adequate comprehension of their most facile points of connection with us. An analysis of the elements of the highest influence over others, whether insensible or direct, and whether in the mere forms of ordinary intercourse or in high governmental relations of any kind, will always detect these two as chief: rightness of principle or thorough reason, system and science in the positions assumed, and kindness in one's feelings and manner in taking them. All who excel in generalship, statesmanship, education, or parental duty, do so by holding these two elements in full combination in their work. Kindness means treating others, as belonging to the same kind. This is the origin of the word; as of humane from human, and of generous from genus: all indicating a disposition in full acquaintance and sympathy with the race at large. But what room is there, in employing the elements of power over others already mentioned, for ever-varying additions of patience, tact, skill, plan and prayer in the mode of reaching the desired result, both by way of not evoking any passions, prejudices, or suspicions against us, and also by way of introducing the influence which we wish to exert in the most insinuating and winning manner. The knowledge of human nature can be best communicated to another, by the constant exhibition of its practical use. Opportunities of incidental instruction, also, in its elements occur perpetually in teaching the philosophy of history, and in traversing the rich and ever varying field of study in the classical authors. And if there is one spot of all the earth that furnishes, beyond any other, incessant occasions for discovering and watching the developments of human nature, it is the school room ; and here too if anywhere, a skilful acquaintance with its principles is in ever new demand, at all times.

(2.) The knowledge of human history.

By knowing what man has been, during the ages that have gone, under every variety of climate, education, religion and social development, we are best prepared to learn what he is in himself, without reference to any outward conditions. It is man that gives to every mountain, river, sea, ocean, or continent, all its value, as these are but his surroundings, and contrived to be as they are, only to make his nature all the more super-eminent.

The study of history is one of the most liberalizing of all studies. It gratifies the curiosity : it furnishes endless food for thought ; and it multiplies our own experience for breadth and value by as many fold, as the area of our observation is extended outwardly from ourselves. All human character and conduct, fate and fortune, are covered up within its ample folds. The older the thinker or writer, the larger his stores of thought and the wider the scope of his powers, the higher always is the estimate, that he sets upon the value of historical knowledge.

History must be studied philosophically, and its lessons conned over and over again, or its rich harvests of truths will be only looked at, but not reaped by the student. The true history of a nation is its inner, not its outer history: the history of its courses of thought, purpose and achievement. Its external show of bustle, pomp and pride may please children, who like noise and glitter, but not a real man, who looks beneath the surface after the hidden springs of all that at any time appears upon it. The track of historical investigation that every truly educated man should traverse with care, beside that passing through the dimmer regions of antiquity, in Egypt, Phoenicia, Judea, and western Asia : beginning with Greece, where the historic muse first combined exactness and fulness of record, with high elevation of style, passing through Rome and the Middle Ages and modern Europe, as such, branches off into separate lines of special interest, through Germany, Holland, France, Italy, Spain, England and America ; with all of which countries the developments of modern progress are greatly connected. It is singular, indeed, that our scholars are so generally contented, to be ignorant of the history of Germany and of Holland ; to which two countries we are more indebted than to all others of the present day, except England. To Germany we owe, to a high degree, our blood and language and reformed faith and scholarship ; and, like England, Germany deserves from modern society at large, for its intellectual explorations and discoveries, for its many practical inventions, and for its general spirit of progress, the highest possible appreciation and gratitude.

History should be taught so as to hold up the facts and principles of our natures, as men, in a clear magnified form before the eye ; to show in general the onward movement of Humanity from age to age, as well as the particular steps of its progress ; to interpret the slowly unfolding scroll of Divine Providence ; and to make indeed the whole gorgeous past move as a vast connected drama, with its different acts and scenes, from one fixed beginning in man, to an equally fixed issue in God, of whom and for whom are all things on earth and in Heaven.

(3.) The knowledge of human language and literature.

Language is, for all its uses, the chief of earthly studies. It is in itself alone, as a piece of mechanism, of the deepest interest ; and with such endless connections does each language run into and out of others, before, around and behind it, that no one can be studied with any adequacy by itself alone.

Language is our first intellectual want ; and there is nothing next after our limbs, that, to the end of life, we use so much. There is no such other mode in which we are always doing good or harm. Life and death are in the power of the tongue ; and therefore by our words we shall be justified, and by our words we shall be condemned.

There is no intellectual discipline at all equal to the study of language, for variety and force of stimulation to every faculty. No one is really educated who has not made it a study ; and no attention to it can be called a study which is not analytic and philosophical, and which does not centre in the classical languages, as its great fountain of interest Variety and fulness of linguistic culture are specially demanded, in the American system of education, beyond any thing yet generally conceived. All those languages should be embraced in our system of education, with which as such our own language is most fully connected ; and whose history and literature have attained to any large growth and maturity.

The whole system of female education in this country is, in this respect, radically deficient in its style. Its foundation is mathematics, and should be language. Woman has special endowments and qualifications for success in the mastery of language ; and, next to the power of her character and disposition if lovely and refined, there is no instrument of such great and constant potency within her grasp, as skill in the use of language. Elegance in conversation, and the skilful .use of the pen in correspondence and composition, are intellectual ornaments, which every cultivated lady should obtain and keep with diligence. Many a woman, capable of exalted usefulness and happiness, now walks through her earthly history with little strength or zeal or joy, unconscious of her own real undeveloped nobility of mind ; because untrained to the clear, definite, earnest expression of thought, and to any high sensibility to the charms of beautiful language.

The so-called female college or university, that shall revolutionize the present basis and mode of conducting female education, and mark out for its pupils a thorough, persistent course of wide and high study in the languages, ancient and modern, will do a work for the age and the female sex and the world, for which the centuries have been long waiting.

Philology has recently, by a wondrous series of explorations, brought to light a wide array of most curious and valuable facts, concerning the different languages of the world, whether viewed singly or in combination. There is no more inviting field of research now open before an earnest, deep-searching mind. Here is a land abounding in mines of gold and precious stones. Labor is sure of its reward, and glittering prizes on every side await discovery.

There is a true high Christian method of teaching the classics, worthy of the name. In the elegant contributions of ancient authors to the poetry, history, literature and philosophy of the world, we see as in a mirror, the social ideas and habits and manners of their times ; and in what grand delightful contrast to the wants and woes of heathen civilization, in its most refined form, do the laws and institutions, the customs and comforts, of modern Christendom reveal themselves to view. Perpetual opportunity is here furnished for tracing the directions, degrees and processes of human advancement. And how can the wants of our moral nature be exhibited, and the need of special divine revelation for the right shaping of our opinions and our lives, when wandering amid such a vast collection of intellectual and spiritual ruins ! In contrast also with that corrupt mythology, amid the sensual imagery of which so many love to tarry, as if pure poetic idealism and moral impurity could, by any possibility, be truly and beautifully joined together, how does the innate loveliness of Bible-truth appear : as the prophet of the old covenant, and the apostle of the new, make the pontiff and the augur of heathen Rome appear side by side with them, like savages, standing rough and grim in the presence of men, whose faces are illuminated with sublime thought and sweet benevolent feeling.

Literature and its history also furnish a large and fruitful field of study and instruction. Here language is employed, not as in the daily intercourse of life, for present uses, but as the guardian of the precious treasures of thought and experience, laid by in the past for the benefit of all succeeding ages. Here are to be found, alike, the selectest monuments of human genius, and the most enduring memorials of human toil.

The historic literature of the world hangs together, in a connected chain of sequences, from first to last. Modern literature is but the broader and fuller efflorescence of the higher growths of thought, that have appeared on the summits of each preceding age. This age is what it is, and English literature has become what it is, because Greece and Rome, and Italy, Germany, France, Spain and Holland, from whom in various degrees it has derived its substance, form and features, were each respectively what they were. There is no one body of literature of such majestic proportions, and of so many beautiful and divine aspects, as our own; and this, according not only to our own view which might be unconsciously perverted, but that also of the great men of other nations, as loudly proclaimed in many directions. Our own literature, I have said ; for we are richer in literature than even England herself, as we own all hers and ours also. It is a great defect in our common style of personal self-improvement, as well as of our system of public instruction, that so little account is had, or rather in most cases no account at all is had, of the vast continent of literature to be found in our language : excelling in breadth and variety and the luxuriance of its growths, all the literature of the world, present and past beside. Surely here again, "the prophet is without honor in his own country." There ought to be, in all our Colleges, a professorship of English literature, whose function it should be to unfold its history, in rich living discourse, with ample sketches of the leading literary men of England and America, accompanied with a broad and generous spirit of criticism upon the substance and style of the great works in our language : a professorship, the text-book for whose recitations should be Shakspeare ; which ought to be for its own worth and the value of its influence in training our young men to the highest style of native growth, a classic held in the greatest honor, by those of Trans-Atlantic and Cis-Atlantic English blood alike. In connection with our own literature, the man of any thing like full education will acquaint himself with Grecian and Roman literature also, without a thorough knowledge of which, indeed, he cannot understand or appreciate our own ; as well as with German and French belles-lettres, especially German, so full of all vital energies of thought and feeling. Æsthetical culture brings great rewards to its possessor, both in respect to his high personal enjoyment and in respect to his influence, as a thinker and writer over others. No eye can gaze unmoved upon structures of beauty in the world of thought, or see them rise as if by magic like fairy castles, under hands skilful in rearing them, without admiration.

To this department of study, criticism and rhetoric belong, the two chief forms of literary art ; which are of the highest value when supplemental to previous courses of thorough mental discipline, but are never to be, as they sometimes have been, substituted for them. As well might one think of filling the parts of a huge edifice which should be occupied by solid masonry, with the light ornamental work that belongs only to its finishings.

(4.) The knowledge of human wants.

The true object of education is, to acquire the power and the disposition to do good to the highest possible degree. As the will is made sovereign in the constitution of the mind itself, so the moral is the crowning glory of all the powers and faculties of our entire manhood. It is the law prevailing throughout the whole universe of minds, that he who has obtained treasures of any kind must share them with others ; or be made miserable by withholding them. It is as logically and practically necessary for a man to know the actual state of the world in which and for which he is fitting himself to act ; and whose demands upon his thoughts and labors he is to meet rightly, or his life will be a failure : as for one who is constructing a steam engine or a telescope, to understand well the principles to be followed, and the ends to be gained by his mechanism, when completed. Many make in education the same mistake that others do in religion : in treating it as if having a distinct existence by itself, separate from its relations. But all things are for their uses ; and all the wonders and beauties of their being are found in their many and marvellous adaptations to those uses ; and so among the whole army of intelligent beings, he that would be the greatest of all must be the servant of all. To do good as we have opportunity : this is the law that is not only appointed of God, but reigns self-ordained also over every being that possesses reason and conscience. So many have lack-lustre eyes in their studies, because they have no great controlling object of thought and interest in view. The mind is made to lay out its force upon the objective world, as upon it also that outer world is made to pour perpetually all its myriad influences.

Each is made for the other ; and as in the partnership of kindred hearts in life it is not good for either to be alone. The reason why so many fail in the various professions : as indeed well nigh the great majority do : is because they make a wrong selection for themselves ; and this, because their ulterior aims are such as to pervert their judgment and their action.

Another of the general forms of intelligence to be gained in the higher education, is,

2d. Acquaintance with science.

All sciences and all branches of knowledge have been interwoven with each other into a beauteous garment of praise to their great Author ; which like a royal robe of many colors he has dropped, as if with purposed carelessness, among his earthly children, that they might in disentangling its materials learn to know him in the greatness of his power and the goodness of his love.

The sciences, so-called, are the exact sciences, (or the mathematics,) the natural sciences, and mental, moral, legal and political science, or the science of political economy. Some knowledge of the mathematics is absolutely necessary to the most ordinary transactions of business. The utilities of mixed mathematics, from simple arithmetic up to any and all of the applications of trigonometry and conic sections, are obvious as a matter of practical profit to those who employ them. But pure mathematics, from algebra through all parts of the calculus, have in them a higher value still to the mind itself, in the inward wrestling to which they summon it with difficulties, in that invisible, wondrous thought-land, where an intellect of bold, strong tread most loves to wander. The higher walks and visions and exhilarations of mathematical science, must of course be reserved for that little circle of minds, which are so charmed with its abstractions, as to leave every thing else neglected by the wayside in order to seek after them. Great absorption in this one field of investigation, as indeed in any other, can be had only at the sacrifice of inquiry and progress somewhere else. For the general purposes of education, the mathematics do not compare at all in power of drill, and variety of mental exercise, and so of consequent mental growth, with the classics.

As to the natural sciences : they are all, more or less, and generally in the most intimate manner connected with the mathematics, according to whose principles the inward elements of matter are mixed together, and its outward forms are constructed. No education can be complete, which passes by the laws and forces of nature : as with them every man is connected, in some way, at every moment. He acts on them, and through them at all times. By new combinations of some of their most subtle agencies, or new uses of old combinations, some of the highest points of progress in our age have been reached. And certainly that science, which concerns itself specifically with the human organism, and with the vital elements of its health and growth and force, claims with more imperativeness than any other the earnest attention of every educated man.

Many of the natural sciences are of very recent discovery, as geology, chemistry and physiology; and yet these are among the sciences that are now most influential upon human thought and progress. Geology has given eyes to men which can penetrate the surface of the earth, and read the mystic contents of its dark bosom; so that, like Le Verrier before the observer pointed the instrument toward the new star that he could himself announce but could not see, the geologist ere the laborer lifts his spade can point with a sure finger to the mines of coal, or iron, or gold, that lie deep out of sight beneath. Chemistry, also, has broken the seals that before held the secret essences of things together; and taught us how to loose or bind, at our will, the hidden ties of their connection. The very lightning, the most untamable in itself of all God's ministers among the winds and flaming fire, has been made to come and go at our bidding, on errands great and small, and to quietly spell out our various human alphabets : sounding distinctly every letter across seas and continents in the hearing of all nations. From the science of physiology, what leaves of healing, as from the Tree of Life, have been scattered over all this generation ! It has given additional honor to the body and to our life in it, and poured streams of gladness into all the fountains of our earthly experience. Many of the natural sciences, also, have made such great advancement during the last century, as though possessing the same name to have yet become themselves quite new sciences ; as natural philosophy, in all its departments, especially in electricity and galvanism ; astronomy, in its improved instruments and discoveries ; mineralogy and botany, which have been wondrously enlarged in their contents and beautified in their arrangements. The pursuit of the natural sciences, beside the general advantage which it furnishes of enlarging the boundaries of knowledge, and multiplying greatly the topics of thought, and the materials for analogical reasoning and illustration, has also a high value as a special variation of the best mode of mental discipline : furnishing, in connection with all the other elements of educational improvement for the young, a wide and diversified range of appeals and stimulations and rewards to the spirit of study. But, adopted as the sole path

5

of intellectual development, as if having any sufficiency in itself to compass all the ends to be gained, it realizes but a very partial benefit to the student: giving him large information and pleasure, but robbing him of all those higher growths of strength and beauty of mind, which can be acquired only by the wide, philosophical and artistic study of language. Here is the great defect of the French university system, which not only rests on the mathematics and natural sciences as its base, but confines almost its whole amplitude within them. The German system which lays its foundations in linguistic culture, is right in its great fundamental idea, but inadequate in the structure which it rears upon them. Their whole education, as such, is linguistic education. In France, science, and in Germany, language, is pursued as an end and not as a means except for the mere purposes of a livelihood. The end sought is the pleasures of intellectual conquest, or the rewards of honor; while in every case the only objects to be aimed at in an education are, on the one hand, to develop in full perfection the secret germinal forces and elements of the mind, as such, and on the other to prepare each individual to pursue through life the most high and manly course possible, of purposed toil for God and his fellow-men. Neither the French nor German system have the impress of humanity and Christianity upon them. Utility is not the law of their being. In the English, and particularly the American system, when enlarged and perfected in all its details especially in the department of language, is the truest model yet conceived of what the people that are to be will ere long erect as their standard of general education in all countries and ages.

The natural sciences ought to be taught, so as always to show the great architect of Heaven and Earth, manifestly revealed in His works. Those works are everywhere full of mechanical principles and adaptations, and press in many varied forms perpetually the argument of design upon our hearts ; one of whose first and deepest intuitions it is, that design everywhere presupposes, by necessity, a designer. In the adaptations of anatomy, one to the other, and the wonderful conformation of man's structure in all parts of his nature to the elements and resources of the surrounding universe, from which he is to draw his experience, and on which and through which he is to work his will : himself, though so small, yet the actual counterpart of all that is without him and around him ; how plainly do we see the skilful loving mighty handiwork of God ! And, in the minute mathematical and dynamical proportions and analytical discriminations of chemistry, as well as in all the vast, and yet well-defined records of geology, what secret, and at the same time what intelligible and unmistakable proofs of God's presence, amid the forces and essences of nature, to guide them to His own high ends and to man's uses for His kingdom and glory! Since the assent of the mind is so instant and instinctive to the necessary connection between every contrivance and its contriver, that no two things can be jointed or framed together, however rudely, without creating the feeling, as infallibly as if a matter of vision itself, that it is the work of some designing human hand; it is wonderful, that such a pile of multitudinous appeals should be set up everywhere before the human mind by God, to this so instinctive quick and necessary conviction. Geology of all the sciences is foremost in necessitating the admission on the part of all who know its facts, that every thing now living upon earth has had a recent beginning, and so a recent origination in the will of some great Contriving Hand. Animal Physiology too shows, in each animal structure as in every other one of the same species, and in the last as precisely and wonderfully as in the first one of the kind, the same numerous inward specialties and harmonies of plan and correlation: part with part and each part with the whole. Here God, the great benevolent Creator of man, shows Himself as plainly to the eye of Reason as well as of Faith, as when first entering upon the execution of His great world-plan. Here therefore science should show Him and His footsteps to the view.

Mental science, or the science of the human mind, bears in its very designation its title to the first rank of human studies. With logic, the science of reasoning, it forms one of the best of all modes of strengthening the intellectual faculties, when in their higher stages of power and progress. In metaphysical studies, indeed, the loftiest minds in all ages have delighted to dwell, like eagles in their mountain homes. The greatest forces that have moved the world in any age have been metaphysical. To a mind at all addicted to coasting around the shore of things invisible, and hovering about its secret wonders, to one that knows the mystic spell of abstract thought, there is a pleasure, a rapture rather, in philosophic speculation, which is to be found outside of the realm of holy work and worship, nowhere else.

Moral science, or ethics, must have also its proper place in the course of the higher education. This is the science of human duty. It determines the sphere of right and wrong for both individuals and communities, in all the relations of life. Its facts and principles are much more plain, than those of metaphysics; and the profit of the study is, rather, distinctively moral than intellectual.

Legal science pertains to the whole scope and

sphere of human laws, whether founded in natural equity, common custom, or positive statute. Here is the realm of nice distinctions and close definitions, and of strong argumentation, welded and clamped and riveted together. Both as a matter of mental discipline and of personal information, the study of the general principles of law, that is, of its great elementary facts and features as a science, is, if not as a matter of absolute necessity yet as one of very great value, worthy to be embraced in the specific course which deserves to be called that of the higher education.

The science of political economy, although of but recent establishment, is one of the noblest of the inductive sciences. Its deductions are large indeed, having applications as wide, not only as the boundaries of national development and prosperity, but also as those of humanity itself, in all the mutual bearings of international exchanges, and the social stimulations and advantages of general commercial intercourse. In a country, where each man directly decides who shall rule its interests and according to what policy ; and where, at any moment, he may be elevated himself by popular suffrage to offices of trust and service of the highest kind, the science of political economy, at once so profound, engaging and profitable. should be of course included in a high and true style of preparation for the duties of life.

From the rapid survey now taken of the sphere of knowledge to be possessed by the true scholar, how obvious is it that the prevailing ideas on the subject of academic, collegiate and professional education alike, are altogether too narrow! The time is coming because it is needful that it should, when the lad of ordinary endowments and attainments, at twelve, shall be led for six short, not long, successive years through a preparatory course of earnest, vigorous, ever-triumphant study: in the classics, through all the vast variety of rich, delightful fields of investigation that they open in ground forms, syntax, prosody, etymology, grammatical and lexical, both special and comparative, antiquities, geography, biography and history: in the mathematics, up to the broad and glowing plane of its higher elements and formulas: in geography and history, ancient and modern, over all their wide enchanting fields of interest; and in the ancient and modern languages, especially the French and German, to the point of a full and facile possession, not only of the languages themselves, but also of much of their best literature. With such an outfit secured, and made permanent by the most accurate and energetic drill throughout, especially in grammar in all its full scientific elements and relations; with the superadded advantage of a complete comprehension and appreciation of the facts of physiology, so as to know and to keep the rules of health: the young academician of a future day will be ready to enter upon the more advanced stage of university-education, which will then be opened before him. Into that higher form, our present, low, collegiate style of education must ere long be raised. Through six, instead of four years, the eager student well accoutred for his work, fond of intellectual labor and panting to conquer new difficulties, should be led in this part of his course also: beginning for his first year with those studies which are now assigned to the second or third year of the college course, and mounting up along a path of much more complete daily toil than is now assigned for him, year after year, into one region after another of the highest and broadest, most analytic and philosophic study, in the departments of language, science, criticism and art, throughout the whole range of the ancient classics and of the modern, especially the English and German. With three years more of strict professional study, studying both the science and the history of it; deeply and gladly involved in the precious toil of original composition, and in inspiring converse, all the time, with the elect minds of all ages bending in holy silence from the thrones of their written thoughts to greet him: what a preparation for entering on the work of making thought for others, and guiding their actions to great issues, would such an one have! What young giants at twenty-seven would then be found among us, instead of the pigmies at fifty, not a few of them covered with titles to conceal their nakedness, which are now quite too abundant over all the land.

Another of the higher kinds of intelligence to be gained is,

3d. Acquaintance with nature.

Nature is the home of beauty; for it is God's pavilion among the sons of men. Here, as Adam heard the voice of the Lord God walking among the trees of the garden, the man of true thought and feeling meets everywhere, and almost in open vision, the great, good Father of lights who seems to be, as he is, everywhere waiting to be gracious unto him. Here is perpetual refreshment for the eye and the heart. Many have indeed managed the sublime work of education in a way that divorced the victims of their perverted ideas from nature, and art and man and God, and left them in an intensely isolated state, at the best, of mere elegant good-for-nothingness; but a true education ends in the marriage of the soul to every thing great and good and true in the universe. As poets delight to gather garlands of flowers from the fields, and hang them around the necks of the muses; as kings lavishly adorn their walls within, for their own eyes, with pictures of the beauty that is without, on which every one can gaze nor ask permission: as divine revelation comes clothed to us in a garb of many colors, taken from heaven and earth; so, of all places in the world, the silent, meditative walks of the student should be carefully festooned with beauty; and his cloistered chamber should be fragrant with the scent of Eden. As Truth is his attending Genius in the world of thought, so should Beauty be in that of sight. What vivid illustrations can one who loves nature himself, draw to his work as a teacher; and with what perpetual relish and profit by his pupils, as did the divine Saviour, who so loved the mountains and the sea, in his instructions to his disciples! Their imagination craves such food: it belongs to them; and he who negligently or unconsciously withholds it from them, robs them of something far more precious than food or raiment.

A youth should be taught both at home and in school; and for this reason, life in the country is so much better than in the city; to observe the ever-changing forms and scenes of nature, around and above him. Fine landscapes, sunrises and sunsets, the ever-varying clouds, majestic storms with their thunder-trumpets, the moon and stars by night, mountain heights, dells, and gorges and deep caves, the solemn hush of the forest, and its more solemn moan, the calm hour of twilight, the noise of waterfalls, the laughing stream, the placid lake, the surging sea, the universal chorus of birds, as the gates of day open at dawn and shut at eve upon us, and all nature full, in high keys and low, of the voices of happy creatures summering away their lives in gladness : what endless food do these all furnish for the inspiration of thought and feeling !

Beauty of form or outline is to be seen and studied in nature, as also beauty of color or of light and shade ; and not alone these mere external aspects, but also the inward order of mechanism, and the designs of love that they reveal, and of which the glittering or elegant exterior is but the fitting enclosure.

It is surely one of the most surprising proofs of man's inward blindness, that nature, the very book whose letters are largest, and which God holds most closely before the eyes of men, and the only one containing the lessons of His wisdom and love, which is ever opened to the mass of mankind, is still the very one, in which the great majority of the race read not a lesson, and see not even a single letter.

Let no student feel, wherever he is, that he is denied a high and true intercourse with nature. There are walks for meditation, and heights for prospect even in the crowded city, where swarms cover every open space, and where all original variations of surface are carefully evened ; and the scenery of the sky is there, and of the sea or of some mighty stream hastening towards it ; whose bosom is ever heaving with the burdens of commerce, and within whose arms its sails, like doves whispering to each other, gather themselves together. And in the want of all material stimulations to poetic sensibility, there are yet books full of thought-pictures of the selectest beauty, which indeed have been nearly always drawn with the most effect by those, who amid the cares of city life have pined for the remembrances of a youth spent under more open skies, and on broader fields, and under the shadow of the everlasting hills.

Another of the higher forms of intelligence to be gained, is,

4th. Acquaintance with art.

Among the elements of the higher education, should be instruction in the principles of art. By art is meant in the abstract the theory, and in the concrete the faculty, of rightly executing, or expressing, the more tender, beautiful, or sublime conceptions of the human mind. Art is therefore the revealer of the best moods of humanity on the one hand, and of the highest capacities on the other, of the objects on which the artist works, to receive and to keep the image of himself and of his thoughts, that he would stamp upon them. Art has its great generalizations and its grand ideals, and may be taught and studied in the sphere of its general relations and uses, without centralizing one's thoughts on any one specific department of it. The careful study of Reynolds and Ruskin, than whom no modern writer displays more power and beauty of thought, will open the eye to see and the heart to feel, through what a world of wonders our path of daily life, however common, passes. In what heathenish neglect is the art-side of our natures left by almost every one, who assumes or ventures upon the holy work of educating them, whether at home or at school! Man has indeed an organism of susceptibilities and capacities, vaster than it has entered into the hearts of most men to conceive; and the work of leading him up to glory and to God is the grandest work, for height and breadth, in which the efforts of any one can be employed.

But there is a still higher form yet of intelligence to be gained: higher in itself, and higher in its results.

5th. Acquaintance with the word and character and plans of God.

The grand fact of the universe absorbing all others in its vast dimensions, is this: God is. Any and all finite creatures, however numerous or mighty, and all their affairs are but mere motes appearing in the universal blaze of his being, and made visible by it. Every thing pertaining to him, or his ways, is immediately aggrandized by the connection. The Bible, as his word, is rightly denominated in its very title, The Book. No other on earth has such heights in it to climb, none such depths to sound. No book has such power in it to educate the intellect for force of logic, beauty of conception, breadth of view, tone of feeling or sweep of thought; for it is God's book. It is the great enigma of our educational system, devised as it has been by Christian men, that this sacred volume not only does not occupy a conspicuous central place in it, but not even for educational purposes any place at all. The Mohammedan bases his whole system of full long school-instruction on the Koran, the Hindû upon the Vêdas, and the Papist on the interpretations and traditions and perversions of the fathers; but we who alone have the glorious word of the great God of heaven and earth, instead of bearing it with joy and triumph into the recitation- and lecture-rooms of our high schools and universities, keep it well bound and gilded as a cabinet curiosity in our houses or our hearts. But the Bible is yet to have free course and to be glorified, in our colleges and academies, as in all the world beside. Its history and literature should be studied and made familiar, by the educated youth of our land. Its geography and antiquities should be mapped out clearly in their thoughts, as are the marvels of foreign countries in the memory of travellers who have visited them. Its great men and their great deeds, its many poets, orators, prophets, apostles, and heroes should ever people their imaginations, as an army of light, moving with the Lord's banners over the highway of the past to the land that is above. It should be made the book of life to them, by making its truths a living fire on the altar of their hearts. The character of God as our Father: his intimate presence in fact and at heart with us; and his high governorship over all our thoughts and ways; and all the fulness of his many great and loving relations to us, should be joyously and flamingly held up as a torch of sacred light before the young, in all our courses of education. In his personal, watchful, ever-brooding care for each one of the race is contained the whole mystery of life, as a matter of his ordination, as well as the whole doctrine of its work and worth to us. His plans in behalf of man, or the great scheme of redemption which contains them all, should ever stand clear and high like a pyramid of light, before their thoughts. It is because of his designs of mercy, that the world stands at all, and that the generations of men come and go one after another upon its surface. And ought a young man to be so educated in a Christian college or school, as to know and think a great deal more about the Acropolis at Athens, or the temple of the Parthenon upon its brow, or the statue of the goddess within, and even its ornaments of gold and ivory and the sacred peplum upon its limbs, than about the very object and end of his own formation, and of that of the world itself? No muse, or grace, or nymph, could so adorn a Grecian grove, fountain or poem, as the genius of religion will beautify any fireside, school or heart, in which it is invited to make its abode.

Our attention has been confined thus far to the department of education called intelligence, and the elements immediately connected with it, because for space and time it is so large in itself, and because it is the foundation of all the rest, as containing the facts on which and with which our minds are to act.

The next point to be gained in the plan of the higher education, beside the right kind and amount of intelligence, is,

II. Aspiration.

Man is placed at the outset at the bottom of the scale of intelligence and development, and taught to look ever upwards. Voices from above are perpetually calling in love to him, Come up higher! Every thing that can be done to inspire the soul to desire and strife and hope for what is beyond, is among the selectest bestowments of either heaven or earth. No part of the work of a true education is more neglected than this. When once the mind becomes fully awake to the consciousness of itself, and has a true sense of what God is and what life is under him, and for him; when it feels the powers of the world to come, breathing like a wind from Heaven upon all its being, and it sets all its faculties astir to fulfil its whole destiny, what loftiness of purpose! what strength of zeal! what energy and constancy of action will it evince in its high calling! No man has any credentials from God for assuming the great work of a teacher, who is not himself full of the new wine of love for his work. His mind whether resting or moving any where must be so occupied with great thoughts at all times, as to be surrounded perpetually with a contagious aura of vitalizing influences, into which whoever comes will find his nature kindling at once into a blaze. And no one has really obtained a true education, who does not wear "zeal" for all high and good things, "as a cloak." This is the very meaning of the word industry which, like the words endue and endow, comes from the Latin induo, to put on or wear. It must be as much a part of the man in all his public life, as his very garments, seen by all men wherever he is seen.

Another great end to be secured is,

III. Not only the power but the habit also of constant, full, disciplined application of all one's energies, in right directions.

Information and aspiration are valuable ends to be secured, only as they shall become helps and means to the true work of life and the right development of the soul itself in conducting it. As a fountain is constructed to receive the streams ministered unto it, only to bestow them copiously upon those who need ; so the mind is made capable of receiving, merely for the purpose of giving. Work is the law of life to all intelligent beings, from God to the lowest creature made in his image. "My Father worketh hitherto," saith Christ, "and I work." And our work, like that of God, must be for others. "No man liveth to himself; and no man dieth to himself." Each man is appointed of God, in his very constitution, to be a light-bearer to the world. Different indeed are the forms and degrees of light, that we are made capable of bearing ; but yet our work is, for each and all of us, everywhere the same, to "shine, that others may see our good works :" luminous with the inward light of a true noble character, and with the outward glow of God's manifest smile upon us and presence with us. Do men need discipline, drill and application, earnest and true, in order to accomplish ordinary useful ends, in social development and enterprise ; and how much more, in the matter of distributing best to the world the divine resources of their own immortal natures, over the wide area of all their physical, intellectual and moral activity, in behalf of their own age and of all succeeding ages. Men are made by their Maker to excel in different kinds and degrees of work. What work any one can perform, and therefore was made to perform, and in what style of thoroughness and finish, can never be known, except by the fullest possible preparation of his powers for working, the most vigorous outlay of them when employed, and the steady holding of the highest of all possible objects of desire and effort before the mind in their employment ; together with that earnest, importunate looking of the soul to God in faith for his blessing upon every effort, which secures the addition of his strength to our own, in our enterprises.

IV. Full power of communicating the treasures of light and love possessed, unto others.

The real end of all true education is objective, is benevolence : the distribution of thought and truth to those that have them not, and the outlay of one's self for the world's good in every form of action, in a more intelligent, effective and beneficial manner, than otherwise. A miserly spirit of self-appropriation here, which is universally pronounced miserable in the very sense of the word miserly itself, is more base than in the use of money ; as light and knowledge are of so much higher value, and their bestowment is so much richer in its results.

Men once ruled others by the club, the sceptre, or the sword ; and emblems of such a sort are still placed everywhere in the hands of titled nobles and magistrates ; but the rulers of the world now, where thinking men are found, are those who wield that little but mighty instrument, the pen ; and these are they whose hearts and tongues are most vitalized with truth and thought and love. Living hearts, living tongues, and living pens : these are the modern names for the weapons of which Paul spoke, when he said "the weapons of our warfare are mighty." Mighty indeed in all ages and places is the truth spoken in love : the mightiest power on earth, next to the Spirit of God himself, whose word it is.

Speech is the noblest vehicle of human thought and feeling, and not of human only, but also of divine. "The tongue is a little member, but boasteth great things." Well did the great generals of antiquity know, that the swords that flashed with thought struck sharpest and deepest, and remained unbroken longest ; and therefore relied quite as much, on what words could do beforehand to put a living spirit within the implements of battle, as on what the arm could do at the time, in wielding them. He who remembers what the two great leaders of the Church, in the two chief epochs of its history, were, and how they executed their work: Moses in the Jewish world and Paul in the Christian ; and so he who comprehends what such men as Demosthenes and Socrates and Cicero did, each in their own land and age, and how they did it ; or in more modern times what Luther and Calvin, and hundreds like them who have battled for truth and freedom and God, aimed to accomplish and in what way ; such an one will see and feel that simple, earnest, loving speech from one overflowing human heart to another is the most powerful instrumentality that man ever uses upon his fellow-men. The great Saviour himself when upon earth sought to do little else, because that alone was so much, than to stand up and speak meekly and yet powerfully of God and truth and heaven and the soul, to all men wherever he could find them, in public or in private.

System, mechanism, organization and contrivances of all sorts, and every kind of policy, outward and inward, he left to others and relied on the simple, living contact of his own loving heart in open, constant converse with the hearts of others. The commission, Go! preach my gospel! is the only order given to his followers, for the mode of spreading the knowledge of his name; and in all ages it has pleased God, by the foolishness of preaching to save those that believe.

Who then can over-estimate the value in our courses of education, of thorough attention to the cultivation of high and true forms of expressing thought, or rather of communicating one's whole self unto others for their good. When all the other advantages of a true education are obtained, then the results of thorough training in composition and declamation, so as to secure the power of uttering one's thoughts in the most vigorous, earnest, tender, moving manner possible, must be superadded to complete the finished man.

This part of a full style of high and true education for the real work of life, among those who are by their education to become the leaders of society, is greatly underrated, in nearly or quite all of our Colleges. How little is actually required of each one, throughout his entire course in this direction! How often is left to the student's own immature valuation, the question of the loss or gain to him of one of the most essential of all modes of preparation for active life!

And what gifts are squandered by so many; and what high faculties for impressing others with great truths and influences, remain voluntarily although unconsciously dormant; faculties which rightly employed might set the hearts of multitudes ablaze with divine truths for ever!

V. Artistic execution.

God is a perfect artist in all his work. Whatever he looks upon, when finished by his own hands, he always sees to be very good; and this pleasurable survey of all his works is no small part of his boundless joy. The more nearly, at whatever distance, any mind approaches his in style of character, the deeper, fuller, richer, sweeter is its sense of beauty, and its capability not only of enjoying but also of executing it. The highest of all forms of art, in respect to the grandeur and variety of its subjects, the diversity of its uses, the number of its beneficiaries and the splendor of its results, is the art of composition: or the art of making, arranging and expressing thought, in a manner that shall best answer the true end to be attained. Here not only do all previous knowledge and training and study find their appropriate outlet, showing perpetually both their fulness and their quality; but also in no way can one so perfect himself in exactness and power and beauty of thought, for the growth of his own mind or the increase of his usefulness, as by the careful and continual practice of the art of composition, upon great themes and for high ends. And while art in general should be greatly magnified as such, in all our higher courses of instruction, this one art itself should be specially taught in all the departments of criticism, taste, and style, throughout the whole breadth of their historical, logical, and rhetorical characteristics. As the utterance of language reacts upon the very processes of thought themselves, establishing and enlarging them, so composition, which is not only the studious elaboration of the outward expression at which point so many stop in all their conceptions of it, but also of all its inward contents, serves wonderfully to heighten and perfect the native vigor of the mind.

Thirdly. In reference to the heart.

The habit which so many have in the work of education, of systematically dealing only with the intellect, or rather of confining their attention and labor to even the most narrow part of its vast dimensions, is morally abnormal and absurd. A man is what his heart is. His faith and hopes and purposes : these are himself, both the foundation and the superstructure of his entire personality. All education in heaven begins and ends with the heart ; and so must it on earth in the family and the school, ere God's will shall be done here as it is above, or man be educated as he designed in making the strange and varied organism of his capabilities, that he should be. The most impressible of all things in this world to outward influence and culture, is man himself. The air and sea, which are perpetually in such a state of flux, are relatively immobile as if made of iron or marble, compared with the intensely vital instincts and impulses of his nature. By insensible imitation almost, he will become what men and things around him claim, invite, or even suggest that he should become. The power of a right example, clothing as in a garment of light all true principles, and of a heart set on fire of heaven and earnestly at work by design to spread the sacred flame among others, is morally irresistible by the young, whose nature has been everywhere purposely thrown wide open by its Maker to all right influences from without.

In the character of its educated men, society has the greatest possible interest. The more mighty for good is an engine, when properly used, the more terrible for evil is it when perverted. The same education, wielded as an instrument of great efficiency by a heart deeply in love with God and man, or by one of only narrow, selfish aims and purposes, will be potent to produce an earth-wide difference of results. How in working iron or steel or harnessing any of the forces of nature, must they be tempered and gauged, and harmonized at the outset, according to the character of their future uses! But how much more necessary to the proper and required issue, is that great neglected and even forgotten work, in all true education, of tempering the heart aright and adjusting all its inner forces to the appointed work of life. From either a perverted, paralyzing sense of the greatness of man's natural propension to evil, or a self-excusing unwillingness to assume and maintain at all times an energetic spirit of duty and effort, most who enter upon the holy office of instructing and forming other minds, neither bestow any earnest, connected labor, nor seem to know that they ought, upon the divine work of rightly moulding and beautifying their characters.

The great points to be gained by the true educator, in the character of all who drink inspiration from his heart and life, are such as these: elevation of thought, refinement, delicacy and tenderness of feeling, self-forgetfulness of aim, energy of purpose, and all pure, bright, joyous religiousness of spirit. Many are the forms in which these may be skilfully and sedulously cultivated; and many the opportunities, in which they may be employed by the teacher, who is himself their possessor. He who diligently seeks them as the treasures of his own character, will by the natural fire and heat of his heart, its spontaneous, ever outspoken fulness of desire, overflowing at all times into every kind and degree of expression, perpetually teach and invite and allure his pupils, to enter with him into the same "pleasant paths of wisdom." Such an one will not need in order to meet in a formal way the sense of duty, to hold up with mock earnestness the dry forms of didactic precepts, as if to discharge his obligations with a will. Men are as little moved to action by skeletons of doctrine, as would be an army, or an audience by the skeleton of a general or of an orator, instead of the living, breathing man of their hearts himself.

Any education which is not thoroughly and delightfully religious, in its whole inward spirit and outward aim, is not only false, but abominable. False preaching and false teaching are the two great masterpieces of Satan's art, in his work of ruin. Man was made wholly for God ; to reach out towards him as a child to its parent, to run lovingly in his footsteps, and to abide in festive union of heart with him forever. For if any man, saith Christ, hear my voice and open the door, I will come in to him and sup with him and he with me. To call, therefore, such treacherous treatment of a youth as terminates not merely in his being indifferent to Him, but even in his not knowing him at all, education, what barbarity is it not only of language but also of sentiment! And so, also, not to see and to feel, in undertaking to fashion the future of the pupil, the fact of his immortality; to stand in the presence of his great soul, with no sense either of its greatness or even of its presence, and much more to sow daily the seeds of eternal joy or sorrow in it, and not be awed by any just conception of the solemn grandeur of such a work; what is such ignoble conduct but absolute contempt of both the present and the future, of time and eternity, of man and of God! Christ, not a dead Christ such as papists hang up as a curiosity in those great mausoleums of souls called cathedrals, or such as hearts unacquainted with his presence may yet describe with all the glow of poetic inspiration; but the living, reigning Christ of heaven and earth, living and reigning in every human heart that opens its everlasting gates to this king of glory, should be cherished universally by the wise men of the West, as, when a babe, the wise men of the East brought unto him gifts and gold and frankincense and myrrh. The odor of his garments, which smell of cassia out of the ivory palaces above, should be in the halls and corridors of all our schools and colleges; and every teacher in them should delight to bathe his feet with tears and to break all precious ointment upon his head. In every form and degree of human culture, Christ is the Model; and constant, earnest, joyful labor: the more joyful the more directly it is laid out in his name: is the rule of service for him and to him; while prayer and praise will ever prove themselves to be to all who try their power, the very wings of successful toil.

The power of Christianity is in its principles, and not at all in its outward conditions; and, therefore, the apostle knew Christ after his departure, no more in the flesh. The power, also, of any human life or character lies in the fact and the degree of its conformity to those principles. The secret of Christ's influence, as a teacher, upon the men of his own age who did not know him as we do, lay in the truths that he uttered with his tongue and represented in his life; and similar results have never failed and can never fail to reappear, in the history of any one whose heart is all aglow with the same fire from heaven.

All systems of education that are not vitally Christian are doomed, like all perverted forms of government, science, literature and religion, in their essential constitution to perish; and as in these other departments of social life, since the Reformation, false ideas, many of them once of giant height and strength, have been melting away in rapid succession, so that infidel poetry, philosophy, and letters have entirely lost the deceitful glitter that they once possessed ; so all ungodly principles of education are, in the end, to be still more clamorously rejected and abhorred. Man, universal man, is yet to come into full, deep, warm sympathy with God, in his estimate of the glory of our nature made in his own image, and, therefore, of the high responsibility of him who undertakes to lead it forth, upon the pathway of its true development.

The earnest use of positive religious influence in the work of education, is neglected by many, on theory or by blind impulse, who yet profess to acknowledge its amazing value ; by some, from a foolish fear of being regarded as hyper-denominational ; by others, from a blind sense of the fact, that in the economy of modern society the office of religious instruction is assigned, in its general division of labor, to the ministry as their special work ; and by others still, from the feeling, that the art of right religious stimulation and guidance is one, in which they hardly know where to step or where to stand. It is, indeed, one of the greatest of all arts, as also of all modes of usefulness, to know how to bring completely one's whole personality into bright and burning contact at all points, with the natures and wants of others. The right use of religious power over them is not, however, to be of a formal and fixed character, or occasional in its seasons ; but, spontaneous, perpetual, and ever-varied, according to the everchanging aspects of nature and of life and of each soul, that gives or receives the blessing of communicated love.

The teacher, if possessed of intellectual and genial personal qualities alike and fully devoted to the cause of God, can do a work which, if neglected, the ministry with whatever weaponry of truth and love may ever afterwards attempt in vain. The recipients of his influence are exceedingly impressible, and as never again in subsequent years. He not only teaches but trains them, if faithful, to walk in the paths of uprightness. And, yet, his is the calling so noble and divine, which is commonly so lightly esteemed, and whose honor, most who undertake its vindication would determine by some of its higher positions so called, instead of by its own great intrinsic merit, as a vocation: as high in itself, as any mortal can presume to enter uncalled, or feel that he has received a commission from above to undertake.

III.

THE TRUE CHRISTIAN TEACHER.

III.

THE TRUE CHRISTIAN TEACHER.

There is no relation in which God stands more conspicuously and constantly before His intelligent creatures, than that of a teacher: ever showing himself to them, as the Infinite Counterpart of their being, in respect to all its capacities and all its wants; and summoning purposely, by every possible variety of object appeal and influence, in his works and word, every faculty of their natures into full exercise. The highest also of all Christ's offices when on earth, except in the very article of death as man's atonement, which expresses indeed his dearest relationship to man, was that of our great Teacher. And so fully is the whole universe, which is everywhere pervaded with God's being, pervaded also, almost equally, with His sense of the value of the high work of education, that all the forms of matter around us are astir with mute eloquence, "uttering speech" of Him. Voices of the day and night are ever crying to each listening ear: God is good and man is great: each hour is precious and the future is unending! It is a holy office indeed to teach. To guide a weary traveller through the pathless woods; to conduct an invalid to the fountain of perpetual health; to restore a lost child to its parent's arms; and much more to plant the feet of some poor wanderer from his God in the pathways of virtue again: is there any class of deeds, to which the universal heart of Humanity more instinctively and sympathetically responds as noble? And yet these are but separate, occasional symbols of the higher service of the teacher, who is ever systematically, artistically, patiently and prayerfully at work, to lead each pupil upon the highway of glory and honor and immortality for himself; and to prepare him also in the best manner, in spirit and power, to lead as many others as possible in his train. In tender watchfulness and care, he combines in the prosecution of his plans, all the devotion of a gardener to a favorite plant, of a nurse to a sick friend, of a physician to a cherished patient, and even of a parent to a loved child, with the study and taste and delicate execution of an accomplished artist, rejoicing in his art.

But consider more minutely,

I. His spirit.

II. His labors.

I. And what of his spirit? Much in every way.

1st. He loves his work.

Others may move, as so many do, discontentedly through their daily duties and experiences; as, in the days of Horace, " Said the soldier, oh the fortunate merchants; and the lawyer praised the farmer; and the farmer cried out that they only were happy who lived in the city." But he, as each new morning opens its golden gates before him for action and enjoyment, comes forth from the chamber of his repose to his loved work, like a strong man rejoicing to run a race. How can one, on whose neck his daily employment, and with it his daily existence, hangs as an unwilling weight, stand up worthily in his appointed lot! Both God and man love cheerful givers and cheerful workers. The true teacher, like the true poet or preacher, who cannot but speak the things that he has seen and heard from above, teaches because he must. Woe is unto him if he teaches not, as said the apostle, woe was unto him if he preached not the gospel. Although many wonder what charms he can find in what they deem so laborious and thankless an employment, all its heights are to him of Alpine grandeur; and all its breadths of ocean-width. His very estimate of the exceeding glory of his calling, is itself his special anointing for it from on high: the fire that is in his heart, has been kindled by a hand divine. He not only sees a vastness of dimensions which others do not comprehend, in the sphere of happy toil to which God has beckoned him, but also an infinite fulness of details, ever inviting his attention and pleasure, which their feeble vision cannot traverse. They having eyes see not, and having ears hear not, the things which rivet and ravish his thoughts. As with all men sent of God on a special errand to the world, his impulse to action in his chosen work is not that of a cool determination, to make in his life as it were a geometrical demonstration of some theorem of duty ; but a spontaneous, native, ever-glowing force, divine alike in its origin and in its aim. Not more naturally, by the very necessities of its own germinal outgrowth, does a plant hold brightly up to view, on the very summit of its strength, its appointed flower where all its forces of life and color and fragrance are concentrated ; or a bird carol by the sweet compulsion of its nature in a tree the song which has been given to it to sing, than his soul delights in all its joyousness to empty its riches bountifully, as if by the force of a heavenly instinct, into the hearts of others. The proper governors, and leaders and great men of the world are made by the same great Being, who made the mountains and the seas ; and who certainly would be quite as apt to provide society with an abundance of its higher resources and endowments, as to furnish, as He everywhere has done, any of its separate and subordinate elements and appliances in such a way; which yet themselves exist only for its sake. Happy is that community which knows how to find and to use the leaders, prepared for it of God. They carry all their ensigns of nobility within them and not upon them, for mere outward show. Yea! happy is that community which does not, by artificial restraints, repress their native consciousness of their true position in their age or lead them away by false lures from their designated work of high and holy leadership to their generation. In the day when kings shall be nursing fathers and queens nursing mothers to the church, kingly minds and queenly hearts: what an universal outburst of mental and moral vitality will then be seen over the face of the whole world! and how will the kindred offices of the parent and the teacher appear, like two pillars of light rising from earth to heaven and connecting them forever, as with bands of beauty, to each other! So thinks the true Christian teacher of his calling. He loves it: he rejoices in it: it is his very meat and drink, to do his Father's will in this high form of holy enterprise for Him.

The relation in which the teacher stands to his pupil, is in some respects higher even than that of the parent himself. The mind of a youth is, at the first, but a vast sensorium of impressions, as his heart is of influences, vital in every part and always in inward motion from one form of conception or perception to another. On his soul in its native openness, unperverted by abuse from himself or others, every cloud casts its shadow ; every tree shakes its leaves when green and drops them when dead ; every flower breathes its fragrance ; and the hills and dales, the summer-fields and the quiet streams, image themselves in ever still happy repose. He is prepared in all the sensitive, receptive and emotional elements and adaptations of his nature, to be influenced at the outset almost wholly, as if only susceptible and passive under impressions from without, by the whole, grand, imposing array of things and beings around him ; while yet in the end, when accoutred for the work with strength and experience and disciplined skill, he is to react upon the surrounding universe, and to use time and space and opportunity and men and matter, with all its outward forms and inward forces and laws of gravity and momentum, and its capacities for the composition and resolution of its elements and agencies in every varied way, to carve his own ideas and plans upon the world and upon mankind, before leaving them.

What now is to be done to this easily moved

and mightily moving nature ; and what is to be done for it, in the sublime process of its right development ? Is the stream of its sensations and impulses, its ideas and intentions, to flow on in a wild flood of chance experiences and issues ? Or, is impulse to be put under the check of principle ; and energy to be led into right directions ; and discipline to bring forces, otherwise blind and ruinous in their action, into powerful subserviency to great ends ? The intelligent parent trains his child to, at least, apparent obedience, and to the forms of polite intercourse with others ; and here usually the scale of home-education begins and ends, although with an elect few it is held to be a high angelic art, of many diversified ends and appliances, demanding at all times thought and effort and grace, in their best degrees and modes. But, however high a parent's estimate may be of the greatness of his duty as an educator, the teacher has still a work to do which the parent has not : to train the mind of his pupil to true, full, constant self-productiveness, up to the entire strength of his resources natural and acquired ; or in other words to fashion and fix his working faculties as a steward of God and a man among men, according to such tastes and habits, that from his whole active life as a thinking, willing, busy being, there shall actually come to mankind the greatest possible tribute of service, which God has made him capable of rendering.

2dly. The true Christian teacher loves his pupils.

He loves them personally. A man may love his employment, as an anatomist loves surgery ; or a painter his studio ; or a soldier the hour of battle ; and yet take no interest in him who is affected by it, except as furnishing him an opportunity of new professional labor or skill. But the true educator, not only feels himself towards each pupil, but makes him also feel it, that he is his personal friend. This conviction is infallible in his pupil's mind, and comes swiftly and strongly in its course, because he really is such, and shows it therefore in all his looks and tones, his words and plans and deeds. The sentiment of personal consecration to their good possesses him, as an ever-present inspiration ; and the perpetual manifestation of its light perpetually entrances their eyes and hearts.

Love begets love : this is its normal product. The love of the superior must precede that of the inferior, and call it into life. This is God's mode of vitalizing the universe with the power of love ; and it must be man's. "Speaking the truth in love" : this is the Scriptural, the philosophic and the only practical way of influencing minds in any right direction. Truth and love, if employed to their utmost strength, what results could they not accomplish, in blended beauty and power, in the family and the school, the church and the state! Mighty indeed are our weapons, tempered and edged above for our work.

The path of the true Christian teacher is that of the just man, shining more and more unto the perfect day: ever ascending from earth to heaven into more and more light and into more and more joy. Mounting himself with transport, upon such a path of ever new progress and expanding vision and beauteous discovery, he never ceases to be eager that those who are behind should hasten on with flying feet, and share with him the continual rapture of his life. Compared with such an one scaling height after height of knowledge and pleasure, and stopping at each new point as he rises, only to shout his joy with eagerness, to those who are toiling on after him below: in what a pitiable contrast does he stand, who, instead of climbing upwards to new attainments, sits quietly down by the roadside and amuses himself and his pupils with those cheap trinkets, the petty prizes of a school or college, or even of the larger world beyond them, as the chosen incentives to toil and aspiration. But how, one may well ask, how can ye believe or how can ye become great, who seek honor one from another. And flattery to which so many resort as a substitute for love, expecting to accomplish by it in a word, what much, patient, loving labor only can achieve, what a breath of poison does it spread over all the tender fibrils of the heart! It is the bane of all piety, eloquence, action, poetry, music, art, business or personal development in any form, to begin or end in selfishness. Under such an overlying rock nothing that has any life from Heaven in it, can grow. Deeply does the true teacher feel this great fact, and does not content himself with working upon any perverse or even merely superficial elements, in the character of his pupil. He breathes and moves and acts at once, only and for ever, upon the deepest and strongest elements of his being.

His love is the same in kind as that which stirs an angel's heart and harp; for he is engaged in the same high work, ministering unto candidates for immortality, health and strength and joy. As his pupils stand before him veiled in mortal flesh, he beholds them in their inner nature rather than their outer, unrobed of all the meannesses of their temporary, earthly state; and feels that his appointed work, to lead them to glory and to God, is august indeed beyond his vastest conceptions.

And as, in the review also of the means and appliances adopted for his own education, he sees and feels most deeply what might have been done by higher skill and finer art and greater labor and warmer love, in unfolding and beautifying his intellect and heart; he carefully and lovingly undertakes to avoid himself all the mistakes which he can discover, and to add to his work every new and higher advantage, which his own experience or reflection can suggest.

With no such weak theory to mislead him, as that God has constituted minds all of one original mould and grade in power and brightness, he studies with keen relish and discrimination the peculiarities of each pupil committed to his care, and his capacities, susceptibilities, idiosyncracies, habits and all the elements of vital force or feebleness, that enter into his composition: so that each one, instead of being lost in any general aggregate, stands before his thoughts in his own, clear, individualized personality.

3dly. He loves his Master.

He has chosen his calling, as his highest mode of serving Christ. Christ set before the soul by its own choice, as the great commanding object of its life, will fully, yes! alone, draw out all its hidden powers and resources into action. How often is what is true only of direct love to Him, as the great motor-force of one's being, ascribed to a spirit of self-sacrifice, which is but one of its many products. Self is but the mere point of an endless circumference. Self has neither breadth nor depth enough in it in any form, positive or negative, as an atmosphere for our thoughts to float in. The highest form of unselfishness is absolute self-forgetfulness, in which state of heart as in the blaze of a furnace, all ideas of self-denial and self-sacrifice are immediately consumed. Christ, only Christ : in this sentiment is the highest vital energy that can walk up and down, whether in kingly robes and aspects or not, in the family, the school, the pulpit, the press, the halls of legislation, or the courts of justice.

True teaching, like true living or true feeling, is and must be religious : not theoretically, formally or negatively alone, but actually, designedly and earnestly. With what a train of sweet influences, does one who thus zealously labors for God, move among his pupils ? Light from above is in all his features ; and the scent as of a garden of spices is in his garments. The eyes and ears of the young are made to be tenderly and thrillingly touched, by looks and tones that are filled with the Spirit of Heaven. He who bears these elements of moral energy in his person, because filled with them in his heart, always finds the young bending with sweet responsiveness to their influence, as if under the magic spell of some strange invisible power, constraining their thoughts and feelings to its will. How beautifully is childhood conformed in all its opennesses to the selectest social and religious influences, and in all its aptitudes for faith and love and joy, to the idea that the highest forces of the world are moral. How vividly, in this dawning freshness of our being, are the practical lessons of life imaged to our view! that this world is but the seed-plot and nursery of the next; that the family-institution is normally a school of Christ; that the parent is God's representative in his household, for truth and law and every thing great and good; and that the true discipline and development of our brief earthly state is that of faith.

The true Christian teacher feels in his work the inspiration of these great facts. His very love for his Master leads him to desire the office of a teacher of minds and trainer of characters under him, and to value childhood as the most inviting of all fields of labor in His cause.

But consider,

II. The labors of a true Christian teacher.

Labor is to him joy. It is on the wheel of toil that every thing in this world moves. Work is the very law of intellectual, as of agricultural, mechanical or commercial, life. The progress of history, all human improvements and the whole steady movement of each generation above the preceding, are all but so many chapters of the results of labor. To multitudes toil is either practically or theoretically an abhorrence. Next to serving Him who perpetually exemplifies the power and the pleasure of ceaseless activity in his own high being, as the great fountain of his constant enjoyment and beneficence; and who has ordained this law of mental and moral life, as one of the very necessities of existence over all his intelligent creatures: there is nothing that mankind dislike so much to do, as to maintain a life of laborious industry. There are many who speak and more who think of labor as a curse. This is indeed the common, thoughtless and yet willing interpretation of the curse upon Adam: by the sweat of thy brow thou shalt gain thy bread. And in the same way, those of such sluggish natures look up languidly in their thoughts towards Heaven, as a place of inactive rest, as if God himself could be in a state of dull repose, or as if any creature could be dormant in the intense glory of his immediate presence. No! work is no curse, except to him who curses his own nature in thinking so: to a right mind and a true heart it is perpetual pastime. The spirit of labor is one of man's highest honors, as its results are his highest rewards. Not labor was the curse, but the direction in which it was appointed: to obtain the elements of bodily subsistence, to extort from the earth, before yielding its bounty unasked but now covered with thorns and briars, food and raiment; and thus to devote to physical things that attention, which might otherwise have been fixed by man as by the angels, with intense gladness upon higher employments and pleasures. Such was the curse : to return to dust again and to spend the brief interval of life here in the dust, serving the wants of that body in yielding to whose cravings our first parents sinned. And the rest of Heaven is rest from toil for physical subsistence, as well as from all conflicts within and all foes from without : the rest of high thought and of deep love, that perfect balancing of one's whole being, in the full harmonious exercise forever of every susceptibility and activity of the soul towards the greatest of all objects, and in the best of all ways, which leaves no room for any want and no sense of any wearisomeness.

Such a sublime course of effort as that, to which the true Christian teacher has consecrated his life, will demand for its right execution, the most earnest, constant, thoughtful, skilful labor. The spirit of work also is one of the very first elements, that he must set in motion, and ever keep alive in the hearts of his pupils.

There are two separate spheres of toil in which he must be viewed, in order to be rightly comprehended : at home and at school.

Behold him then

1st. In the midst of his labors at home.

§ 1. Here, as a physician or lawyer, who is elsewhere completely involved in the practical duties of his profession, studies the facts and philosophy of his cases, so he carefully analyzes and defines to his own eye the condition and wants of his pupils, and the most efficient mode of meeting them. In the noblest of fields one surely cannot work blindly: in the highest of arts, he cannot reach success on a pathway of guesses. It is the trained eye and hand that hit the mark. The laws of matter are not more exact than are those of prosperous labor, in things spiritual alike and intellectual.

§ 2. At home also he strives to enlarge his own foundations perpetually, as a scholar and a teacher. The greater the breadth and fulness of his own attainments of knowledge, the better will be his capacity for appreciating and selecting the true elements, for kind and number, of the higher education. The larger his own acquisitions of mental discipline and power, the more competent will he be to lead others through difficulties and deserts, into the realms of thought and truth, the land of light and harvests upon earth, which is like to that above. The fresher his own spirit with gladness from constant triumphs of discovery and conquest, the more will his example flame as a guiding star, to those whom he would animate with a spirit of lofty endeavor. By energetic labor at home he has made himself what he is ; and in the same way he will keep ever rising into new attainments.

(1.) One of his felt duties and efforts at home will be, to keep himself fully informed of passing events : so as to be in complete sympathy with the great community of those who are living in the same age.

Each man needs for his own sake to feel the pressure of his age upon him, as in it and for it he is required to conduct himself, as a true man. Here is the horizon of his earthly being ; and amid its circumstances, forces and movements he is to live and grow and act, as in his native element. This age has in it the strength and fulness of all preceding ages. In it they find their culmination and consummation. How is a whole volume of history often suddenly unrolled at our feet in a single day ! Each new age makes its own special demands on the men that belong to it ; and each man belongs in fact as specifically to his own age, as any race of men or animals or plants to the zone in which they occur. And how can one prepare others in all the elements and forms of a right educational outfit for life just as it is, who does not well know and deeply feel the actual condition and urgencies of the times. So many mischoose their proper occupation in life, and is not the number legion, because not having seen themselves, nor having had teachers who saw before them and for them, what it was that God and man would have them do while upon the earth. The common charge and much more the common fact if it be such, that our educational appliances fail in the result, of any thing like a real adequate preparation for life as it is, should lead to a careful examination of what can be done, what ought to be done and what in fact is done, in so high a sphere of action and influence.

(2.) The true teacher will also employ himself, at home, in close earnest study. Every day will be fruitful to him in new ideas. To study is his joy, as it gives delightful employment to his mind, which must otherwise fold in its powers in dull passivity upon itself; and as also wherever he turns his eye eagerly, to find something new above, around, beneath or within him, every effort is rewarded with discovery; and the whole universe he finds is full of ever new, unthought-of riches, awaiting his research.

Do not many of even our so-called higher professional teachers, like the mass of our other educated men, come to be quite stationary in all elements and forms of mental advancement, at a very early period? How few grow as continuously and rapidly, from thirty-five to sixty as from fifteen to thirty-five; and yet with the larger facilities of study, and the higher powers of intellectual movement belonging to full manhood, and all the stimulus to be derived from the pleasure and profit of past acquisition, and the advantage of trained habits, and the wider scope obtained for the practical employment of new knowledge and new inward augmentations of power, ought not a higher rate of increase to be expected of our intellectual men at this period of their lives, than ever before ? The awful difficulty is, that, such is the vis inertiæ of most minds, so small is the felt pressure of the great unrealized future, vast and wonderful beyond all conception as it is, when a comfortable livelihood is obtained, the energies of multitudes at once stagnate as if the end of life were gained, and as if they themselves, with all their apparatus of sublime faculties, were after all but well-appointed machines for grinding out a certain modicum of earthly comfort, or of earthly show.

The field of labor opening before the true teacher for perpetual acquisitions, is twofold : that of the study or class of studies, which, from his peculiar taste for them or success in them, he considers his specialty and that of general scholarship, in which, in common with all educated men, he desires to obtain as much knowledge as he can, in the direction of the great wide all-embracing drift of his general thoughts and efforts, as a man. He who would fire others with a spirit of progress, must possess that spirit himself. He, who would lead them to seek for great acquisitions, must have large wealth of his own to use. The teacher's ideals, in repect to the style of his work and the measure of his successes will become, whether with his desire or without it, the ideals adopted by his pupils. In the study of painting, sculpture, music or any high mechanical art, men act wisely in seeking only those to instruct them, who themselves excel in the practical execution of that art. And so, in the sphere of personal education, he who comes into full, warm communion of soul with one who is ever rising eagerly himself, from height to height of intellectual progress, is blest indeed ; for he has a leader in spirit as well as in form, a living, active, zealous guide to the great things of heaven and earth. But where are such men, of fervid interest in their own constant improvement alike and that of others, to be found ? Is any profession more disgraced by abounding indifferentism among those who have ventured, unbidden of God or man, within its sacred precincts ? A man filled to the full with knowledge and thought and high desire, is in his looks and postures and motions and words, completely antipodal to the style of manhood to which he could otherwise attain, and to which the mass around him of even so-called educated men do attain.

The unuttered language of the eye, the mien and the manner, breathed out from the whole manifest purpose and conviction of the soul : this reaches more quickly and vividly the inner ear of the mind, than words spoken to the outward ear, which often never pass, at all, out of its chambers into those of the heart.

The greatest want among the working forces of our educational system, is the want of men of lofty purpose in the profession : men determined to take possession of its broadest and richest fields, and to scale its grandest heights. There are not giants enough among our scholars : a class indeed including multitudes more in name than belong to it in fact. But the greatest glory of any people, next to general religion and general liberty, is true, thorough, general scholarship ; with such heights of private scholarship swelling and rising upwards out of it, as shall give to society everywhere in things intellectual and moral an abundance of bold mountain-scenery, and of clear strong mountain-air.

But consider the true teacher at work,

2dly. In school.

Here is the spot where he brings, joyfully, all the riches of his heart, and of a life spent in labor and prayer, with much purpose and plan and hope, and lays them down, lovingly and trustfully, at the feet of his Master as a tribute of love to Him, and at the feet of his pupils with deep holy longings to do them good. He comes not hither, therefore, as a laggard who has found life full of cheats ; or who works against his will, because the curse of work is upon him. Not with slow and measured steps of feeling, does his heart return to its daily toil, as a captive held in bonds ; but as a deer when unconfined would bound away exulting to his forest-home, or an eagle would fly aloft from an open cage into the upper air. Is there, one may ask, can there by any possibility be, such food for strong thought and exhilarated energy in a mere school-room, when surrounded by children, altogether unripe in years and knowledge, whose eyes are quite unopened yet to the vast and beautiful universe around them ; and whose ears are so deaf to all its higher voices and all its profoundest harmonies, as not even to hear them yet at all. Yes ! give me but one child of the Highest, into the living chords of whose being I am to breathe thought and feeling ; the light of whose spirit I am to kindle ; and the tread of whose footsteps over this dark world and into the gorgeous future beyond, are to be shaped by me, and you put at once the crown of a king upon my head, and the wand of a prophet into my hand ; and you commission me to do a work the sense of which, if I have any true sense of it, will give a divine energy and dignity, at once, to all my movements, because it is the highest of all work on earth for God.

In order rightly to appreciate the teacher, as a workman, in reference both to the style of his work and also his own genius and nobleness in rightly conducting it, we must consider briefly the natural preparation of those, for whom and on whom he is to labor, for his plans of effort in their behalf; and look also, in contrast with the true teacher's style of influence upon them, at the frequent and indeed common way in which they are mismanaged and abused.

Children have certain special characteristics, as such, adapting them to receive, just at the period of his contact with them, his full formative influence. What then are the preparatives of childhood and youth, for the reception of deep determinate influences into the character? Behold them! they are elements of susceptibility and activity, that are always reaching, blindly and yet instinctively, after a supply of their wants. They are these: inquisitiveness, or a great desire to know more; acquisitiveness, or a great desire to own more; great sensitiveness to others' thoughts and remarks concerning them; a restless love of action; delight in every new conscious exercise of power; special confidence in their natural guides as appointed of God for them, their parents and teachers; a spirit of constant imitation ; buoyant, ever-bubbling sportiveness of feeling ; and, in general, a full broad openness of nature to receive whatever person or influence that approaches them, in a genial stimulating persistent way. These elements enumerated all belong in special strength to the period of youth as such ; and are so many open avenues to action and influence over the heart, at the first, which are soon afterwards closed one after the other, by selfishness or suspiciousness, to all access from without, except by formal and cautious permission.

But, in what terrific ways are these tender sensibilities of childhood to right influence generally abused ! The uprisings of curiosity are battered down by ridicule : the spirit of acquisition is unnoticed, or led aside from the pursuit of knowledge or of excellence, to shrewd and sharp ways of making gain : the delicate susceptibilities are ruthlessly trampled under foot : the desire for activity is allowed to run into a love of mischief, so that it is deemed by many complimentary to a child to call him roguish : the disposition to confide in those who are his superiors is so often thrust at with marvels and tricks and deceits, that even the young child ordinarily learns early to be suspicious : his love of imitation, instead of being the silken chord that God designed it to be for leading him towards heaven, becomes a chain of darkness in the hands of false guides leading him to ruin, who yet laugh constantly at the deceptions that they practise upon him and at his own short steps and many falls in following after them ; while all the glad impulses of his young, laughing heart, are so deadened by stolid indifference to him or by vexatious teasing or by constant interdicts upon his own appropriate pleasures, that a large proportion of our youths have old faces and dry hearts and dull pulses, while yet in their teens.

How different from such foolish, false and cruel treatment of the young, is that other mode of dealing with them and their interests, which is inspired by just views of their immortal natures ; and, which, ever flowing in a strong stream from a heart full of joy itself, abounds in such beautiful elements of influence, as these : constant sympathy with them in their joys and sorrows : glad attention to their wants and ways : readiness to overlook little offences, and to interpret all things in them generously ; and unbounded devotion to their improvement and happiness at all times.

That the true teacher may be seen as he is in school, we must look at him, in the four great modes of labor which there open before him : instruction, government, personal influence and direct religious effort.

1st. Instruction.

To instruct, from Latin instruo, means literally to pile up or upon, to prepare, to furnish ; and this indeed is real instruction : the right and full furnishing of the youthful mind for life as it is, for its duties and experiences, its toils and pleasures. The true teacher has a definite aim in his work, by which it is all shaped, and with the spirit of which every part of it is animated ; and that is the procurement in each individual of the systematic and symmetrical development of his entire nature, as both a receptive and active being of high endowments, invited and commanded of God to spend all his powers and resources, as best he can, for Him.

§ 1. His first and constant effort is, to get each pupil vigorously at work for his own self-culture. Application is the lever of all his plans and hopes for the student. He has no idea of overlaying his mind with learning, as a gilded external accomplishment ; or of ministering, in any way, to the petty conceits of a weak and idle nature. He is ever intent therefore upon stimulating his pupils, in all possible ways, in season and out of season, to wakefulness of thought, loftiness of aim, and energy of purpose. Whatever new ideas or influences he can set in motion at any time in their hearts, concerning the value of knowledge, the preciousness of time, the glory of man's mental and moral constitution, the magnificence of the universe, as the field in which his thoughts and plans are to range, the greatness of the future, and the ineffable majesty of God, as his King and Friend and Father, he is watchful and eager to communicate. All his looks and words and deeds are full of the light of these great truths, ever burning with intense heat upon the altar of his own heart ; and the holy fire he cannot keep pent up, if he would, within the narrow chambers of his own single soul.

In these views is contained the true commentary upon the remark so often made by parents, and true as far as it goes, which is only however half way of the whole reality, that a given boy can be readily coaxed but not driven ; and that he needs to be encouraged. He does indeed: he needs to be encouraged to what is right ; and as truly and as earnestly discouraged from what is wrong.

§ 2. The true teacher also continually sets obstacles, of set purpose, over against each pupil, which he must overcome or be overcome by them. This is God's mode of training men in his providence to greatness of intellect and heart ; and although so many object to it, as so full of mystery in Him and of trial to themselves, it would be difficult, it is certain, to invent any other system which would be equally effective in habituating men to strong thought and action. In every conceivable way beside, the mind would be left to the drift of its own caprices : forever floating, as an inert mass of consciousness, upon a sea of chance or fate. But if such be the plan of that great Being, in guiding his children to the greatest possible enlargement of their powers, who made them on purpose to educate them ; any, surely, who are engaged subordinately in the same labors, may well imitate His example. This is indeed the perfection of art, of mechanical skill, of parental duty, of statesmanship and of all high and true educational treatment of men, to watch carefully how God accomplishes, in the mighty sphere of His activity, the same kind of results which we seek ; and then carefully and prayerfully, although at such great distance, to tread in his footsteps, according to the measure of the sphere which we are to occupy, and our capacity for filling it.

§ 3. He aims to establish, by regularity of arrangements, requirements and practice in his work, perfect method in the working of the student's powers, as well as in his own chosen use of his time. The absolute method, established by God in all the movements of the masses of matter, constituting the physical universe, as well as in the many chemical and vital processes, that are witnessed in every part of them, is among the most noticeable and amazing wonders of His hand. Absolute method is one of the essentials of absolute perfection ; and an ever-present necessity for absolute success in any direction by the finite mind.

§ 4. He aims to establish, by the exact comprehensive, and critical style of his requisitions in the recitation-room, the highest and truest ideals possible, in the scholar's mind, of what real study is and what are true scholarly attainments. Great is his sense of responsibility about this part of his work; for here is the secret fountain of its largest issues, for good or evil. A recitation such an one does not consider as a piece of vain self-exhibition, on the part of the successful, and much less as so much drudgery to himself, made necessary for the sake of obtaining a livelihood or meeting the mere professional demands of his calling; but as the time and the place in which he with his trained powers, is to sit in judgment upon a series of mental researches and decisions, made deliberately by the pupil, and offered to him respectfully and confidingly for his endorsement or condemnation; and in which he is to apply all kinds of tests, chemical and mechanical, to the quality of the intellectual work presented, as a specimen not only of the native and acquired power of his mind when at work, but also of its conceptions what the style of that work should be. His criticisms, whatever they may be, will all be not of a destructive but constructive influence, not depressing and humiliating but guiding, inspiring and warming in their style and tone. From under such searching, kindling treatment, a mind of good quality for power and responsive to it in its moods of feeling, must come forth in the end, like gold from a furnace seven times purified, bright and beautiful.

What the pupil studies under a faithful guide and master, he studies until he learns ; and what he learns he learns to keep and to use, to use familiarly with the same freedom and effect as a part of his inward self, with which he makes use of his bodily limbs in his outward nature. While the true teacher will not despise, but rather highly value, a vast capacious memory : unlike many shallow revilers of this noble faculty, who, from either not possessing it themselves to any great degree, or not having ever freighted it with any thing but cheap wares, do not know its worth ; he will yet strive with all earnestness, to reach and fire perpetually all the higher faculties of the soul, and to find a permanent lodgment in the reason and the conscience for as many ideas and principles as possible. In teaching the pupil ideas as such, and leaving him so far as possible to express them in his own words, instead of using the forms and formulas which others have devised for their utterance, you teach him to acquire power of language and self-possession as a thinker, in the presence of others ;

while at the same time training him to make all his labor definite in his studies, and all his conquests sure.

How simple therefore and yet how precious are the secrets of the true teacher's success, in the office of instruction! They are, on the one hand, the thorough intellectuality and spirituality of his labors, and, on the other, such effective elements of action in his work as these: constant stimulation; exact method; close critical requisitions; and thorough patient drill, connected with frequent systematic reviewing, so as to make secure and familiar all acquisitions that may be obtained.

In the specific act of instruction itself, what various elements of power can be employed by one earnestly devoted to their use, in the form of exposition, illustration, collateral information and broad philosophic generalizations!

The philosophical mode of instruction, in whatever form, is the only true one: as it is alone adapted to the wants of young inquiring minds, that need for their right inward growth principles rather than mere facts, which are always relatively superabundant in their comprehension of things. On a thorough framework of principles, every other form and element of knowledge communicated or acquired can be laid up in its true place and for its true use. It is also necessary on the other hand that the student should be taught the practical habit of making constant application of all principles furnished him by his author or teacher, to the real utilities of life ; for principles like every thing else are valuable only for their uses. Some err in one of these directions : some in the other ; and many in both.

There are three classes of studies which, from the special scope that they furnish for the full and yet varied use of the best resources and talents of an instructor, deserve a distinct consideration here : history, science and language.

Many rob each and all of these departments of instruction of very much of their profit and pleasure, by a slavish confinement to text-books. An author, in the hands of a true teacher, furnishes but a leading string, by which his pupils may direct their footsteps in the hour of study to a general acquaintance with the subject ; and which he may take up afterwards, in common with them, for their guidance to a better acquaintance with its treasures. The author is only therefore the teacher's servant ; and he who treats him as his master, establishes at once thereby his own utter disqualification for the high office that he has assumed.

Some also, and generally without consciousness of the fact, teach the various knowledges, each as an end by itself, and not as a means to the end of all education : which is the proper development and equipment of the pupil, for achieving the greatest possible results for good, throughout all his life, to God and his fellow-men. It is astonishing indeed, how few living influences seem to exist in our fountains of education, where of all places upon earth they should surely most abound. The uses of education are multitudinous ; and all of the most vital practical kind ; and how can one who undertakes to dispense its blessings, think of aiming at any other object in all cases than the pupil's good ; or thinking of that to some degree dole out his love in any stinted measure to him. A slow-paced, dull-eyed, effete teacher ! can any monstrosity among all God's works appear like this, to those who dwell in Heaven !

And is it not true also, that many undertake to teach others who themselves should be learners, not only of the first principles of so divine an employment, but also of the very substance of the things themselves, that they teach. The idea has been quite common in the profession of education,and in this alone, that a man of slender preparation might enter, at once, into even its highest offices and then qualify himself afterwards specifically for its details. And indeed the neglect and abuse with which this exalted vocation has been long visited by the multitude without, have been attributable to the wide-spread practical indifference manifested toward all its higher claims, by so many within its precincts.

(1.) History is the most suggestive of all the great elements of instruction. It covers the whole field of human activity and experience, and furnishes endless materials for profitable thought and remark. Historical composition is itself one of the highest forms of literature, for both strength and beauty of style ; and from its wonderful combination of the means of mental excitement and information, with all the resources of argument, sentiment and taste, it appeals, beyond any other form of written thought, to the interest of the old alike and of the young, as well as of the learned and of the unlearned. Standing on the high and broad platform of historical instruction, a teacher who is himself inspired with the love of it, can exert an exciting, elevating and controlling influence over his pupils, equalled nowhere else in his work, and spreading its rich benefits like an overflowing stream, over all their other studies and endeavors. The whole additional power of the lecturing system of teaching, should here be mingled in detail by the teacher with that of formal recitation by the student : both instructor and scholar mutually combining their interest and action in the recitation, as can be done nowhere else not even in the sciences, so well. Not Socrates nor Plato had nobler opportunities, for their searching questions, or glowing disquisitions, or any of their special modes of contact with the minds of those who waited for knowledge at their lips. A man, whose mind can lie flat upon the field of historical vision and exploration, has in his nature an amount of stupidity which nothing can disturb, and to undertake to remove which would bring but little gain to its victim.

The true study of history is one of the most important, of all the appliances of a high educational system. If the foundations of a thorough acquaintance with its lessons are not laid in youth they never can be laid on any great scale, amid the cares and labors with which after-life is crowded. To be rightly pursued, it must be not merely read but studied. Slowly and repetitiously must its paths be traversed ; and carefully must its facts be collected. Haste will surely, here if anywhere, bring but scanty harvests.

It has in its depths, like honey in the comb, a rich deposit of philosophy : the philosophy of human life, of the rise and fall of all greatness and of the causes and courses of failure and success in all earthly undertakings. It is for their use in displaying the real forms of human excellence and honor, directly as the principal figures to be seen : or indirectly, by some dark background serving to bring them into clearer relief, that all its pictures are so carefully drawn to the life. This inner sense of all the outward circumstance and show of so much recorded action must be thoroughly seen, or the wide stream of the past will be made to flow before our eyes but in vain. God in history: this is the key to all its philosophy. As well might one think of comprehending a steam engine, by merely looking at it as a piece of wondrous mechanism, without knowing its adaptations and uses; as of understanding any thing, beyond its mere surface, of the great organic past, without the perception of God's plans within and around all human events. History is, externally, an account of what man has done and undertaken to do; but, internally, it is full of the hidden life of God's thoughts and feelings, restraining, counterworking and directing the influences, that man has set in motion. It is therefore, like so many other things, double in the elements that compose it: being, on the one hand, the development of man's agency on man's part, and, on the other, of the great scheme of redemption on God's part, including in it his daily providence as well as the plans of his grace and the work of his spirit. Rightly taught therefore history, like nature, becomes a grand volume of theology. The key to its secrets and its marvels is to be found, in the Jewish prophets; and to such a wonderful degree, that prophecy might be defined to be, history written in advance, as history itself might also be called the prophets verified.

(2.) In connection with history, instruction in science is one of the teacher's highest fields of labor. Here are many and open channels for the outflow of his strongest thoughts and feelings ; and abundant opportunities for accomplishing the highest intellectual and spiritual ends, at which he can aim. Science, like history, leads directly unto God. He who stops in teaching it at the mere outside fact or arrangement of facts presented, without inspecting its inward mechanism of adaptations, abuses his own nature as well as that of his disciple ; for science is but man's collection of a few of the specimens of God's skilful provision for the activity comfort or improvement of mankind, in some of the physical, intellectual or moral aspects of his being. It is therefore the ever-present duty as it is the pleasure of the true educator in teaching science, to show, wherever he himself can see it, the contriving hand of that great Mechanician, who, in building the universe or any part of it as the home of his intelligent creatures, purposely left its tracery of design open to their discovery, appreciation and grateful recognition. The sense of God's existence, and goodness, and watchfulness over all his creatures, can be nowhere obtained away from the closet, the secret place of his manifestation to the sons of men, as among the open demonstrations of science ; where the revelation made is as near that of vision, as is possible without it.

In teaching science, reference must be had also by the instructor, at all times, to its practical uses. Every thing that has value upon earth derives it from its connection, in some way, with man ; and here is the value of science, in its ultimate uses. The tendency to divorce study and learning from the wants of every-day life, is neither divine nor human. The two grand terms of every thing on earth, and in the universe and so also of the whole universe itself, are God and man. From God to man, this is the direction of the scale : the secret alphabet of all the hieroglyphs of Time and of Eternity.

Instruction in science in its higher forms and degrees, will, rightly conducted, establish in the diligent student such mental habits, especially, as quickness of perception, thoroughness in exploration, careful scrutiny, close penetrative analysis, exact method, and skill in analogical reasoning. At such results in his pupil's mind, baptized meanwhile with a deep religiousness of spirit, the true teacher will earnestly aim. Around each lesson in the text-book, as a nucleus, he will gather delightedly all his own stores of thought and treasures of feeling, and lavish them upon his pupil, as his tribute of interest in the science and in him.

Many, even Christian teachers, by a heathenish way of speaking of the facts of science, as the laws of *nature*, her preparations provisions and compensations, quite exclude God from His own universe in their instructions ; as if nature, which is but the product of his will, were herself God or had given birth to her own self, as an independent, self-originated existence, in his creation.

(3.) Right instruction in language, also, in respect to the number to be influenced by it and its bearing on all the intellectual ends of education, is of very high importance. In what a dry and spiritless manner is it however generally furnished? Who could imagine, in looking at the languid air of many self-appointed teachers of the ancient languages, and hearing the dull drawling recitations of their pupils, that in their slow movements as a company of drones, with heavy hands and steps and eyes, they were all the time passing through a land, full of odorous perfumes and gems and mountains of wealth. The true spirit of study in the department of language, sweeps with living energy, over many fields of deep enchanting interest, as grammar, prosody, specific and comparative etymology, antiquities, history, biography, geography and literature, out of the materials of all of which the accomplished teacher can and will, in various combinations, weave the web of his daily instructions to his pupils. What a place of earnest strife can one, who is himself zealous, make a school-room to be, which is full of youthful linguists, not indeed of strife with each other for a selfish triumph, under the power of unholy ambition, but of conflict with ever new difficulties, each for himself; which, like bold adventurers climbing up a mountain's side with shoutings, they shall pass over in succession with exulting footsteps.

In whatever department of instruction the true teacher is engaged, his conception of his relations to his pupils is ever the same, that, from his own spirit as a powerful battery, the whole life and character of the school are to be daily and momentarily derived.

But look now at the true Christian teacher, in another department of his work.

2dly. Government.

This is one of the highest of arts; and natural genius for it is as shining a gift from God, as inborn capacity for any other lofty style of action. The faculty, when native to a high degree, involves in its exercise a full and quick comprehension of human nature in any of its forms, an immediate intuition of the demands of every crisis, facility in making provision for them, and alertness in mental action, as well as a natural sense of the beauty of order and a natural force of will ; which, combined, make it as easy to govern as to think or act in any other direction. In discussing this part of the subject, I shall consider the general style of management which the teacher should adopt toward his pupils ; and yet management is not the word that will rightly figure to all minds the full orb of our idea : as so often, in other things, it implies a mixture of craft and cunning. If we call it treatment, the phrase will have perhaps too much of a medical savor about it, and call up thoughts of the student as a patient, if not even as a victim : a conception, which, as there is so much traditionary nonsense in common speech and in some of our best literature, about study as a task and school-boy days as days of sour experience, we are over-willing to avoid. Let us call it then the high and skilful ordering of all those influences which serve to arouse, determine and prosper, in every form and at all times, the whole activity of his whole nature ; or in other words the full, designed outlay of the teacher's labor, tact, art, taste, genius, strength and time for the greatest possible enlargement and refinement of all that constitutes the real manhood of the pupil. So much of this part of the subject as belongs, strictly, to either of the specific topics of personal influence or direct religious effort, will be reserved for subsequent consideration.

§ 1. The general discipline of the higher Christian education must be exact. In its realm of toil, Law must sit, although unseen herself, upon a throne of light and wave her silent sceptre over willing happy hearts: law, that great invisible abstraction born of reason and the conscience, which pervades, like God himself, all the works of his hands with its mighty presence. If in military tactics, in order to secure power of motion and action in the body, such attention must be given with long and constant repetition, to the procurement of entire subordination to authority, manly endurance, regularity, precision and swiftness of movement, and all the other elements of effective warfare: if, to accomplish by mechanical agency any great material results in regard to either force or finish, spring and valve and wheel and cog must all be made to play with absolute certainty of time and strength, each in its proper place, and all the more silently all the more beautifully; how much more, in the higher sphere of great intellectual effects, must order reign: order, not of that negative spiritless form which is the mere absence of disorder, the order of a desert; but that sublime marshalling of active forces to a grand unity of results, which, while it brings out of them the highest possible advantage, requires in him who thus undertakes to harmonize their agency to so productive an issue, the greatest possible use of skilful and watchful energy. Such a style of order has a momentum in it, a ground-swell, that bears forward every thing else that rests upon it. The quality of the discipline to be found in our schools and colleges, is not often what it should be, to meet either the demands of Christianity or those of the age. If the potency and preciousness of the voluntary system of public life and manners, and so of the entire democratic framework of society, be what they are claimed to be, the nearest possible approximation to a perfect social state, then, properly, the fact should be quite manifest in not only the relative but also the absolute superiority of our educational institutions and appliances. But is it not true that in multitudes of instances there is not as much order secured, or attempted to be secured, in reference to the high ends of mental and moral training, as the general government readily obtains of its sailors and soldiers ; or a mercantile house of its clerks ; or a manufacturing company of its operatives ? The reproach so often uttered abroad against American democracy and Christianity alike, that they fail to sustain before the bar of the world's judgment, their claims to superior excellence, on one of the most important of all test-points, the home—

and school—education of the young in respect to their intellects, morals and manners, is surely too well founded to be either denied or excused. And yet, in the real type and spirit of our institutions, civil and religious, fully developed and employed, there are capabilities for attaining great results, that no part of monarchical Europe, however cultivated, ever has possessed or can possess. Their discipline of the school, like that of the state, is the discipline of physical necessity and of fear: outward in its bearings rather than inward, mechanical rather than personal in its spirit: that of compulsory requisition, rather than that of stimulated self-respect and well-acquired self-government. Whatever results are obtained, are gained under the pressure of the doctrine, that might makes right; while under our system of government, religion and education, the opposite sentiment flames forth everywhere, as our guiding star, that right makes might. And although the working of such a system of influences, where ideas are the tools to be used and each mind is to be made a law unto itself, involves much more labor than the little effort required to bring the wheels of previously organized social machinery to bear on a given point at hand, yet the toil is well spent, as the product is of so much greater value; and the observance of the universal rule of heaven and earth, that the more valuable the result, the higher and harder we must climb to get it, will always bring with it its own reward. To establish in any one habits of self-respect, high ideals of personal character, lofty aims and aspirations, and the deep true elements of all manliness and godliness, which are rather one than two: being the same state of heart as manifested variously on its under and its upper side: is a work worthy of an angel's hand.

§ 2. The discipline of the higher Christian education, must also be genial. The youthful mind is as has been said remarkably responsive to sympathy and appreciation. He who makes much of a pupil's excellences and little of his faults; who, forgetful of the past, is always summoning him cheerfully and inspiringly to new aims and efforts, exerts an almost magical influence over him for his good. Alas! how ungenial are most teachers towards their pupils: interpreting them and their conduct from the stand-point of selfish feeling, and ever fretting their own thoughts with a pitiful sense of the self-denial, required in their noble calling; instead of becoming elastic and heroic and mighty in their work, from a cherished sense of its value, if rightly executed, unto their pupils. A selfish, materialistic, worldly-minded teacher of youth is as great an object of pity, or rather of contempt, as can be found in this lower world. He, on the contrary, who acts in such a way as to deserve at all times the respect and affection of each pupil, yea! rather his imitation also, is a giant in his position. He is not indeed himself above law: as no one in the universe is, not even the Great Divine Being, the very effluence of whose thoughts and feelings is all according to the law of love; but he is the law itself impersonated.

There is wonderful profit and power to the teacher in the habit of treating his pupils at all times, with the same consideration in kind, with which the intercourse of older persons is stimulated and gladdened, in cultivated society. Childhood is remarkably susceptible to all such kindly influences. Polite attentions from a superior in age and attainments combined have a wonderful charm to them; as to men of low estate, similarly, the gentle condescension of those who are greatly superior is so delightful. Even pleasant, sympathetic playfulness with them will open the way, effectually, to almost every other influence upon their hearts. It grieves one to say, as it does so many to see, that in some if not most of our colleges, there is such an amount of cold formalism of management and manner, on the part of those whose hearts should be all aglow with the most intense interest in the young minds, divorced from the strong constraints of home on purpose to obtain the greater benefit of their teachers' company, example and guidance, that not only in college but through all their subsequent life, so many speak to each other of their college-teachers, as men to whom they feel no personal attachment or even indebtedness, and whom they always avoid or at best fear, rather than love. But if anywhere in the world the place or the occasion can be found, in which one may naturally and successfully occupy, instead of the parent, his very position, both in his own thoughts of his adopted relationship to his pupil and in his hearty reception by him as "his next friend" on earth, it is in the holy work of education, yes! holy, in which all the privileges and powers of all other offices of trust and honor among men, are united in one.

The two great component elements spoken of above, are, as already mentioned, those of all true government at home or at school, in the state or in the church, on earth or in heaven: complete scientific strictness of principle and plan, mingled with real personal kindness. The beautiful definition in the Scriptures of proper spiritual labor for others, in the work of the gospel, "speaking the truth in love," would be, if duplicated to both speaking and acting it, an exact description in a word, of the high art of all worthy intercourse in any form with each one of them. Justice and mercy: these are the two chief attributes of the Deity, for wonder in himself and for their productiveness of all things great and good to his creatures; and they are the two highest manifestations of humanity. To combine them in full proportion; to know when to be firm and when to yield; to carry the conscience of the pupil in its full strength of judgment and feeling always with you, so that your acts shall be at all times but the voice indeed of his own deepest unuttered thoughts: this is an endeavor in accomplishing which every faculty can find full play; and every resource of one's whole vast complex nature, can be brought into complete employment.

At the bottom of all other attempts for the right training of the young, lies the careful formation of thorough habits of industry. Activity, constant, true, mental and moral activity is, as really, one of the great primary laws of life in the soul, as breathing in the body. An unemployed mind, or one employed but feebly and partially, is not in a state in which any high growths of thought and feeling can be planted and prosper. As well might one expect to display in rich abundance the fruits and flowers of a luxuriant garden, on hard unbroken ground. If necessity is the mother of inventions, certainly industry is still more the mother of virtues. The requirement of lofty, vigorous, sustained effort the student's conscience will always sanction, as right; and if led to it with no more even than ordinary tact and earnestness, as well as required to undertake it, he will show at once in his looks and words and deeds, how well he understands that at last he has found the proper element in which, like a bird in the air or a fish in the sea, he feels that every thing around is strangely adapted to him, and he is as strangely adapted to it.

In arrangements, requirements and appeals, directed to the constant procurement of earnest application by the student, lies not only the best but also the only preparation in his mind for the administration of true discipline over him. So far as the teacher is concerned what he specially needs, over and above the qualifications already mentioned, without which indeed he is disqualified for any part of his business, as love to his work, to his pupils and to his Master, is tact. Small is the word, it is true ; but great is its meaning. It is one of those few words that are almost undefinable : their sense is so varied in varying circumstances. Those apt movements and happy hits and quick inventions, which characterize real tact, make it seem more like a sort of luck alive, than any thing else : they involve in them such a fine mixture of good sense and good feeling and of shrewdness, as well as alertness of mind. If also the Teacher combines with abundance of tact abundance likewise of bright glowing cheerfulness and even of warm playful mother-wit : so that all the most quick responsive susceptibilities of the pupil's heart are perpetually stirred and swayed by his magical influence : he moves about as a governor bearing divine insignia of office, among the happy hearts that perpetually obey him, without ever thinking of the reason why, and seem· to themselves to do by instinct without requirement, all the time, exactly what they know that he would have them do.

One of the chief points of tact, in the government of a school, is to keep always in motion, as an offset to the ever-present working of depravity in each heart, a thorough system of anticipative and preventive influences. To break the certain force of temptations, by ingeniously excluding them : to ward off the occurrence of junctures and crises in one's work : to so occupy the pupil's heart with the high aims and enjoyments of earnest self-improvement, that the fiery darts of the tempter shall at once be extinguished, as if falling into the tide of a deep strong stream, the moment that they reach him : this is tact, that is worthy of the noblest intellect. One of the most desirable of all feelings, that the teacher can possibly create in each pupil's mind, in undertaking to work effectually such a high preventive system of influences, is that which may be called a sense of his personal ubiquity. Real or supposed publicity is a wonderful damper to wrong action, in one who has a character to keep or make. And far-sighted plans, quick movements of body and mind and clear intuitions, with strong executive energy, are as valuable qualities in the school-room as in the battle-field. Military generalship is, indeed, when of a high order, as is statesmanship, more akin in the assemblage of qualities which it includes, to those required to be united in the true mastership of a school, than any other form of governmental administration.

One of the highest sources, and indeed forms, of tact in a Teacher consists in what may be called, talent in reading character. Some, although otherwise competent, are disqualified almost entirely for entering on this noble profession, at least with any high success, because of their want of intuitiveness in interpreting character. While having outward eyes, they are from inward blindness like persons of imperfect vision, in the management of the young, whose personal inability to comprehend at a glance all their movements perpetually tempts those over whom they are placed to practise all kinds of dupery little and great upon them. But keen-eyed perception of character, when combined with unsuspicious openness of conduct and prompt executive habits of action, gives a teacher a felt position, one felt by his pupils as well as by himself, of almost unlimited power over them.

Another of the special kinds of tact displayed

by the true Teacher, is seen in his subsequent treatment of the erring. Like his own Master on high, he is royal in forgiving and forgetting all past offences, if he can only see a new spirit for the future ; and this he is constantly seeking in every way to originate and cherish. Forgive means to give away or put away out of sight : so, he strives like God to "remember their transgressions no more": "he upbraids not"; but ever keeps the way wide open, for one who has in any manner lost his position with him or with the school, to regain it.

Many make rules, for their selfish ease, in the school-room, which if God were to make for this world would empty it at once of all its inhabitants : they will receive or keep only those who are exemplary at the outset. The cure for the undeveloped or wayward with them is, expulsion, not reformation ; because it costs patience, skill, time and prayer to work effectually on such untoward materials. But the genius and the glory of Christianity, whether its energies are employed by God or man, consist in its power to renew and elevate those who need its full renovating influence upon them. No greater pleasure on earth belongs to the heritage of a faithful earnest Christian teacher, than that of an entire and lasting remodelling of the habits and purposes of those, who before went astray. The school, like the church, is after all a moral hospital, where all kinds of infirmities and evils must be expected and brought under skilful curative treatment.

In connection with these aims and characteristics and kinds of tact, the earnest Christian teacher, who fears God and loves man and feels the pressure of "the powers of the world to come" upon his heart, will give effect to all his requirements and plans and varied forms of tact and all the many kinds of moral influence which he may employ, by the use of the rod when necessary. But how different in meaning and in effect, will his use of physical appliances for the good of his pupil be, when originating from such views and pervaded by them, from that of him, who is fitful in his plans and passionate in his feelings! The true Christian Teacher punishes corporeally, only as a last resort: he punishes because he must, or else must let his pupil go on unchecked to ruin. Alone with him, he talks in earnest loving tones about his delinquencies and their fearful results; tells him of his own love for him and much more of God's; urges him to a new style of effort for the future; and then punishes him because he must as his true friend, and punishing him on principle does it thoroughly: every stroke of the rod from him being answered by a corresponding stroke within, from the conscience of the culprit upon himself.

The government of a good school is so good in itself and in the apprehension of those dwelling happily under it, that, like that of our own peaceful democratic government, no one has any reason for desiring to change it: every thought of disobedience or even restiveness under it is forestalled by its own perpetual pleasurableness. The sunshine of universal satisfaction is spread everywhere around.

Another of the principal modes of labor opening before the true Teacher at all times, is

3dly. That of personal influence.

This is in all men of two kinds, unconscious and designed. The greatest influence which any man exerts upon others, is that of which he is insensible: it is so all-penetrating and all-surrounding like the very atmosphere, in its action upon them, when they are in contact with him or even in his presence. It is the influence of character, of one soul directly upon another; exhaled in the breath; streaming through the eyes; and animating every motion; rising up out of the deep and secret fountains of the heart; and finding its way through the most subtle and invisible channels, into the hidden recesses of others' being. Well does the very word character, which is but the Greek χαρακτήρ anglicized, express the fact described. It means alike a graver and the thing engraved. Character has in it the fixedness of a stamp itself and the power of a stamp on others. Although life and death are in the power of the tongue, yet actions speak louder than words. The power of example is greater than the power of speech. No energy reveals itself, whether in repose or in action, so instantaneously as character; and not more quickly is the eye sensitive to light, than is our whole being responsive in every part, to its influence. Who does not feel at once, that in the days of Washington or Napoleon a speech, welling up with a full overflow of thought and feeling from their hearts, would have a far different effect upon their soldiers, and ought to have, than the same speech containing the same good sense and earnest appeals if made by a subordinate would exert. Every act of a great man is ennobled by the elevation of his position. What is overlooked as common in others is watched and studied, as of special interest in him. His table-talk is reported; his correspondence published; his manuscripts and even his signatures are bought and sold; his favorite haunts are visited; and his intimate friends are looked at with admiration, as children walk about with a soldier to stare at him. And so, words of counsel and encouragement from a friend, compared with those which are just as true and wise and precious in themselves from others, are like luscious fruit plucked ripe and fresh from their native tree, compared with the same fruit when dry and stale from heat or age.

As face answereth to face, so does the heart of man to man. This is true, not only of the natural likeness of men in body and soul to each other, wherever found ; but also of the influence of man upon man, face upon face and heart upon heart, as of the sun on the earth or the moon on the sea. This is the great, unappreciated, unconscious influence exerted by every man, of which the Bible speaks in the declaration, that we are epistles known and read of all men, and in the command to let our light shine, so that others may see our good works. If now the teacher, as he moves among his scholars, can always appear to them clad, as in a vestment of light, with bright and pleasing associations : full of the sweet majesty of thought and love : bearing in his face the image of Heaven ; and himself the very exemplar to their conceptions of all that they themselves would fain be ; how will all his unuttered wishes become at once loud-voiced commands to them, and his secret feelings find deliverance in their happy pursuit of the ends which he seeks and sets also before them, for their attainment ! The heart of a child has been naturally prepared by its Maker for just this willing captivity to those who are appointed to train it: in the general simplicity of its feelings, its easy trustfulness, and the conception, so universal with children, that their teachers are of vast attainments and infallible in their decisions: a mistake better made for its influence on the young than unmade; and while innocent in all its bearings upon the objects, towards whom it is extended, it is yet capable of being employed by an enthusiastic teacher, with the highest stimulating effect upon the young themselves. Confidence is as necessary in the mutual relations of teacher and pupil, as in the monetary world between the borrower and the lender; or, in the household, between husband and wife, parent and child. Nothing but the direct abuse of this highest privilege of his position by the teacher can prevent him from leading them as he will.

As for designed personal influence, as well as that which is unconscious, there is wonderful scope in the teacher's work, for all possible ingenuity and faithfulness in its exercise. "Study to show thyself approved: a workman, that needeth not to be ashamed:" this is the sentence written by the finger of God, which he must write for himself upon his own banners, as he leads on his pupils to glory, honor and virtue. Certainly one engaged in an employment, in which he is to touch perpetually so many living springs, of character, fortune and fate, in all that he does and all that he leaves undone, can afford to study well the bearings of every movement which he originates ; and to combine in the practical conduct of his plans the results of all the thought, experience, science, art, enterprise and religion, which he can possibly blend together. The only way in which to appear to be good, is actually to be so ; and of all forms of goodness that is of the highest and most enduring power and beauty, which flows forth in a full stream from a cultivated and commanding intellect.

A man, besides, can do almost any thing in this world, who sets earnestly about it. The positive qualities which characterize an earnest nature, its determination, hopefulness and daring in various degrees and mixtures, according to the duties and emergencies that it is to meet, are among the specimens of human character that every man admires most, in every other man. Hence the strange electrifying power of boldness, whether in opposing or leading men. The earnest men are so few in the world, that their very earnestness becomes at once the badge of their nobility ; and as men in a crowd instinctively make room for one, who seems eager to force his way through it ; so mankind everywhere open their ranks to one who rushes zealously toward some object lying beyond them.

Next to the great constraining power of the

teacher's personal example of goodness in every form, and that of his manifest personal love to the pupil, there is no influence that he can exert for his good, like that of frequent earnest conversation clear and full and warm with him, about all points of danger or duty, and every thing pertaining to his regression or progression, in his course.

But there is still another mode of labor, in which the true Christian teacher is ever glad to employ his skill.

4thly. Direct religious effort.

He feels in teaching youth, even his own children, that they are all God's children and not his or man's, but placed by his Father in heaven, solemnly and lovingly, under his care to be trained for Him. A company of his pupils, therefore, always stands before him as a company of immortals, in whose very features he seems to read these words, in lines of light: these are from God; and let them be to God.

Religion is most truly presented to mankind, in any department of life or action, when made the living in-working principle of every thought and plan and movement in it: like the light, revealing itself by revealing every thing else in its true colors and proportions. In the very act of separating religion from the business and pleasures of life, as if a mere doctrine or form or institution or convenience, "its occupation is gone."

But while religion should transfuse its deep sweet light, through not only the whole character, but also through all the minutest parts of the entire work of the teacher, as the great ever-present source of all his ideas, feelings, words and deeds; there should be also direct specific effort made for the conversion and sanctification of each pupil. Is God a God of law, in things material, mechanical, agricultural, commercial and intellectual; then, how much more in those highest of all relations, for which these others are appointed! A man who strives rightly for the overthrow of Satan's kingdom anywhere, and most of all among the young, may labor justly with more hope and assurance of the result desired, than he who furrows the ground and sprinkles it with seed and prays for the early and the latter rain: as the interests involved in his toil are, in themselves, so much more precious on the one hand, and so much dearer on the other to God himself.

Religion is seldom presented to the young, in its true light: as a glorious privilege, a delightful treasure and a source of perpetual gladness. All the cheerful, hopeful, buoyant instincts of childhood are purposely set by their Maker, so as in their right use to appreciate and crave the beauty of His works and of himself and of a religion, so full of all ministries of peace and pleasure to its intelligent possessor. But how is our great good Father above made to appear distant and cold and forbidding to the young ! and how is love to him spoken of as a mere duty ! and how are all its most precious quickening truths converted into a mass of bare, portentous doctrines to their apprehension !

It is manifest therefore in what way a school or a college is to get and to keep a deservedly high reputation. Its only policy should be the policy of absolute merit. With simple reliance upon God alone, its whole effort should be to erect a lofty pile of good deeds in its work upon the earth : such as the great Judge himself shall pronounce to be good. The highest scrutiny for which one can prepare himself, the only one of which he should have any apprehension, is God's. Not he that commendeth himself is approved, but whom the Lord commendeth, and they who seek not the honor which comes from God only can be accepted of Him neither in their faith nor in their works. The idea is quite common, not only in matters of business, politics and fashion, but also of education and religion, that there is after all some pathway of success beyond and beside that of striving in all things to please God. Would not Christ, were He to appear on earth again, say everywhere now with sadness, as when He was here, Oh ye of little faith ! and with the same intense irony as then, "when the son of Man cometh shall he find faith on the earth ?" The mass of men still expect to prosper best, without God. They do not believe in his providence over them, or in his presence among them. And how is that sweet conception of him, as a Father: the brightest and best of all the thoughts, that can ever be taken into the human heart, and breathe out its perfume there : utterly lost to them, as if they had no inner sense to which its beauty could be revealed !

Nothing can take the place in the management of our educational institutions and appliances, one and all, of work : honest, earnest, skilful, constant work. How contemptible is reliance, in the place of such work, on public examinations, for which to the neglect of all scientific treatment of his real interests, the student is so often stuffed and crammed with zeal, only for the sake of the desired result to the institution, instead of any absolute profit to him, who is in fact sacrificed himself while being carefully tricked for show to others ! The object is to make capital of him for the future benefit of the institution, instead of developing him perpetually, to the highest degree possible, as a thinking active being of many and great natural faculties and resources. Public exhibitions also are, on the same principle, quite in vogue in many places ; in which handsome declamation, prepared by mere imitative drill, and compositions, abundantly interlined, enlarged and adorned with all sorts of superadded excellences by zealous teachers, are prepared for the glorification of the institution and its officers, in the eyes of superficial observers : which yet are all shams, since they do not indicate at all the real mental condition of the pupil, and since therefore he could not, if left to himself, produce any such speech or composition again. Skill in composition is one of the last attainments of an educated mind ; and, therefore, when it appears in early youth, betrays at once its foreign origin.

The results of true teaching will be those of high advancement to every pupil, individually, of whatever style of disposition or grade of character, that comes under its influence. In no employment is there greater versatility, in fact, in the objects and ends of the toil expended ; and in none is a more varied and elastic style of adaptation to those ends demanded. A true teacher never settles down upon average modes of dealing with his pupils. Such men, and they are numerous in all kinds of business, are themselves but average-men. Often, if not well-nigh always, the medium-grade of talents and attainments is selected, both at school and at college, as the uniform gauge for the amount of toil and rate of progress appointed for all. Those, accordingly, of maximum-power: made of God to be the very ornaments of the institution, as in after-life of society itself: are either left to the waywardness of their own untutored impulses, or, while being open at more points of their nature to assault than others, are exposed by utter neglect of their special wants, as if on system, to evil influences tending powerfully to disorganize all the inward elements of their mental and moral vitality. Those of minimum-force of mind, who need to be aroused and cheered and inspired, rather, than like the preceding, to be provided with adequate work and to be guided skilfully and earnestly into proper directions, for variety of effort and height of achievement: these are abandoned, on the cold and heartless plea of necessity, to their own habitual self-discouragement. The same requisitions are made of them as are made of others, whom God has made capable of doing much more than they.

It may be, in some respects, convenient for selfish minds, to equalize their work, and so make it mechanical instead of artistic, by resorting to short-hand processes, and doing things by average. But is it right? A school should be so conducted, that no one in it is ever at a loss to know, what to do next, and no one ever ceases to feel, that he is under the pressure of immediate necessity and of immediate obligation.

Perpetual effort should be the ever-present rule of action for each: effort for such things as each severally needs; and perpetual victory should be the happy history of one and all. It is the rule in God's kingdom that "of those to whom much has been given shall be much required;" and the rule really enforced by the true Christian teacher, if not always observed and watched by the pupil in its workings, will be the same. One of abilities decidedly superior to the others, should for example not only recite in three or four lessons, as Latin, Greek and Mathematics, &c., like the rest of those with whom he is otherwise wrongly classified; but in another recitation also, with another class pursuing some high English study or some Modern Language. There is no difficulty in working such a varied system of appliances and demands, according to the varied talents of the pupils, on a large and free scale, and with great pleasure and profit to both teacher and pupil. It is impossible to see how one can do his daily work without it, so as to satisfy either any high ideas of educational art or of educational duty. Those whom God has made leaders in mind, should be so developed at school and at home as to fulfil their destiny, from the very first, among their associates young or old. Their endowments have not come by chance from God, and it is left for men to say that they shall not be in vain. But how are boys of genius everywhere sacrificed both at home and at school by foolish flattery, by weak, blind, educational treatment and even by such pitiful theories, as, that smart children must be held back lest they die before their time, and that genius will carve its own way without the necessity of much early discipline, or of much toil in subsequent life. As the world goes, it is about as unfortunate, with here and there a noble exception, for a youth to possess native genius, as for one of the other sex to be gifted with great physical beauty. By positive abuse on the one hand, and by under-development on the other, he never acquires or early loses the spirit of work and all zeal for mental progress and becomes, instead, the victim of a ruinous spirit of self-conceit, destructive of all thoughts of toil, all intellectual conquests, all usefulness and all real benevolence. The atmosphere of a true educational establishment should be and will be genial and tropical: exactly adapted to force onwards all high growths. Every thing good will break out in it into larger fulness of life: what is great will become greater; while every thing evil in it will be subordinated and mellowed and under the accompanying dews of divine grace changed into forms of varied beauty and excellence.

It is right for parents and guardians to expect great and continued improvement in their sons and wards, at school and at college. They should expect more than they do ; and the higher the class of institution, the more should they expect and claim. Here, certainly, is not only a fair field for close, vigilant, perpetual scrutiny ; but it is demanded by the real interests of all parties. Both pupils and teachers should be made to feel, that they are surrounded by a multitude of eyes, burning with intense interest in what they do.

Such characteristics as these should begin to show themselves at once, and in ever enlarging degrees of strength and beauty, in each pupil : a new sense of order and a new love for it ; a new spirit of work ; higher aims and purposes and plans ; loftier ideals of attainment ; increase in daily happiness ; and greater refinement of feeling, both as a matter of artistic sentiment, and of a deeper moral sense. The nobler the style of boy by nature, the more should such intellectual and moral fruitage be required, and the more regularly under true educational culture ; while the more backward is any pupil, the more should we secretly pity him and labor patiently and continually for his advancement : regarding his backwardness, as in nearly every case it accords with the truth to do, as the result of voluntary, although unconscious torpidity of mind on his part : a dulness self-imposed by a will hitherto unawakened, because hitherto unsolicited or unpressed to work; or of early abuse, stifling its first beginnings of growth, by ridicule, or neglect, or at least want of earnest, loving kindness and care in some form.

But how different from the views here expressed, are those represented in the current style of education! According to these it is of no advantage to the world, that there are different orders of talent among youth, and that young giants appear among them in advance, as among men in the higher employments of life. It is as if one were called to train a multitude of quadrupeds theoretically for their own best development, and, instead of adapting the style of education assumed, to the size strength and capacities of each, he were to put all, of whatever stature or form, into one style of harness, and to require of all, of whatever step or gait, one uniform style of movements. Is it any wonder, that so many feel utterly disgusted with the prevailing modes of instruction of whatever name, as well as with their results; while others laugh at the whole thing as a pitiable though ostentatious farce.

Does any one in conclusion ask, what is to encourage and sustain a teacher, of the highest aims and efforts, in his career of constant, noble toil? Faith in God! this, and this alone! Leaning on this staff, given to him from above, he can walk triumphantly, through flood and fire, onward and upward, in abounding usefulness. The one man in modern society, little as he may be so recognized, that combines in his own person the offices of the prophet, the priest and the king of ancient days, is such a teacher, walking with God, and ever looking up to him, and working for him with all his might of body and of soul.

IV.

THE TRUE CHRISTIAN SCHOLAR

IV.

THE TRUE CHRISTIAN SCHOLAR.

THE word school, Greek σχολή, meaning leisure, repeats itself, under various euphonic modifications, in all the languages of the civilized world. And leisure it is, or freedom from manual labor, that those devoted to learning enjoy; and freedom, not only from the mere care of the body, which makes life to most men such a series of burdens, but also from a multitude of other dusty experiences, connected with a material and sensual heritage of the world. The classic sense of the word, as of the word scholar, had reference to adults: to those who gathered, from principles of elective affinity, around the great inquirers and reasoners of elder days. The Latin word, ludus, which was also used like schola to denote a school, and which does not seem to have been transferred to any other language, signifies sport, games, strife: presenting the idea of a gymnasium, where earnest combatants struggled with each other for the mastery. The "contentio corporis" of the one corresponded to the "contentio animi" of the other. The view of the scholar's life in the one word is objective ; while in the other it is subjective.

The name scholar has ever been a name of honor in the world, and he who has been worthy to bear it has been sure of respect in all ages and countries. The priests who ruled in the inner world of faith, in the first beginnings of historic development, as among the ancient Egyptians and the Celts, were the scholars of those times. The thinkers, who, in after ages in Greece and Rome, kept open court in the temple of reason for crowds of admiring attendants, and sent forth from their secret place of power all the vital influences and energies that originated within the bosom of society in their day, were the men of thoroughly trained habits of mind : the men of vast scholarly powers of exploration and discovery, for their age, in the realms of truth. How much of the intellectual history of Greece, full of all great things as was the stream, flowed forth from the fountains of thought in Plato's and Aristotle's heart ! Scholars were often, in those days of thunderous strife, appointed also to muster the hosts of war. Pericles, Demosthenes, Thucydides and Xenophon, Cicero and Cæsar, were all generals.

The structure of ancient humanity was reared on the basis of physical strength and martial bravery. Giants, heroes, chieftains and kings then ruled the world. Modern society, so far as it is normal and Christian in its type, is all upreared on the great doctrine of right, not might: a mental and moral basis. Thought not force now holds the sceptre. The paraphernalia of power and its blazonry are put away out of sight, or gazed at, wherever they are found, only as the tawdry relics of the past. Power itself is latent, like the great invisible forces of nature, but all the more real and mighty. Scholars are the nobles that now walk the world, without indeed any regalia, but bearing the stamp of Divinity upon their brow. The aristocracy of mind is the only aristocracy, that envious Time cannot destroy.

The common classes once everywhere looked askance at men of study and learning, as those, who, in lacking stout, hard hands like themselves, were thought to have of necessity but weak heads: being regarded but as accomplished drones, who were willing to see others gather the honey of life, that they might dwell in ease and consume it. But educated men have so evidently carved out all the features of modern society, and led the nations forward, step by step, on the great highway of human progress, that every mouth is now silent against them from conviction. The study, the laboratory, the office, are the places where the modern rulers of the world sit in state. And yet, strange to say, the school, the great original fountain of all the education of the age, the spot whence its quickening influences all flow, is practically regarded almost with indifference by the mass of educated, and more still of even Christian men.

What a magnificent procession of worthies, each bearing a serene front and holy light in his eyes, would the great army of scholars in all ages and countries present, could they pass together before us! What a galaxy of stars and of constellations of stars in the firmament of History! Numbers without number of such men, in the church, as Moses, learned in all the wisdom of the Egyptians, Solomon, the wisest of men, Paul, brought up at the feet of Gamaliel, Augustine, Jerome, Wickliffe, Luther, Calvin, Pascal, Fenelon, Cudworth, Larned, Chillingworth, Edwards, Chalmers, Neander; and, in the world at large, as Plato, Aristotle, Cicero, Cæsar, Bacon, Leibnitz, Milton, Newton, Porson, Herschel, Berzelius, La Place, Cuvier, Gesenius, Niebuhr, Passow, Bopp, Grimm, Liebig and Agassiz, in all the departments of science, literature, history and language.

Will it not be both pleasant and profitable to consider, what are the characteristics of the true scholar, and in what way he can best promote his own highest development.

I. His characteristics. By these are meant,

1st. His loves and pleasures.

2d. His liberties.

3d. His habits.

1st. And what are his loves and pleasures ?

He delights in solitude. He is freed in it from the interruptions, temptations and tumults of life : secluded from the noisy world without, so as to be all the more free to range with giant-steps the bright world of thought within. He is least alone when most alone ; for then, as Plato beautifully defines thinking, "he holds sweet dialogue with himself ;" or goes forth through the golden gates of the past, which open of their own accord before him, to greet the venerated men of all ages that stand waiting, with crowns on their heads and censers in their hands, to minister to his gratification. The closet and the study : these are the two corners of Eden still left to this world, and the two radiant points from which the light of Heaven most streams out, over all the earth.

But it is of the scholar's pleasure in his own acts and states, rather than in any thing pertaining to his environment, of which we design here to speak.

(1.) He delights in gaining knowledge.

There is great pleasure in mere acquisition. The very faculty itself, as well as the impulse to use it, now wasted by so many upon the pursuit of money and power, were made a part of our original mental constitution, on purpose that we should employ them in securing the riches of the mind and of the heart.

The more that one increases in knowledge, the wider becomes at once his conscious relationship to the universe within which he is placed, and on which he is to act. The greater therefore is his sense of the order, worth and beauty of all that is outward to himself, and which was constituted what it is, in advance, with direct reference to the capabilities and wants of the soul; and the higher and the broader becomes his own consciousness of himself, as the appointed lord of this lower world. "He that increaseth knowledge," saith Solomon, "increaseth strength;" or, as Lord Bacon hath it, "knowledge is power." To gain new knowledge is one of the highest pleasures of life. The constant excitement of the eye and the ear, and of the whole sensational nature of childhood, in the reception of new ideas from every object in every quarter, is one of the chief sources of that spontaneous, joyous hilarity, with which early youth is everywhere so radiant. Not only "is the world ruled by ideas," as is often said; but idcas are also the well-spring of all the joy or sorrow of our mortal life.

Were more men addicted to acquiring new ideas through all their life, in grand and glowing succession, so many would not say as now that in youth they had their largest experience of pleasure. He who desires to be a child again, pays certainly a poor compliment to the quality either of his mind itself, or of his general treatment of it. Ideas ever new and ever great are obtainable in whatever direction one turns his eyes, or his feet, to obtain them It is one of the greatest results of modern civilization that, while money can be obtained in all ages by but few, and is in every age obtained by far more than ever make a right use of it, the treasures of knowledge are made open to all, in forms and ways that are of perpetual recurrence, and at prices that can be met even from the shrivelled purses of the poor.

That higher style of mental toil and attainment, which we call scholarship, may be of two kinds: general and special. General scholarship presents one of its chief charms, in the wider view which it furnishes of the great harmony of analogies prevailing in all sciences and knowledges, as constituting one vast sisterhood of mutually according witnesses, that they all had a common origin in the will of one glorious Divine Being, and all have a common end in their benefits and uses to his creature, man. It has also the advantage of giving greater breadth to the development of the mind itself, greater range to its researches, and greater volume to its thoughts. Special minute scholarship also has its own individual pleasures; and they are great. The field of its operations is infinitely diversified; and the subdivisions of which earnest mental labor is capable are endless. There is enough wonder in any minute department of investigation in nature, science, art or language, to occupy fully one life-time after another spent in Herculean toil. The greatest beauties of art are those which are minutest: the greatest marvels of nature are those which are microscopic; and the greatest blessings of life are those momentary benefits, the aggregate of which makes such a broad stream of bounty, ever flowing unto all men from the great heart of God. "He that is faithful in that which is least is faithful also in much." Nowhere is this more true than in the realms of scholarship. Nicety of knowledge is as essential an idea of a scholar, as nicety of execution is of an artist. And, as the Divine mind took great pleasure in constructing little things, as is evident in the accuracy and harmony of their most minute adaptations and uses, and in all their careful elaboration of form and color, in reference to his own sense of beauty or that of a happy few of His intelligent creatures, who should at some future day of advanced knowledge, as now, inspect them with wonder; so, the finite mind, when most like the Divine in intellect and character, is most fond of searching the hidden riches of His wisdom and goodness, and most appreciative of them when found.

It is no part of real greatness, God's or man's, to slight what is little, and invisible either on account of its minuteness or of its vast distance from the view. That proof of genius, of which we so often hear, carelessness about trifles, while rejoicing in a vaulting, brilliant style of mind, in certain speculative or imaginative directions, is but a proof of a perverse heart, neglecting its duty because of its irksome details ; or of a perverted intellect, expecting to gain the desired result without heeding God's appointed law of work, which is : that, according to the quantity and quality of the product, must be the quantity and quality of the labor expended. What greater folly, than to expect to have the whole without having each of its component parts.

The pleasure of investigating minute facts, principles, relations and uses is very great. It has in it the excitement of busy research, and also of perpetual, ever-widening discovery. It furnishes, besides, deep, philosophic gratification in the larger comprehension afforded by it of the analogies of nature and of providence for one's self, and in the ability obtained, to verify or modify the theories of science, to extend the boundaries of human knowledge, and to multiply the many uses which man can make of his own powers or time, or of the outer universe to which all his functions of action and enjoyment are so exquisitely adapted. The difference between modern and ancient scholarship, as between ancient and modern philosophy, lies in this one thing chiefly : the greater minuteness of the modern, and so its greater universality. Superficial theorizing took the place, in the ancient, of close, repeated, patient investigation, in the modern. And the reason why men now-a-days have so many more comforts and appliances of every kind, personal and social, than those of former times, lies very largely in the fact of the revelation which minute modern scholarship has made of the hidden elements, resources, energies and agencies laid by in the great store-house of nature, for the benefit of those who shall search after them and find them.

(2.) He delights in finding truth, as such.

Truth is the natural and appointed aliment of the human mind. To an angelic mind, or a human one in its true normal state, all truth of every sort would seem, whenever found, but a part of God's image of Himself in his works. The charm of searching for any truth is to such a mind the charm of seeking for something, anew, that has come from His heart and hand, and therefore is full of the beauty of his skill and love. And if the undevout astronomer be truly mad, what must be said of the scholar, who, by turning away from God, makes all his wisdom utter foolishness, both in His sight and in fact ? Much of the scholarship of the world has been indeed hitherto, under evil preparatory influences, not only in a negative, but also in a positive way, ungodly. Multitudes of students, like so many possessing wealth and power, have used this world as abusing it: turning what are properly but means to its great ends, into ends of action for themselves.

The habits and tastes engendered by true scholarship are favorable to the study and reception of evangelical truth as such. The scholar has indeed a noble preparation for high, religious thought, and for delicate refined sensibility to every thing fitted to lead him to the adoration, worship and service of God. God delights in true earnest thinkers. All his forms and degrees of approach to his creatures, in his works and word, his providence and grace, are alike accommodated to the supposition, that they are to be active and true and earnest in their modes of understanding and appreciating Him and his ways. The whole universe is indeed, rightly understood, but an universe of multitudinous appeals, in high and bright material forms, to thought. If "it has pleased God to save men by the foolishness of preaching," it has not been by choosing fools to be his preachers. Those to whom, having arisen and stood upon their feet: according to the word sent unto the prophet: "arise and stand upon thy feet, and I will speak to thee:"

He has spoken words during the ages, that they should speak again for him to all men, have ever been the greatest men of their times, in genius and learning and thought: men like Moses and Solomon and David and Isaiah and Ezekiel and Paul and John: such men as mankind would have called golden-mouthed, even had they stood up in their own names, alone, in their day and generation. The highest style of piety can be exhibited only in a mind of the largest dimensions for power and attainments; and, as faith rests upon reason, so does all lofty religious energy and joy upon high strong thought. The quality of the piety, exhibited by such men as Paul and Edwards, presupposes by necessity the quality of intellect, with which it is always found connected. The influence of Christianity, in developing scholarship, has been quite as remarkable, as in developing public reforms, enterprise, art, or civilization, in any of its specific departments. "The living creatures," now astir within the wheels of all our modern movements, are the busy, earnest, studious thinkers of the day.

The true scholar will be then, legitimately, observant, appreciative and studious of all the great aspects, bearings and issues of evangelic truth; and, just in proportion as one is entitled to the high designation of a scholar, will he exhibit subjectively, in spirit and aim, an exact correspondence with the influences and claims of all objective truth with which he comes into definite relations. He is intellectually at one with the universe as it is, receptively, in welcoming its lessons, influences and benefits to his heart, as was God, actively, in making it for his own pleasure and for the good of his creatures. The truth it is, that he everywhere longs to find : the truth as it is in Christ : in nature, history, art, or life, and throughout the wide range of the present, past or future. And how delightful is it to find the truth ! The discovery is substantial and abiding. The mind has now something on which to repose with confidence : it has obtained a new stepping-stone on which to go up higher ; and it has a deep, glad sense that its great powers have now found their true use, and its highest efforts their true end. The human mind is as plainly constructed for the pursuit, apprehension and enjoyment of truth, as is the eye to bathe in floods of light, or as are the chambers of the ear to reverberate with sound.

3dly. He delights in using his own powers.

So exquisitely has God fashioned both the body and the mind, that the mere use of their powers, without reference to the object on which they are employed, gives great pleasure. What gladness does simple motion give to the bird, the quadruped, the insect and the fish ! Which of them all is still, except for short periods of necessary repose? The more complicated the structure of an animal, the higher the style of his capacities, and the broader the range of his being; so much the higher will be his enjoyment, in the natural use of his functions. From the lowest forms of vermicular or larva life, through all the most varied complexities of animal organism, up to man, as rises the scale of multiplex energies and uses, in the construction of the being, so rises, correspondingly, the scale of his pleasures in quality, variety and number. Man, as he stands at the summit of the ascending series, in the fulness and finish of his powers, should also appear, and in his completely developed state will appear, as the crown of all God's works on earth, not only in the height and breadth of his capacities, but also in the overflowing abundance of his pleasures.

The true scholar in his highest form is the Christian scholar; and his proper appointed portion of good on earth would be most of it sacrificed, if the temper of his heart and the aims of his life were not divine. The scholarship of the present day is far more Christian than in any preceding age; although, with remarkable uniformity, the scholars of every land and age, Heathen, Papal and Christian have occupied, as a class, the advanced posts of morality, religion, and theology in their times. And, just as surely as the commerce, enterprise, art, literature and jurisprudence of the world are to become thoroughly Christian, and all the drift of the past and present is manifestly and powerfully in that direction, so ere long is all the scholarship of the world to be only and completely evangelical.

And what are the pleasures to the truly Christian scholar, of the full earnest use of his powers? Great, very great in every direction. The mind was made for incessant thought, for seeing, comparing, analyzing, arranging and deducing facts and principles; and exalted indeed is the joy of the mind, when at work with all its might upon great objects, and for great ends. Not more sublimely sweeps an eagle around a lofty mountain-peak, hovering, as if intoxicated with delight, over the vast abyss below, than circles the excited soul of a noble Christian thinker, in the full equipoise of all its powers when in their highest state of exaltation, around the loftiest summits of truth that are visible to mortal eyes. The pleasure which others have only in momentary gushes of splendid excitement, from the irregularity of their untrained mental action, he, having learned, by long and careful self-discipline, to sustain consecutive and concentrated habits of thought to any desired period of protraction, is able to keep in a full ocean-swell in his heart: ever

10

breaking grandly like a sea of glory, whose waves are all waves of light, surge after surge, upon the shore of his inner being.

The Christian Scholar's thinking, on whatever special theme employed, is always as such devoted to the greatest of ends. The two ends of his scale of thought and of life are God and man. From God to man : this is the next of sentences in his thoughts to that sublimest of all utterances : from eternity to eternity. Whether ascending or descending on such a scale, his movements and his pleasures are godlike. The true Christian Scholar is a sort of intellectual mediator between God and man : revealing to human view the hidden stores of God's wisdom and goodness, otherwise as much undiscovered to ordinary passers-by, as if indeed they were not at all in existence. While the sense of power is one of the most delightful, natural senses of the mind, from the experience of a little child who knows enough to blow out a light, and laughs at the feat, to that of him who can build a telescope or an ocean steamer, or write a great epic, it rises to its greatest height, when the end accomplished is one that brings lasting, moral advantage to the race.

But let us consider

2dly. The liberties of the true Christian Scholar.

To other men the great bright outer world is a mass of confused unmeaningnesses. Nothing is seen as it is, in reference either to its origin or its uses. All the real relations of things, whether outward or inward, are not only unappreciated but also unwitnessed; and the wonders with which every moment's vision or experience is crowded, appear to them, if they look at them at all, like the words of a strange language to one who is rude in knowledge. The books of thought and truth and life and love which lie with large, open, glowing pages before the eyes of the Scholar, for his constant rapture in gazing at them, seem closed to them with seals that they cannot break. But to the Scholar, the deep, earnest, patient, right, thinker, of wide horizon and high range in his style of thought, all passages of light through this world, or from it to another, that God has paved for any but an angel's feet, stand ever open, in full, clear, broad, illumination before him.

He has the range of all the many approaches to the secret places of His skill and love, which God has prepared with such royal munificence for man's appreciation of Him and His ways. Others are ruled almost inevitably by circumstances: he in a great measure rules them. They wait for outward opportunity: he is instant in season and out of season, in thought, effort, plan and attainment, and in always trying is always succeeding; while, in always looking to God for His blessing on what he does, he enjoys at all times doubly whatever he obtains, as the fruit both of his own labors and of God's co-operative beneficence.

Like distinguished men, who, when travelling in foreign lands, are presented with the freedom of the cities through which they pass, he has received in the very enlargement of his mind as a Scholar, and his investiture as a Christian by God of "all things" as "his," the freedom of the universe; and to him alone is realized in its full sense what is meant in this world by that phrase so characteristic of the gospel: the freedom of the Sons of God.

He is free from the errors, limitations and disappointments of ignorance; from the misleadings of superstition; from conscious subjection to others' neglects or frowns; from the power of foolish fears, presentiments and morbid imaginations; and from the gross temptations which so often assail effectually other men and surprise every one by their overthrow; as well as also from the lusts of other men, as the lust of gold, of power, of flattery, and of all the varied gaudy show of pride. No men work so much and so gladly, for so little compensation, as Scholars; and men looking on, say: "Well! if the reward be small, the honor is great, and this makes the balance even between them and the rest of the world." So indeed writers on political economy say in form in their works. But not such are the secret thoughts of the Scholar himself. He of all men feels that honor is not a matter of any man's calling merely, but rather of his own actions in it. It is not the outward glitter of his style of life, that reconciles him to the narrow equipments with which society furnishes it; but the inward satisfaction of it, as meeting the deep interior wants of his nature, as a thinker and a doer upon the brief stage of life, and as providing him with treasures for his own enjoyment, far richer than those that can be measured in gold or silver. He is free likewise from others' regrets, who feel not only dissatisfied, without thinking why, with life as it passes; but also at its close generally feel their own self-condemnation, for the frivolity and emptiness of their whole previous life, resting with the weight of a mountain upon their hearts. He is free too from the wants of others, who always pine for something that they have not yet obtained. They crave novelty, change, excitement, and seek it where if gained it cannot last, or even pass away, as it must, without reactive sorrow. And he is free from the accidents of others. In the peaceful, sequestered vales of thought he walks; and the tumults and the uproar of those, who are involved in the conflicts of life and their hazards, are to him in the far-off distance. No class is, as a class, so long-lived as thinkers, especially earnest, joyous Christian students. Their powers remain unbroken to the end. They have inward stimulations in high objective aims, mental activity and sweet perpetual joy, that of themselves tend most powerfully to prolong life. And the more really that they deserve the name of Scholars, the more do they walk by rules and principles established by God himself, in respect to both outward and inward elements of happiness and prosperity : as they see their existence and their scope more clearly, and appreciate more instinctively than other men, their beauty and their force.

Others possess, in the natural endowments of their being, an immense amount of what is in their hands but unproductive real estate ; while in his case his education, in its full, Christian type, constitutes a great and splendid capital, which he keeps with gladness ever invested in man's wants and God's claims. And at the same time, in the objective resources with which it furnishes him, he holds in his hands the keys of Heaven and earth and of all their untold riches ; and every door on every side, that he fain would enter, flies open, as if by some inward magic of its own, at his approach, as if his very looks were keys to turn their bolts.

The Scholar's occasions for employment, moreover are of his own making, and they are of perpetual recurrence. He determines his own sphere of activity. What he is or has or does is under God self-appointed. The habit of his mind is therefore that of strong, conscious self-direction. The more of a scholar that he becomes, the more does each new degree of elevation isolate him, in respect to his elements of thought and feeling, from the mass around him, who are quite unsympathetic and indifferent to his high pursuits; and without the counteracting influences of true piety, so outward and communicative as it is in all its efforts and effects, the strong centripetal tendency of his life would serve to make him not only isolated in his experiences, but also seclusive and selfish in his feelings. The attitude of his mind towards all surrounding objects: his apprehension and appreciation of them: his standards for judging them and his desires in relation to them are all directly relevant to his own special position for viewing the universe. What others see not he beholds, and what they gaze upon he often does not see at all. Indeed, as each man's sight of the sun or of any object that its light reveals is his own, and can be no other man's; so, the universe is to each of us what his eye for perceiving it is, and what his heart, for appreciating its beauties and treasures and glories.

3dly. The habits of the true Christian scholar.

These are twofold: his habits of thought and feeling about his work, and his habits of application to it.

(1.) His two characteristic moods of mind toward his work represent well, not only the double polarity of his own thoughts, but that also of every right heart toward its duty: patience and enthusiasm.

§ 1. His patience.

He accepts, not only contentedly but also gladly, the law of labor, against which others in such numbers are, either in spirit or action, at perpetual variance. He loves labor: an acquired taste, which he has slowly but surely obtained, as one of the great, ruling elements of his daily life. He has schooled his heart to keep a steady eye upon the future. All heroism begins and ends in the habit of making the future present to the heart, as containing in itself all the great realities of life. His heroism is not, as is the bravery of a soldier, or adventurer, that of a crisis: impulsive and temporary; but the heroism of a whole life, steady and true, by day and night, in summer and winter, from youth to old age: not issuing from caprice or excitement for a little time or space; but ever flowing in a full stream from the fountains of reason and of conscience, wherever it can find a channel for its tide. He has faith in the future, in the steady sequences of cause and effect, in the positiveness of Divine Providence, and in Time as the great Ripener of all things thought or done by man.

There are no preparatives for patience, except those of grace, like those of thorough classical study. The first requirement made by the genius of scholar ship of a student, in his very novitiate, is self-control. Peace is the atmosphere of the secret place of study, as of that of prayer. Almost all the self-government of society: its equilibrium of thought and its great all-pervading stability of feeling, even under the reign of Christianity, are, rightly interpreted, but the results in one form or another of the thorough, intellectual discipline of the leaders of society, in this and preceding ages.

Often is the scholar thronged and almost suffocated with difficulties. He must have indeed steady nerves and a persistent foot. His eyes must look right on, and his eyelids straight before him. Often, after long and eager wandering through some narrow winding path, to find the object of his hopes, he comes, when most excited with the expectation of success, to the verge of a precipice, or to some high, perpendicular obstruction, and must retrace all his steps again to the very place of beginning. Critical scholarship is full of such experiences. Ever and anon badgered and baffled in its course, but always erect in its spirit and earnest in its work, it holds on resolutely to its undertakings. Trials are its needful discipline, as they are of religion: hardening, tempering and purifying its character. The true Christian scholar is energetic and hopeful. Some trial and trouble must be accepted, he feels, as a part of the necessary wear of life. For the rest: and this is the greater part of all the fretted experience of men; which is self-determined, from over-sensitiveness to it or from want of earnest effort to remove it: he ever bids his heart remember, that there is a way out. For every temptation, saith the word of God, and so for every trouble there is a way of escape. This is a cardinal part of his great, practical philosophy of life. Others allow themselves to think and say that they cannot do, what yet they see some around them do, for their own improvement or the good of others, and content themselves with a paralytic philosophy of their own powers in theory, and of course practically also of their duties.

Men honor only what appears upon the surface and strikes the sense with its glitter. Parade and noise, if well supported in the rear, make an essential front to all the shows of human greatness, that men are disposed to admire in their own age. But the true forces of society that inspire and control its movements, like those of nature and of the universe itself, are out of sight to the multitude and revealed only to the eye of thought. The true noblemen of the world move unknown among the men of their generation. They are the toiling, earnest, persevering students of the times, ever busy in penetrating into the recesses of nature and the mysteries of life and the wonders to be found in the invisible realms of thought and truth : lovingly bent on bringing forth to the view of all men whatever beauties and riches they can find, for their use and enjoyment. And, as a tree has received its present growth and shape, from myriads on myriads of distinct minute influences, from sun and soil and wind and rain ; so, the final results of their efforts, which the rest of mankind find of such practical advantage to themselves, are the sum total of multitudes of separate thoughts, examinations, experiments and labors, patiently encountered and added to each other, pile upon pile for years. It is in their very patience, their long, calm, bold waiting for the desired end of all their labors, that their power lies, and with it their honor.

What a demand does all true, high scholarship make upon its votaries for patience ! It never ceases to require continuity of effort. Genius, wit and speculation may flourish on happy hits ; but scholarship is the preparation and growth of years. Its results are not like those of a battle, achieved suddenly and once for all, but rather like those of a huge edifice, carefully planned and constructed from the corner-stone without to the last finishing stroke within. Beside mere continuity of effort, which might have in it the variety of constant change, scholarship demands a great deal of repetitiousness of aim and toil; because sometimes the end to be gained is a large collection of many details of the same kind, and at others repeated failures to obtain the full result in every desired particular perpetually stimulate the mind to new efforts to avoid them. A frequent, critical review also of one's supposed achievements is not the smallest, in some instances at least, of the forms of patient toil that the true scholar is ever willing to impose upon himself. And so also the element of time is one of the most fundamental elements of all broad and high scholarship, as of all broad and high character. Slowly, although surely and majestically, rises day after day the vast pile to its completion.

Patience in its higher forms is bravery. This the Romans understood and therefore described a brave man as fortis (from fero to bear), one who could endure the worst. So Paul speaks of charity, or Christian principle, as "bearing all things:" it is brave. One of the finest of all preparations, accordingly, for real bravery in the battle of life and even in the actual thunder-storms of war itself is obtainable by long-protracted, thorough, mental drill in study. An army of well-trained Christian scholars would certainly be, in a war of principle, the most formidable army that any one could meet. And that higher bravery of daily life that is needful, to go persistently and triumphantly through all the labors and troubles of every-day experience, to the end : higher, because demanded on so much larger a scale and without the aid of great occasions and great crowds to animate it : can, next to religion, and in conjunction with it, be best obtained from a high and true and large style of mental discipline.

As most schools and colleges are at present conducted, a young man runs a complete gauntlet, consciously or unconsciously, during his whole course in them. His destiny is left wholly, or nearly so, to his own unenlightened judgment and his own unsupported courage, to keep steadily at work for benefits that are out of sight. Nothing therefore does he need more than persistent patience to the very end

§ 2. His enthusiasm.

The word student from studium, eagerness, zeal, implies that he, who deserves this honorable title, is "fervid in spirit." Zeal is an essential part of the character of a scholar. No two ideas more perfectly antagonistic to each other could be combined, than those united in such a phrase as a lazy student. Not more absurd would it be, to talk of sluggish lightning, or obscure brilliancy.

Character is so little cultivated in this world in any direction; and all ideas of artistic development are so foreign to this subject in the thoughts of most men; that patience and enthusiasm are both regarded commonly as natural endowments, where they are manifested, rather than as virtues prepared and nurtured from height to height, in the heart that possesses them. But they are voluntary excellences which each man is required to have, as truly as honesty or purity of heart. They appear also at first sight to be contrary, the one to the other; while in fact they blend as harmoniously in union, as the subjective and objective elements of things, which are everywhere sublimely paired together, and which in fact they respectively to a great degree represent. The virtues of patience and enthusiasm are body and soul to each other. Patience is the response of the soul, on the passive side of its nature, to stubborn things without, that press upon its consciousness; and enthusiasm is the response of all the many active elements of its being to the opportunities for effort, progress and usefulness, which it beholds around and before it in its onward pathway.

The Christian scholar, when in his full development, has an inward sense of the beautiful, the true and the good which other men lack: so that they are blind to the vision which perpetually enchants him. He seems to himself, almost even when walking amid the dust of this gross world, to be passing over fairy ground. Forms, aspects, colors, that others never see at all, are always glowing in his eye and burning in his heart. The fire of his thoughts is celestial and never goes out or even goes down, but is always blazing upward to its native source. The impulses of a true Christian scholar are of a high origin: his labors all have a noble end. He so reaches upwards and outwards as always to long for power to reach farther. He so fills up the measure of his opportunities, as to feel ever constrained by the want of more time, to do what he aims to do and longs to do in his brief day upon the earth. His habitual consciousness is that of a soul full of daring, looking out for new fields on which to employ it: full of strength, and wishing to use it; and full of all accumulations of knowledge and goodness, and wishing to bestow them upon others. Time, therefore, never hangs as a weight upon his neck, in the race of life; nor does melancholy sit brooding, like a bird of darkness, upon the altar of his heart. The world always seems to have so few laborers in it, really addressing themselves to its true wants, that there is at all times an abundance of room and work for him. His field of view is earth-wide: his sense of God's presence with him now is strong and quickening; and the thought of his continued existence in that Presence forever is full at all times of grand inspiration to him. His highest taste is for deeds of love ; and his strongest passion is to please Him, who made him and has bought him with his own precious blood. The wants of others are ever sounding like the surges of a sea of darkness in his ear ; and life is full to him of splendid opportunities for the highest sort of moral action. With his own big soul within him : with God above and around him, and suffering men in multitudes at his feet : with Heaven before and Hell behind : how can he be tame in his spirit, or low in his aims, or faltering in his movements ! Whether he moves, or stands, upon the stage of life, it must be as a man of moral grandeur in his thoughts and plans : one, the inward swell and glow of whose feelings will give an air of nobility to all the motions, looks and tones of even his mortal frame.

To an earnest, Christian scholar life appears to be, at all times, a drawn game between himself and the devil. It is not merely Shakspeare's idea of life which he has : that this world is a stage, and all the men and women are actors upon it : as a place for the exhibition of human nature to human eyes ; but Paul's rather and the gospel's : that we are all here upon a race-ground, and compassed about with a great cloud of witnesses on earth and in Heaven, where we must each run so as to obtain, or, failing to do so, lose not a mere earthly crown, but an heavenly one forever.

(2.) His habits of action toward his work, like his moods of feeling toward it, are twofold.

§ 1. It is his habit, to be thorough in his style of executing it.

He is thorough, in the two great particulars, of completeness of plan and finish of execution. Thoroughness is the same as throughness. He traverses with careful exactness the full orb of his subject, or of his department of subjects. He penetrates the hidden recesses of the science, art or language, to which he is devoted, through and through. His analyses are always exhaustive: his surveys always complete. The discovery by himself of real negligence in his work would entail upon him, at once, a sense of guilt. The frequent occurrence of such a fault would justly rob him, by the verdict of his own conscience, of all right to the designation of a real scholar, or to his own self-respect as a man. Blunders anywhere look to him as would rents in a kingly robe or blotches on a piece of art. Accuracy is the very jewel of his honor. He is slow in forming decisions, because so minute in his examination of their proper grounds; but, when formed, they are fixed facts to him, and stand in their places, as if made of iron. He is willing "to take pains" now, rather than to be himself, by and by, taken of them. Care in details, at all times, care in finding them and in discriminating and employing them aright: this defines the fundamental difference between a great mechanician, painter, sculptor, anatomist, or even Christian and an ordinary one; and so does it also between the true scholar and the false. What his taste and his eye demand of him, at all times, in his work is quality, rather than quantity.

§ 2. It is his habit, to concentrate his full force of mind upon his work.

It is an essential idea of the true scholar, that he bends his powers to the utmost upon his occupation. It is demanded by the very scope of his name and office, that they should be made to burn always with intensity, as upon a given focal point, on every part of his work. Other men often pass through life without really knowing themselves or being known of others. They have capacities of reasoning, discrimination, comparison and judgment, of which they dream not, because never using them on any high subject or to any full intense degree: mines of wealth in their own natures, that they have never opened: heavenly treasures which they have never put at all to usury. The true scholar, on the contrary, has asserted his rightful place over things around him as their proper interpreter, manager and owner, and demands of them persistently and successfully to give up the secrets which they hold, for his benefit.

In the use of one's faculties, up to the entire amount of their vigor, there is, when they are in their full combination of action, great joy to one's self and great power over others. The motives which most stimulate the mind to make such a complete outlay of itself, perpetually, are blessed and divine ; and the employment which best evokes, at all times, such a conscious demonstration of one's whole energy of being, is a blissful employment. Not more willing is the fruitful earth itself to yield its riches to him, who will faithfully seek after them, than are the sweet waters of truth or salvation, to run into any one's well, who values them sufficiently to dig down to the depths where they flow.

The accomplished scholar has acquired a power of fixing his attention fully on any subject, at will, and of transferring it from one topic to another ; which of itself alone suffices to open to him myriad doors to all sorts of chambered secrets, in every part of the universe. Power of attention, or of the fixation of any faculty or set of faculties upon their proper object, is the chief exercise of voluntary power, which the mind can employ over its own functions. This it is the daily work of the scholar to exercise ; and whatever other power a strong will has over the native energies of the mind, to intensify their action when in use, he also possesses.

Like all men of high thought, imagination and faith, the scholar holds always in full view a lofty ideal of his work. The elements of his ideal, like those of the painter, embrace, in respect to the style of results to be gained, the following ideas: fulness of outline, completeness of detail and finish in execution. To realize the actual demands of such a comprehensive mass of conceptions, in the form and direction, the quality and quantity, of each hour's labor, day by day through all the year, will require great earnestness of feeling and concentration of purpose and power of will, at all times.

The more real genius a scholar possesses, the more he responds instinctively to all appeals, direct and indirect, to work. That is no fanciful combination of ideas which so often occurs in the biography of great men: "he was a man of great genius and of unbounded industry." Any man who has unbounded industry has, at least, one large streak of genius in him, not to say also of success. Dull natures neither stir up themselves to action, nor respond, with any sensitiveness, to quickening influences from without.

The student needs surely, if any other one does, to be a man of principle or rather of principles, many, fixed and great. Energy, method and patient perseverance must be his uniform characteristics. His hours and places of study he must keep sacred from invasion. Whatever he takes in hand he must master. What he gains he must keep, and be able to use at all times familiarly.

There are especially certain maxims and first principles, worthy to be expanded into a scholar's guide-book, which, for the benefit of the young student, shall find a place, for at least their mere enumeration here.

They are such as these :

1. The method for attaining to the highest scholarship in the end is simply this : while being regular and constant in one's work, to get every day's lesson in first-rate style : as in the construction of a brick edifice, if every brick is itself first-rate and is laid in first-rate cement and in a first-rate way, the whole structure will, when completed, be throughout by necessity of first-rate quality.

2. Whatever is worthy of being done at all is worthy of being done in the best manner possible.

3. There is a very great difference, as in character, art, and even business, so also in scholarship, between being exactly right and a little wrong.

4. Every man makes his own future.

5. Every one can afford to work hard for him-

self; and if so, how much more for both himself and all the world beside.

6. The benefit of all true education is not in itself, but in its uses.

7. Both God and man always help those, who help themselves, and much more those who help others also.

8. In God's kingdom every man reaps exactly what he sows.

II. In what way a true scholar can best promote his own highest development.

1st. He must do really and fully all things for God.

To men who think of God, as but a poetical description of some occult principle in nature, or of the whole material frame-work of the universe itself, it may seem strange that thoughts of him can give any spur to the soul. But conceived of as He is, as a Being before whom all others united, whether for knowledge, power or character, are less than nothing, to whom all the myriads of worlds that he has made, and all their wondrous contents, are but the dust of his feet: the ever-present, tender-hearted, loving God, bending joyously down over each one of his earthly children: like what an orb of splendor beyond splendor, does he glow upon the vision of the delighted soul and fill the whole horizon of its consciousness! Before such light, such beauty, such love, the soul must, by the very necessity of its nature, as born of Him and for Him, arise and shake itself and put on all its strength. Personal love to God, with the sure consciousness of his own glorious friendship in return: what fuel will it not furnish to thought and feeling and vigorous mental effort. Labor, spontaneously generated by such sentiments of affection to him, or purposely bestowed toward him as the formal object of its aims and services, will give to all real scholarship the fullest possible amount of growth and fruitage. Human specimens of intellectuality have been so few and poor, and are so still, because, like plants grown in darkness, they have been reared away from the sunlight of God's sought and cherished smile. All beauty, power and dignity, in any part of our nature, are obtained only under the right ruling influence of the upper elements of our being: the light of reason, the breathings of conscience, the power of faith and the inspiration of hope: all God-ward in their natural tendencies; as in the body all the other members derive their light and usefulness from the head, which is placed over them to guide them.

But, beside the heightened action of the soul itself under the stimulus of a true sense of God, as its object and joy forever, the scholar will obtain, in maintaining right relations to Him, his manifest guidance and blessing. Many see Him only in great crises, or on the stage of national events ; but he is in fact intimately present at all times with us all : more so than was ever any father in his family, when surrounded by his children, hearing their words, noticing their actions and gladdening them with his presence, and being made glad by them. God, who made the palatial chambers of the soul, knows how to walk up and down in them, when he wills, in the glory of his goodness. He, who made the eye, knows how to illuminate it from without or from within ; and he who made the foot knows how to plant it on the paths, where he himself walks in gladness with his children. "Prayer and provender," says the old quaint proverb, "delay no man." Study, baptized with a spirit of prayer, has angel-features even to a human beholder ; but much more to him who made the mind for just such an employment of its time and powers, and who finds nothing among all his works so beautiful to his eye, as a right heart earnestly at work for his sake.

The highest attainable development of science, literature, art, labor or adventure, is its religious development ; and so it is true of men in any employment or profession, that their surest path to success, even according to earthly measurements of its height, is that of religion.

The scholar, who really strives in all things to please God, will feel that a Critic inspects his work, demanding its perfection, far higher than any ideal self or ideal public, before whose fancied verdict against him another may tremble. He will feel that he has ends to gain far grander than those around him desire to secure. His life seems full to him of the seeds of all great things. Each new moment is a new opportunity for some heroic deed. Life is to him a sublime march into an ever-opening, ever-glowing, gorgeous future.

The idea is quite prevalent that real scholarship produces, or at least implies, a cold nature. Classical and frigid are regarded as terms quite synonymous. Many men indeed of a dull, phlegmatic temperament, especially in these modern times, when the temptations to minds of an energetic mould to grasp after the material prizes of life are so great, have consecrated themselves, for their own gratification if not for the world's special advantage, to the walks of study. But a dead-alive scholar, like a so-called Christian of the same type, makes but a miserable figure indeed, in the ranks of honor in which he has placed himself. A cool head is one of the most essential qualifications for scholarship ; but not a cold heart. The only combination, in any department of human labor or experience, that brings to the producer or any recipient the right product of joy or excellence is this: a cool head and a warm heart. Greatness of heart is, as every one knows, the most uncommon symptom of humanity in any part of the world. To be simple, gentle, meek, affectionate, fervid, tender: would to multitudes seem to be weak and womanish. But Christ, who had in his spirit and acts alike all the glory of manhood, and of womanhood, and of childhood, combined, as was meet in Him who was to be the perfect type of the whole human race, is the model of the true scholar. Out of his entire life in all its minutest forms of activity should ring forth loud and clear, as its perpetual, sweet, deep melody to every listening ear: "Wist ye not that I must be about my Father's business?" The only honor that intellectual cultivation possesses in Heaven or on earth, is that of a high means to a higher end. Its riches are either squandered or hoarded, if not purposely used to contribute to the greater beauty and power of a right heart. The more evangelical and glowing the type of religious development, the finer the reactive influence of the scholarship and the character mutually upon each other. The Bible-command to men of all trades and professions, alike, is, "Be not slothful in business, but fervent in spirit, serving the Lord!" In what a meagre, shrivelled form, compared with its proper dimensions, has the scholarship of the world hitherto appeared! When the structure of Human Society shall in advancing ages be completed, in all its fulness of height and breadth of beauty and strength, as a vast temple of praise to God, full of the brightness of His glory: that grand edifice of which Christian scholars are to be, in every part of the world, the chief human builders: what a work will they then be found to have done upon the earth, and what a high commission from above will they prove themselves to have had, beyond others of their race, as laborers with God for man!

The elements of personal character which are most beautiful in a Christian scholar, before both God and man, are these: simplicity, the last attainment alike in science, invention and art, on the one hand, and in human character, on the other; honorableness, which is as beautiful in a scholar, as is gallantry in a soldier; integrity, which, as the word itself, like the word entire derived through the French from the same root, means, is wholeness or soundness, so that without it no man is himself or can be, but is on the contrary only the broken specimen of a man; purity, the want of which sullies him, as it would the minister at the altar or the virgin in her robe of whiteness; self-respect, without which no one else can respect him; industry, but for which he can neither get nor keep the name or character of a scholar ; and active ever-flowing benevolence, according to whose dictates he is to lay out all the riches that he has obtained, natural and acquired, for others.

2dly. He must keep himself in full sympathy with the age.

If any one upon earth ought to be practical in his aims, it is the scholar. He sees, or ought to see, with his purified vision, as other men cannot, the real wants of the world as they are ; and he it is who alone has the materials in his hand for meeting them. The end of knowledge and of scholarship is usefulness to others. Utility is indeed the law of all values, human and divine. The personal life or labor, which is divorced from the actual experience or wants of men, is so far worthless. But how many have turned scholarship, as others have religion, into a mere gilded abstraction. It has indeed passed into a habit with multitudes to jeer, without knowing it, at great truths and rules of conduct in calling them beautiful theories : as if a passing laugh could suddenly change a great commanding fact into a glittering generality.

A man may be as much of a miser in hoarding knowledge, as in hoarding gold. He that would be the greatest of all in the kingdom of thought, as in that of faith, must be the servant of all. Pitiful indeed is any perversion of scholarship to purposes of parade and pride. Real scholarship is as averse to any such perversion, as is real piety. And yet there are many who regard classical finish of thought and style, as the highest attainment possible to be made on earth; and that not as any means of benefit to others, but as a mere shining honor to one's self.

The true Christian scholar however will study his age, as his own legitimate field of action, and strive to communicate the light and heat of his own inward life to it, as one of its great permanent realities. He will not simply feel that he is acting his part in a great amphitheatre, in which the surrounding air is filled with eyes and ears, intent upon all that he says and does; but also that, wherever he goes, he is a seedsman sowing good or evil at every step which shall stand up in the world, long after he has left it, as the lasting product of his life. Of all men in the community the scholar is the most truly entitled to be called a representative man: so many secret wonders stand waiting his beck for the time of their deliverance to mankind, and so many interests of the highest sort and of ever new occurrence are decided by the form and force of his movements. He has obtained light and he should disperse it. He holds the keys of knowledge in his hands, and should open with them the ways of enjoyment, usefulness and honor to as many as possible.

It is a sort of natural habit of scholars as a class to act towards the age as a compensation or complement to its deficiencies, real or supposed. When the tendencies of the community are centripetal, as in monarchical Europe, the influence of the universities is thrown with living and almost instinctive energy and utterance, on the side of democratic ideas and institutions. When the tendency is centrifugal rather than centripetal, as in this country, they, or at least the professors in them, are apt to be of a more centripetal and conservative style of action But to balance the movements of the age, so as to keep the ship of state from being rocked unduly either way, is certainly but a small part of the work appointed for the scholar, as the man who alone among his fellows has had the crown of authority set upon his head by his Maker. He is called, on the contrary, of God, not simply to keep the vessel trim, but much more to steer it safely over boisterous seas, and with bold heroic faith, into "the place of broad rivers" prepared by His covenant for the nations.

3dly. He must keep himself at all times full of work.

Work is the law of success in every thing under the sun. Even those who do not have to work to make money must needs work to keep it ; and he who has tried the two will testify that it is harder to keep money, than to make it. The mechanism of the mind is all constructed with reference to the constant pressure of necessary work upon its energies. This is to give tone and movement and direction perpetually to them. Industry is therefore an absolute necessity to health or happiness or virtue. He who is always employed with all his might on the proper objects of his pursuit will not only find a trail of results accompanying him that will surprise even him ; but he will find also the occasions for fresh interest and labor perpetually multiplying in his path.

Many scholars so-called have indifferent health because, under the influence of the false and pernicious theory that earnest protracted labor of the mind is as such detrimental to high bodily vigor, they restrain themselves with cold and painful pertinacity from the most natural and joyous use of their powers, and spend the time and force thus foolishly withheld from answering the great objective demands of life upon them, in rummaging over their own consciousness and the whole realm especially of their bodily sensations, to find trouble or at least the beginnings of it where they can. A scholar is designed as little by his Maker to occupy his thoughts with himself, as a Christian. Melancholy is God's visitation upon an idle mind: his mode rather of scourging such an one back again to his duty; for the way of escape from any trouble in life is duty coupled with trust in God. Blessed be His name for placing thorns and briars in the way of all, who are inclined to indulge in voluntary mental inefficiency. There is too much bound up in this brief life of ours: the possibilities of our nature and of our earthly relations and circumstances are too great; and the splendors yet to be unfolded in the advancing history of mankind at large, or of any one of its members in particular, are too magnificent: that voluntary torpidity of intellect should be endurable as a matter of duty, or decency, to either God or man.

No man knows what he can do until he really tries, up to the full limit of his opportunities and capacities. It is he who is always trying to do something greater and better than hitherto, who is always achieving wonders. Difficulties vanish at once, like mere spectral terrors, at his approach. Men and circumstances yield before him. He asserts his proper lordship over things around him and finds that they all show at once a willing allegiance. The law of Divine help to human workers is: "to him that hath shall more be given." God's plan of life for each one can be realized or known only as each one makes at all times the fullest possible outlay of every energy, power and resource, in all conceivable forms of duty, usefulness, love and honor ; and so finds in the aggregate results of all his efforts at the end of life, in what he did truly and fully accomplish, the work that he was actually called and prepared to do by his great Maker. The key-note therefore of each man's heart, in respect to every opportunity and responsibility in life should be this, "I will try !" really, constantly, hopefully, ever, "try !" This is the spirit of which all greatness and all high goodness are made.

The great, ruinous tendency of almost all American scholarship, is haste for results and those only of a material kind ; and a consequent narrowness of preparation for any high and broad attainments in the end. The tendency to be unpractical and selfish, in using one's educational resources when obtained, is a fault of perverted human nature itself; but the tendency to satisfy one's self with a narrow and pitiful scale of educational outfit for the many and great demands of life, is one of the special faults of our own country. The student should be early made to comprehend that his platform of research, study, knowledge and thought must be broad. Those who set his tastes and manage his interests at the outset should aim, as the first point to be gained in his proper development, to make him feel that there must be and is, a great and all-sufficient Object fixed perpetually over against his whole, sensitive, active being, for him to see and serve and love : fitted to every want and faculty of his nature, in all the height and breadth and depth of his entire consciousness. He must in the next place be brought under the power of exact and steady drill ; and last of all he must be led firmly on in right directions, over the true fields of intellectual toil, and for a full amount of both space and time.

All this varied work of his appointed guides for him, designed and executed intelligently and persistently in his behalf, has but one real aim : to establish in him the same earnest and fixed habits of self-treatment. All his real growth of mind and character must be, from first to last, high continued self-growth ; and the office of his teachers is but to secure the right processes and directions of it for him at the beginning, and to inspire him at the same time, so far as possible, to carry them on afterwards for himself to full completion. If therefore he has been rightly directed, and responds himself heartily to the moulding influences that he has received, he will go on through life, holding the greatest object of action ever in clear view : full of the feeling and right in the habit, at all times, of thorough self-drill : grudging neither time nor toil spent on his own inward self; and being both wide and far-reaching, in his own chosen style of self-development.

There are two modes of high intellectual self-culture which surpass all others, for both the amount and style of their benefits; and on which for that reason the mature student, who aims at the greatest possible results in ever-abounding continuance to himself, should be always earnestly intent: the study of language, the philosophic, artistic, comprehensive and comparative study of it, in different forms; and the study of the art of composition. Of all just study of language the ancient languages must form the basis, not only in a preliminary but also in a perpetual way. Nor can they be studied rightly by themselves alone: as they are but the lower radical forms of the upper-growing, full-flowered languages of modern times. In these their juice and strength and beauty are all still found. They lived in fact and died for these their successors: as every thing else in the grand procession of events on earth, however valuable in itself, has yet its chief value in its connections, as a matter of profit and gain to those who come after it. One of the chief reasons why the study of the ancient languages is so partial in this country and attended with so little high exultation of feeling is this: that they are studied so much by themselves and therefore out of their connections and apart from their true uses. Who would expect to find any such pleasure in studying a mere mass of base-clefs, separated from the accompanying parts of the tunes whose under-tones they form, as in studying and practising them with a full insight and use of all the correlated elements of harmony?

The study of language in its highest forms and broadest relations calls into exercise, beyond any other study, all the varied faculties of the mind: it feeds the soul perpetually with the choicest thoughts and sentiments of the greatest and best minds in the past; while the taste is perpetually refined and exalted by constant communion with the most elaborate and beautiful specimens of logical and rhetorical art; and the inspiration of the great aims and great deeds of those who adorned the elder ages by their achievements, is breathed through their works into the hearts of those who sit in rapt admiration at their feet.

The careful, earnest practise of the art of composition, according to the highest ideals that the mind can form, both as to the style of thoughts to be expressed and the most effective and attractive method of expressing them, will increase, beyond any other mode of self-culture, both the fact and the sense of the real fulness and readiness of one's inward resources, and of the ever-expanding elements of growth with which his Maker has endowed him as a man. Pitiable indeed is his mental condition, who looks upon this grand employment of all his faculties in combination, as a task which he is glad to escape ; and who therefore from its burdensomeness seldom or never undertakes such delightful labor.

As the habit of regular, right composition is one of the most rewarding of all habits that one can possibly form, we are quite disposed to give the young student a brief homily upon the matter for his good. Have then the habit of writing regularly. Choose a subject that interests you and when once chosen adhere firmly to it, whatever dissatisfaction with it afterwards may tempt you to exchange it for another. Gather together at the outset upon paper the first thoughts that interested you in the subject, and add to them what you can by frequent sallies in the same field after other kindred thoughts. When the pile is large enough for a plan, form one, and one suggested by the thoughts themselves and demanded for them. Then study the plan as such, to make it complete in itself. When this is accomplished : take it up vigorously and eagerly, part by part and limb by limb, to clothe the dry forms and formulas of the plan with full, free, flowing thought and feeling. Make it a rule, from first to last, to think only of your subject and its uses, in unfolding it, and not at all of yourself; and while not rejecting ornament, never to seek for it as such, but to seek truth and strength and fulness of representation first and then to add to your subject, in its exact and earnest treatment, whatever illustrations of beauty naturally occur to your thoughts, serving to illuminate it or to enchant the reader or hearer with it, whose profit and pleasure you are seeking. When thus finished in your best style lay it by, and when it has become quite cold and is to you like the composition of another, take it up for a thorough sifting out of all waste or needless materials, or of everything which does not contribute to its positive clearness, strength or beauty. Concentrate and condense where you can, and finish and burnish the whole composition to a still higher degree of excellence. You will not pursue such a course long, before what you first commenced as a drudgery, or at least as a duty, will become one of your keenest pleasures, and what was at first difficult will not only become facile, but even full of inspiration and joyousness to you.

This general part of our subject we cannot leave, without a word more about the wearisomeness of mental toil. Those who perform the most intellectual labor are commonly those who least speak of its fatiguing them. But if one is exhausted in such a way, it is not usually, when the thing does really occur, the amount of work done that causes the sense of fatigue so much as the associations of the mind with it. He who loves his work not only finds it light, but also finds himself ever fresh and ready for more. How different is a walk for the sake of mere exercise and as an unwelcome duty, from the same walk enlivened all the way with thoughts of some pleasing object to be gained by it, or with the gladsome companionship and converse of a cherished friend! What wonders of fatigue can a frail mother encounter, in the care by day and night for weeks of a sick child, for whom no outlay of strength and money and time seems too precious, provided only she be hopeful and cheerful in her efforts and not anxious and careworn. It is the wear and tear of men's own fretful thoughts that exhaust them in their work, instead of that work itself: like nausea at sea which is said to be when continued rather a mental than bodily difficulty in its origin, arising from the constant resistance of the mind to the motion of the boat, as in the case of vertigo to those afflicted by it in a swing. All the exhilaration and physical profit of a sport is taken away from a child, the moment that he feels that it has ceased to be a sport and is a duty. In the German language, accordingly, our mental states and experiences are truthfully described by the use of reflexive verbs to express them, as self-originated: our doubts and fears, our joys and sorrows. Let then the student be ever vigorously at work, and not only accept the law of work calmly, as a necessity to which he must submit, but much more, joyously, as one whose wisdom and profit he sees and admires.

4thly. He must maintain at all times the most careful, scientific treatment possible of his body.

The body occupies indeed a high relation to the soul, as the outward form of so august an inhabitant. "Ashes to ashes," we say of the body when dead; but the great God, "who dwelleth not in temples made with hands," and "whom the Heaven of heavens cannot contain," Himself calls it when alive "His temple." Without health the finest intellect and the largest, purest, most godly and godlike heart are, with like certainty, limited in the sphere of their action and fearfully shorn of their power in it. The men who have wrought a sublime, abiding work in their age, have been with great uniformity men of abounding health. A man of habitually strong nerves, lively sensibilities, elastic spirits, energetic impulses and ever-conscious force of muscle, feeling, thought and will: what a giant is he prepared to be, in either action or endurance! How can he ever drink, as others cannot, with perpetual joyousness, as from an overflowing cup, of the sweet influences of earth and of heaven; and how can he pour forth the treasures of his own heart in a strong tide of living, loving feeling upon others! No one has a right to indulge in any habits, acts, feelings, negligences or ventures, that can in any way impair or jeopard his highest health, except for reasons that God Himself will sanction as being demanded in His service.

The body is exquisitely constructed, both as a wondrous living organism by itself, and as a complicated assemblage of adaptations for the wants and uses of its indwelling inhabitant. It is the finest piece of divine mechanism upon earth, and the highest form of material beauty witnessed by mortal, if not by angelic, eyes. That great Architect who constructs all organized forms according to perfect geometric principles and proportions, and who makes all even inorganic substances not of simples, but always of different elements mingled together, and that, in each case, with the most minutely exact uniformity of weight, in every element of the compound: He has blended in the formation of the human body all the highest mechanical contrivances and chemical combinations and agencies, to be found among the earthly demonstrations of His skill. Not only in its construction, but also in the daily voluntary and involuntary use of its various elements and functions, law has one of its highest thrones of beauty upon earth. Must then laws be carefully studied and obeyed, in working a piece of human mechanism made of but few parts, and those coarse and heavy, and will a little carelessness here, as in the handling of an optical instrument, chronometer or electrical machine, defeat all the ends that might otherwise be compassed and even ruin the mechanism itself? And how much more will the human body, so manifold in its complications and of such a delicate tempering of all its inward essences and elements together into one strangely united whole, suffer damage from abuse or neglect? But who seems to have any strong, mastering sense of responsibility, about the occasional or even the chronic states of the body? Whose body is not marked with many wounds from needless and wanton thrusts, in moments of excitement and folly, at its tender framework, inwardly or outwardly? No man has a better chance for long life than the student: yea, rather, none so good, if he rightly improves it; and none can get such a rich variety of all kinds of physical enjoyment as he, if he desires them.

The conditions of health and vigor are few, but they are imperative; and it is a maxim not only of human law but also of the divine, that "ignorance excuses no one." They are also all easily ascertainable, and God has placed the privilege of health almost as absolutely within the reach of every one who will keep its plain appointed rules, as He has the opportunity also of a residence forever with Him in the Upper City to all who will seek for it. It is a terrific demonstration indeed of the gross amount of sins against the body committed by each generation, that its average life, instead of being, as it might and should be, a half century and more, should be shortened down to a point but little beyond the half of so brief a period. In the fact that our octogenarians are usually, a very large proportion of them at least, those whose health was originally feeble, and that for many years, and who therefore, in order to enjoy any health, had to husband the little that they did possess, we see on a small scale what might be witnessed in this world, on a large one, if all, weak and strong alike, sought zealously to have a conscience entirely void of offence in this matter, before God. A piece of glass can be kept as long with care, as a piece of iron; and, if kept for a long period, it surely proves that the iron might have been kept, as long and well.

One or two specific hints are all that can be indulged in here. One of them is this: the student must be a moderate eater. He that eats like a working-man may toil with his hands, but not with his head. The habit of eating very slowly, and filling up the space thus allowed one's self with plenty of mastication on the one hand, and of light cheerful conversation on the other, would reveal to many not only new pleasure in eating, but also a new enjoyment of health. Light meals,* especially at the end of the day, when the powers of digestion are most incapable of mastering difficulties, are wonderful helpers to health and cheerfulness and clear thought, and even to religious feeling. A man of thought, whose pleasures are so many of them subjective in their source, as are a scholar's, should find no difficulty in constant abstinence from a full diet, or from one of doubtful quality. But without formal intentions and efforts concerning this matter, he will be quite sure to go astray: as a life of study is quite as provocative of a strong appetite for food in an adult, as schoolboy days have ever been celebrated for producing among the young. Most literary men accordingly eat too much; and hence

* The word supper has come by modern perverseness to bear, as a heavy meal, in its distinctive sense, exactly the opposite meaning to its original signification. Sop, soup, sup and supper are all of one root, and refer to the use of a light broth for the evening meal. Modern invention, not to call it modern depravity, has substituted for such a simple, healthy, hygienic habit the custom of eating, in cake and sweetmeats, the most concentrated food that is used through all the day, and so prepared as to tempt one by its agreeableness to eat more than he needs of any sort of food, and that when the stomach is under its greatest disability.

comes in such cases, and not from a mere sedentary occupation as so often supposed, that special class of temptations before which men of quiet, retired habits of life have so many times fallen. A full bodily habit as such is favorable to no high attainments, in heart * or mind. Some when about to make a great mental effort feed themselves to the full with highly-seasoned food, so as to stimulate the brain the better to action : as Pitt is said to have done with frequency ; and who died accordingly, as might have been expected, of apoplexy, in his early manhood. Others in the same way seek excitation from stimulating drinks, instead of the stimulus of strong, healthy, holy thought. All such expedients are of short-lived efficacy ; and the disposition to resort to them shows, that both the mind and heart of him who does it have lost the virgin-purity of their own conscious duty and power.

On one other point also justice to the bodily interests of the Christian student demands a word here : the use in any form of the filthy and poisonous drug, tobacco. Well does every observing teacher know, who is not himself caught in its snare, that it is a wonderful ruiner of health and character in the young. In one class of cases, it

* Let him who doubts this consult the following passages of Scripture : Jeremiah v. 7, 8 ; Ezekiel xvi. 49.

operates to deaden the vital energies and to make the mental perceptions, the memory and the will, all slow and feeble in their action. In those of another style of temperament it unsettles the nerves, so as to constantly excite the mind to disorderly conduct. Could a true summation be made of all the evil influences of this revolting habit on the health and longevity of each generation that uses it, the sight would be one for frightfulness like a vision of those pyramids of skulls that savage princes in Asia in former days sometimes delighted in piling up, at the end of a life spent in exterminating their species, as their proof that they had not been remiss in their hellish work. But the ruin of health by the use of tobacco is but a faint type of the greater ruin, occasioned to the character and intellect of those who use it. To the young especially, the elements of whose bodily growth and strength are in such a state of flux, and so impressible by slight causes, for good or evil, the use of such an active poison is exceedingly injurious. Teachers, by an extended and constant comparison of many youthful constitutions, and the habits of those possessing them, have experiences and convictions on this subject that fall but little within the range of a physician's observation. They also often see the evil effects of its use by adults, in the sallow faces, stinted forms and languid airs of their pupils ; who thus bear about with them the hereditary marks of their father's folly, and that in growing fulness of manifestation, as child after child of such a parent comes under their care. The devotee to tobacco voluntarily unmans his own will of all its native, divinely-endowed sovereignty over the other elements of his nature, by his self-subjection to such a habit. . He who once felt that he could do any thing great or good, however difficult, now succumbs, with paralytic self-prostration, before this idol-habit, and says that he cannot relinquish it, although he is conscious of its injuriousness.

He who conforms to the principles here advocated may be sure of being able to realize eight hours daily of earnest study, at the lowest calculation ; not only without damage to his bodily strength, but also with positive advantage to it. Study is a thing of zeal : but zeal does not brook the idea of having time doled out to it sparingly, any more than does avarice gold, or ambition, honor.

5thly. He must appropriate to himself, naturally, thankfully and joyously, all the aids, stimulations, treasures and pleasures, which God has expressly and bountifully provided for him, as his portion of good cheer under the sun.

Nature, providence and life are all contrived, with superabounding appliances for such a result, not only to the one idea, objectively to them, of developing man into all "the fulness of the Godhead bodily," but also to the idea, subjectively too, on their part, of furnishing him with every resource for strength, refreshment and triumph, that he can need or desire to find in the surrounding universe. Our powers of attainment are made vast enough, not only to take in that heritage of "all things" which the Scriptures declare to be "ours;" but even God Himself, the All in all, to whom all the worlds that He has made are but bubbles, floating upon the ocean-surface of His being. If any one's heart therefore is empty of living waters, it is because he himself has broken the pitcher; while standing by the fountain overflowing from above. God has given us kindly many wants, that they might be all so many natural voices within the recesses of our being, crying after Him: so that our very wants are purposely constituted, as links to bind us more consciously and strongly to Himself, their willing and their sole supply.

He is always in the lavishness of his beneficence, under perpetual restraint in its outflow: never as gracious as he would be: for want of preparation for his benefits. Let then each one open his whole nature to the manifold streams of his bounty; and the very gladsomeness of God's nature will run through, and overrun all the deep and many watercourses of his soul. If any one upon earth ought to be a man of buoyant spirits, and of vaulting moods of mind, with the very light of Heaven always burning brightly in his heart and eye, it is the Christian scholar. For he sees not merely the exterior of things, as others do only, but also their deep interior, for which all that is without was made, as a mere form for the precious contents within. He is a thinker, searching after all hidden things; and his eye is trained to look beneath the surface and behind the vail. And what numberless springs of perpetual exhilaration has God established in his nature and circumstances, for the daily excitement and refreshment of his heart, in the gratifications of bodily sense, the beauties of nature, the hilariousness of children, the activities of business, the discoveries of the age, the march of public events, the intercourse of friends, the pleasures of thought and of personal improvement in knowledge, character, power and usefulness, the glory, honor and beauty of a life of service to God and of good to man, and all the deep, sweet satisfactions of faith and hope and worship, in the inner sanctuary of the soul.

And is such an one to sit down, weary and wayworn, on the pathway of life, on which prophets and apostles and the Son of God Himself have walked, amid many persecutions, with exulting footsteps, towards the skies? Is this the man to be found moping over the stage of this world, everywhere red with the martyr-blood of the noble men that have been here before him, with heavy eyes and drawling speech, as if nowhere able to find any thing that can captivate or interest his leaden soul!

Some restrain by theory the natural leapings of the heart, whether in the playfulness of sport or in energy of action, towards things without, as well as all its own natural gushings up of life within. More, by cold neglect of both God and themselves, allow the garden of the soul, made to be at all times full of the flowers and fruits and sweet waters and reviving airs and songs of the paradise above: to become a wilderness of weeds, full of all dark, damp places and noxious miasms and hideous noises. Joy, God made to be the very pulse of immortality; and "the joy of the Lord is our strength." Let then the scholar delight himself and honor his God, by always drinking to the full of the cup of sweets which God has lovingly placed in his hands. And let him not wonder if he loses his health and spirits, and reason even, in undertaking to pursue his own pathway, ascetically, through life, rejecting, under the holy name of prudence or religion, the natural aids and stimulations with which God has purposely endowed him for the successful conduct of his interests and his duties.

In the view taken thus far of the true Christian Scholar, he has stood before our thoughts, rather in the strength and beauty of his ripened manhood, than in the more early and formative period of his history. And yet it has been our constant endeavor, to remember also the wants of those who are just beginning to open their eyes, consciously, upon the sphere and work of true scholarship, as they are, and who, seeing them in their real aspects, yet firmly if not eagerly have cast in their lot thither for life. A thought or two to this class of readers and we have done.

Let the student at school or in college cultivate, at all times, the most genial, honorable, manly style of feeling and conduct towards his associates. It is often said that boys, not having learned those refinements of duplicity or disguise which their seniors are often so expert in assuming, under the names of etiquette, policy or shrewdness, show the depravity of human nature in deeper and darker streaks than others. Certain is it that the current inward history, at the present time, of most of our colleges would not enable us to make any improvement in the statement concerning them. How many systematic and traditionary meannesses are rife in them! Close, selfish, contemptuous and contemptible cliques abound. Some of a class-sort and others pertaining to secret societies. Pasquinades, burlesque-schemes and ribald songs, aimed at the students and professors alike, are printed and circulated even on public occasions devoted to the interests of the college ; and the atmosphere of many of our colleges is hot all the time with class-pretensions, society-rivalries, personal bickerings, low and even dangerous tricks on the more simple, and all the terrors, at times, of organized rowdyism. In what style now should the true Christian scholar deport himself, amid such scenes ? He has certainly a rare opportunity for showing the heroic beauty of real self-respect, and of gentle and generous conduct towards all around him. Let him scorn all sympathy with every form of social selfishness, however gilded. If in after-life he would be a true Christian philanthropist, or patriot, or even gentleman, let him be careful to possess the same spirit and enact the same deeds now. For after-life, like after-growth, is but a larger development of the initial forms and processes which preceded it.

Let him in every way escape the first establishment in his heart of that evil egoism, in which one contents himself always with walking in robes before the glass of his own consciousness, and is careless of every thing that does not pertain, in some form, to himself or his image.

He who realizes, whether young or old, the character of the true Christian student in this world, in his own person, will wear a crown of honor here below, and a crown of glory above in heaven.

V.

THE CONNECTION OF THE HIGHER CHRISTIAN EDUCATION WITH THE PROGRESS AND PRIVILEGES OF THE PEOPLE.

V.

THE CONNECTION OF THE HIGHER CHRISTIAN EDUCATION WITH THE PROGRESS AND PRIVILEGES OF THE PEOPLE.

THE people : the good of the people : the progress and privileges of the people : these precious phrases jingle in many ears, like mere words of cant : they have been so often and so cruelly used, to adorn the ostentatious but broken promises of demagogues. And yet they are the chosen watchwords of Christianity, and of all men who are really aiming at the advancement of the species, in whatever nation and under whatever name. One of the most beautiful and touching records of Christ's felt influence upon our common humanity, as he came in direct visible contact with it, especially as contrasted with the fact of his crucifixion by a wicked minority of the religious and civil officials of the day banded together against him, is one indicating the hearty responsiveness of the masses to whom he spoke of his own love and of the

12*

Father's, and showed it to them in his works: the simple statement which so many read, without ever feeling its deep sweet heart-sense; in which he who was "the Desire of all nations" was practically recognized as such: "the common people heard him gladly." Here was earth's according strain of feeling, in harmony with the song of the angels to the shepherds: "Glory to God, in the highest; peace on earth and good will to men;" and in unconscious but appreciative answer to Christ's own joyous statement of the divine character and signature of his work, in the world: "to the poor the gospel is preached." Those melodies, which are the great common beatings of the human heart voiced to the ear, and which every one therefore instinctively loves to hear and loves to sing, have in them beyond all others the soul of music. That poetry, whose strains awaken the most numerous echoes in the greatest multitude of listening ears young and old, ignorant and learned, contains in such a fact the proof that it possesses most of what is truly beautiful or sublime. Those elements of our being, in which we all agree, are far higher and nobler than any in which we differ. That style of religion, therefore, not only but also of education, which is most adapted to every man's wants, and whose results combine at the most points and in the most decisive ways, with the greatest progress of the age and of the race, is most true and heavenly, both in its outward bearings and in its own inward nature.

Diffusiveness of every thing good to the widest possible limits is the genius of Christianity. Its very life is love. Giving is the spirit of all its aims and movements. Its perpetual history is perpetual benefaction. So leavened has modern society become with its influence, in all forms and directions, that the utmost possible popularization of every advantage is the felt tendency of the times, in every quarter. "Knowledge," now, therefore, "runs to and fro," both by the impulse of those who have it to bestow, and the importunate invitation of those who long to receive it. The poor are princes now in power and privilege : "the child dies an hundred years old."

Not by chance, or for fashion's sake, has the title of this closing essay of the series here presented been selected ; but from glad sympathy with its spirit. That high truth placed by God's own hand in ours, as one of the great standards of human faith and feeling appointed by Him for our guidance, that "no man liveth to himself and no man dieth to himself," we do not and cannot gaze at as a stern necessity, from which we would fain escape, or as a mere beautiful abstraction, to be admired for a little while and then forgotten. We rejoice in it, on the contrary, as one of Heaven's own banners, and would bear it exultingly over all the earth.

It has passed into a proverb, from Heathen lips to Christian and from one age to another, that "the voice of the people is the voice of God." Their real voice is His voice: not indeed their vote always; although this, when they comprehend the true issues at stake, is quite sure to be full of the fire and flash of that common sense, which is in man's heart the glow of the same light of truth, that burns with dazzling brightness forever in the bosom of God. But their uttered wants, their universal cry or sigh or desire is indeed His voice. That universal cry is for light. Their universal want, uttered or unexpressed, is love. He who addresses himself with all his energies to meet it, elevates his own nature, in thus striving to elevate theirs; and, as the addition of human labor to any of the forms or elements of matter is what gives them their value, and the connection of man with any thing upon earth is what gives it its importance: so, the effort to promote the greatest possible good of the greatest number is the rule of the highest virtue; and the tendency to such a result is the sublimest tendency of any moral action.

To a careful, earnest, religious spectator of the world's condition and history, two great facts stand forth at once in strong colors and startling proportions. The first is this: that the world has come very slowly to its present incomplete stage of development. Why, he exclaims, such short and measured steps of progress. The present civilization of the world is the grand resultant of the experiences, labors and attainments of countless millions, who have lived their brief day upon the earth, and left behind them each, in departing from it, their share of determinative influence upon its fortune and its fate. And how mournfully small is the aggregate product of so much active human life! The other great fact that astonishes and saddens him, is, that there is now everywhere such a frightful amount of talent and energy lying utterly unemployed in the community. The vast intellectual and moral inertia of the race at large: this is the great astounding fact. How large the harvest and how few the laborers! While the possibilities of human life and of human nature are so splendid, the ever-growing wonder is that so few seem to feel or even to see it. Not a thousandth or millionth part indeed of the latent spiritual forces of society has ever been continually, or occasionally for any considerable period of time, employed on the ends or means of human progress. The machinery of society, it is true, is ponderous enough; but it stands for the most part entirely still, or turns but a few slow heavy rounds, measured by centuries, instead of years, and often, yes always hitherto, backwards in every country sooner or later as well as forwards : so that civilization has ever been migratory, and the genius of liberty, like that of letters, has been from the first a bird of passage in this world, as well as a bird of paradise. Mankind at large are marching, and in all ages have marched, over this earthly stage of their being, like an orchestra provided from above with all bright sweet instruments, tuned in themselves to God's everlasting praise, which however they have borne unused through all the slow, moody, march of life : a great, silent orchestra, trailing in weary languor along the highway of time, bearing even their privileges as burdens, instead of moving in joyous triumph with loud-voiced trumpets and viols, in a chorus of hallelujahs, onwards and upwards to their Father's house above.

If ever the world is to become, as it surely is, for such is the promise, one wide-spread garden of delights, full of the habitations of peace and praise, instead of the habitations of cruelty as now, so great a change is to be wrought by the diffusion everywhere of the benefits and blessings of the Higher Christian Education. The widest range of both the powers and results of Christianity is that lying within the sphere of its educational resources and influences.

The following points are those most worthy of discussion here :—

I. The true limits of the theory of general education, both as to the numbers to be reached by it, and the proper style of their education.

II. The connection of the Higher Education, specifically, with all the lower forms of general education.

III. The necessity and beauty of its being, in all its influence upon the masses, thoroughly and inspiringly Christian.

IV. Some of the chief results already accomplished by Christian Scholarship in the world.

I. What then is the true theory of general education ?

Every man has in him a nature worthy of the highest possible improvement. However humble the lot of any individual, or however menial his employment, there is in his very manhood a beam of light divine that attracts the gaze of angels, and which therefore should not fall upon our eyes in vain. How is every thing external to man overestimated in this world, and all that is inwardly vital to his essence or development, as a man, grossly underestimated ! So great is the soul of each one, and so many and so precious are the germs, now full of life within it, of a vast unfolding future, that the more difficult, hereditary, permanent or organic, the obstructions in the way of the true and enlarged culture of all its elements and resources, the more should the state and the church and the plans of individual beneficence and enterprise concentrate their separate and collected energy upon their removal. It is often said and truly that the first senses of all words were physical, and that all their intellectual and moral senses are but figurative. Alas ! that the moderns have so little, in practice, outtravelled the ancients, in their materialistic use of language, as of the elements of personal experience and of active life, of which it is the reflex image. Earthly-mindedness is a sin of far wider applications than most suppose ; and nowhere has its blighting power been more felt, than in every department of the great work of education. The consciences of but few are at all alive to the claims of the uneducated masses, for the removal of the incubus of ignorance that is upon them, by the helpful beneficence of those, who have received from former generations a better heritage than they.

Those who are educated for unprofessional employments are, with scarcely an exception, educated only so far and in such a way, as is supposed needful or desirable for their best success, in procuring the material advantages of life. Of the little number who enter upon the courses of the Higher Education, but few ever obtain any such earnest inspiring sense of their exalted privileges, as to aim, with full determined perseverance, at those results which are worthy of such a designation ; while the small minority, who may in a liberal construction of the phrase be included among those who have obtained a classical education, nearly all of them choose pursuits in the end that possess the one dazzling, but petty and perishable, element of lucre. In opposition to all such perversions of humanity, we maintain the right lodged in every man's nature, as divine : the patent royal of his birthright as a child of God : to the benefits of the highest possible education of all his faculties. It is often said that every man has an incontrovertible right to subsistence, and in an emergency may steal with perfect moral impunity rather than die. But how much more imperative is the right of each one to all that light, which God has given to others, individually or collectively, on purpose that they should bear it to every creature through all the world. Capital now has its foot on the neck of labor, because it is uneducated. Poverty also for the same reason remains too often hereditary for many generations. Labor itself, which is necessary and honorable in all its innocent variations and degrees, becomes without education a mere brute employment of muscular energy, more or less intellectualized according to the different amount of native mental strength possessed by various individuals, or the haphazard increase made of it, by the force of the fortunate accidents or incidents of their earthly lot. Labor without thought, as its source and guide, is like a blanched rose that has lost its beauty with its fragrance ; and it is changed from a blessing, as it is in itself, into a practical curse, as it is employed. Labor without thought, as its inspiration, is, not merely not work as play, as all true toil becomes to a great man or a good one ; but it is also work without play. There is not an artisan, the daily product of whose hands would not be ennobled, as truly as is an artist's, by the high education of all his faculties as a man, in receiving a deeper impress of his own best thoughts and feelings upon it. But manual labor it is said would become in such cases generally distasteful. It might indeed justly to all those, who are called in the noble gifts of their nature to a higher work, than to make shoes or coats or hats for other men, whose position above theirs is simply the accident of greater pecuniary means, but whose natures indicate that they should be cobblers rather than themselves. In the divine economy of the social state, some have leisure purposely allowed them for the use of their time, in high and noble forms of study, research and discovery, that they may distribute beneficently unto others the knowledge that they have gained for themselves. But none certainly belong to the class appointed of God to such privileges, who, by neglecting them when offered, prove themselves unworthy of so exalted a position. Multitudes there are now in all the professions, who openly declare themselves by their voluntary torpidity of mind entirely unworthy of any place in them : men of low aims, the downward bent of whose tastes shows that they are factitiously placed above their level, and occupy their forced position to the great detriment of society. And so, on the contrary, multitudes follow the plough and wield the sledge, and are never known to be any thing more than clever workmen in wood, or dirt or iron, who might have inspired attending crowds with their eloquence, or swayed the counsels of the State with their wisdom, or led forth the church to victory upon victory through all the earth.

The greatest possible diffusion of true education in its highest forms, for reach and power, is, in conjunction with the utmost possible diffusion of religion, the greatest want of society. These combine harmoniously in the style of their influence and results both to individuals and the community at large. True education when generally diffused levels the elements of society both upwards and downwards. Those who gravitate downwards, with their own free will, should not be held up by official and ecclesiastical supports, at an elevation for which they are not fitted; while those who are capacitated to soar in their tastes and aims and achievements, who have in them instincts all pointing upwards, struggling for free air and free motion in it, ought to have an opportunity to find their appointed range of activity and effort.

Popular education is then, not only one of the greatest of all interests and duties of any community, but also one ever-present in its claims, in reference both to voluntary movements in its own behalf, and also to arrangements and expenditures which can be compassed only by the State. Its elements, likewise, are to be the widest possible universality in its scope, and at the same time, all such preparatives as promise the greatest possible fulness of results.

Not to be misunderstood, let it be premised that the elevation of the mass, of which so much is said as the ultimatum of social enterprise, is to be but a mass of individual elevations. The riches of mental energy and attainment possessed by each person form, when aggregated, the great original capital of society, the whole of which the perpetuation and enlargement of its own privileges demand that it should always employ and improve, as much as possible. The largest, fullest and best education of every man in each age is the first term, on all lines of upward and onward movement, of which the second and resultant term is the greatest possible progress of mankind, in every generation. The man accordingly who has the opportunity to raise himself to loftier degrees of intellectual and moral culture, and either rejects or squanders such a privilege, is not merely a dullard, but a traitor also to his race. He throws away his own birthright, and that of others. also in untold numbers in his own age and in the procession of the ages that are to follow it, whom he might have directly elevated, or at least gladdened with the light of his own beautiful example, as a star that would never set with its inspiring and guiding influences in their horizon. Society is but a grand, divinely-constituted corporation, covering all countries and ages ; in which every member owes by the very implications of its constitution the most zealous devotion to the common interests of all. To one who feels the power of this conception, the voiceless centuries, as they pass solemnly by, one after the other, upon the stage of history, stand before his view, imploring, with an agony of mute eloquence in their very looks, the strongest and warmest thoughts, efforts and prayers of every one upon earth, for himself and for those around him, as well as for all who are to come after him in long succession.

But while such are the duties and responsibilities of individuals to the community at large, society also itself owes great and high duties to them. Duties are mutual; and, the higher the powers and resources of either one of the related parties, the higher its duties to the other. The duties of the State to the individual not only cover the field of personal property, life, liberty and the pursuit of happiness, but also those nobler interests of personal culture, which, although so great in themselves, governments have yet hitherto so perseveringly ignored. Cæsar understands that he must defend his borders from foreign invasion and therefore provides fleets and armaments, which, after possessing them, he has usually shown quite as great readiness to use for purposes of offense as of defense. And what expenditures does the Demon of war exact of all governments? Every ship of the line represents in itself and in its outfit, it is said, half a million of dollars. What a splendid university with large privileges would such a sum provide! and what a great constructive influence for good, instead of one destructive to human life and happiness, would such an appropriation of it ensure!

It would be repeated on its own ground in all time to generations of pupils succeeding one another, while the world should last, and, through each generation itself, over all the earth to multitudes around them, whom their lives and labors should reach for good. Its very name university, if objectively interpreted, would be a symbol of its benign bearing, compared with the Tartarean names, that are generally so aptly chosen to denominate those great floating arsenals of death, over which yet, although costing so much money in fact and so much blood in designed if not probable prospect, not only the State but the community also rejoice with national pride.

The ends of the Higher Education are many and great. Private resources cannot of themselves procure them : they must be furnished by the State. And the State should do it liberally, as a compensation for the services which it receives from educated men in two ways : one general, in the help that they furnish to the stability of the social state as such ; and the other specific, in the fact that nearly all the managers of the affairs of state have been themselves modelled and equipped for their stations in such institutions. The State should therefore also favor and assist the higher institutions of the land, as a matter of its own protection and honor in the future. As in regular military academies are prepared the officers of the army and the navy, so from our colleges and universities are to come in all time the officers of State. The advantages of the Higher Education should then be facile to every one, as, from the great community of all men, are to be developed to the highest eminence under proper private and public training, the few who are really capacitated and called of God to guide, and by their guidance to bless, the rest of mankind. And, while we would not have them presented to the poor, as if they were conferring a favor upon the State to receive them and much more to accept a gratuitous support in doing so ; as if universities themselves and the cause that they represent were reduced to straits and would beg even beggars to pity them ; yet every bar to the aspiring and energetic and hopeful should be removed, who desire to obtain a true and large education, and, at the same time, every stimulating and inspiring encouragement should be furnished them to pursue a high course of personal self-improvement.

Our present college-system has grown up to be what it is, under the pressure of our felt wants as a people, and has in its general outlines the variety and practical adaptedness to the demands of professional and active life in this country, that the progressive experience of two centuries has suggested. Its great defects are want of breadth, as well as of elevation, as a piece of educational structure, and still more the inward want of that living enthusiasm and energy in its management, which can come only from those two grand elements, high intellectual culture and glowing personal religion, combined, and intensified in their action, one with the other. Our colleges are many of them but mere academies ; and not a few are second-rate at that. As some say, they have been multiplied beyond all proper bounds ; but so think not we. In the State of New York, it is true that there are not only two in its chief city ; but that also in every important city, or in its immediate neighborhood, throughout the State from Albany to Buffalo, there is a college existing in full form, or else one either just coming into being or just going out of it. The number in our whole country, now claiming to be alive and to deserve public attention, is somewhere near a thousand. The argument brought against them, by hasty reasoners upon their past history and their future prospects, is the same as that used in reference to the multiplication of different denominational enterprises in small towns : that their very number weakens the working force of them all ; and that therefore the strength of their own resources, and of public feeling towards them, should be concentrated upon a few, which might be in consequence greatly enlarged and perfected. No! a thousand times no! let them be multiplied still more, as surely they will be, from the action of local and denominational causes, if no other; and let their courses of study be extended and elevated more and more. Private enthusiasm and enterprise, and quite generally those of a patriotic and religious source, have founded them, with a wise and earnest forecast of the future. The real fault to be found with them does not respect their number but their quality, as well as the mistake so generally made concerning their appropriate place and function, in the machinery of education. Our colleges, in their present type, which is truly adapted and American, should not be regarded: with the exception of two or three of the foremost, whose history, capabilities and locality admirably fit them for a full and facile transformation into real universities: as answering, in their style of functions and resources, the style of our wants as a people. They should occupy relatively but the place of the German gymnasium, and should be perfected for such relations far beyond what they now are, in fulness and exactness of drill, as well as in the finish of the results obtained by their workmanship; while over them should tower, story above story, the higher university-course of study, in which men, not boys as in the colleges, might ascend to the loftiest attainments, under skilful guides, in all the noblest departments of human philosophy, learning and industry. The scale of our educational facilities would thus become in addition to our strictly professional schools four-fold: as described by common schools, academies or high schools, colleges and universities. One university at least should stand, like a pillar of light, in every State: the glory of the community and the constant object of its care: on which the watchful eyes of the State should be ever set, and to which its hand of bounty should always be extended. Bounty we have said, with all carefulness, instead of patronage: for such an institution patronizes the State far more than the State can patronize it.

The university should thus be distinct entirely from the college, representing in completeness the higher forms of education, as such, and the higher facilities for obtaining them: so that its provisions should be all of the most ample and inviting kind, for those who have run with zeal and thoroughness the previous curriculum of college-life. None but men of really high scholarly attainments should have license to enter upon its privileges. Its gates should be practically so closed against all who have been idlers in their preliminary courses of study, by its inexorable requirements of a certain, high, specific style of preparation, that none but men of glowing, cultivated powers of mind should ever be found dwelling within its sacred enclosure. Here, the topmost heights of science, philosophy, philology, criticism and taste should be eagerly traversed, by those who have the time and the disposition to scale them. Here, faithful earnest guides should have their habitation, full of all large stories and legends even, if you will, about the wonders of the way, for those whose instinct and determination to climb, and in climbing to conquer, all the difficulties that lie before them, is unceasing and indomitable.

The true university-course for this land and age should be no accidental or servile imitation of that existing in any part of Europe, and which has grown up there out of the soil of other climes and other ages, and of forms of government and of society altogether different in their elements, relations and demands from ours. It should be rather the product of our own land and of our own age, and full of the living spirit of the times. So conformed to our present actual condition and wants should it be, that it should seem not only to have been suggested, but required, by them. It should be in other words American and as much above, in the scope and height of its utilities, the institutions of the old world, as our style of government and of social life is above theirs.

Our colleges, also, we have said should be perfected into a state of far higher disciplinary appliances and privileges. They should begin at a point at least midway in their present course : requiring a large, deep and thorough style of preparation for entrance upon it, in previous academic qualifications. Their chief drill should be drill in the study of language ; and the chosen field for it should cover both the ancient and modern languages, which should be thoroughly mastered in all their varied elements, grammatical and lexical, in every possible form of research, syntactical, philosophical, philological and rhetorical. Through six years the laborious student should be led, as on an average from eighteen to twenty-four years of age, through all the mazes of grammar, etymology, prosody and accentuation in the classical languages, as well as through the more comprehensive elements of criticism, logic and rhetoric, and all the higher principles of both philosophic and æsthetic culture in the most effective and attractive forms in which they occur in both ancient and modern authorship ; as well as, for a proper commingling of the abstract with the concrete, through a wide accompanying range of mathematical and scientific exploration and analysis. The great objects ever to be kept in view should be twofold : the most complete and harmonious discipline of all the mental powers as such, and the careful habituation of the mind from the first to great activity and energy, in the highest of all forms of mental productiveness, the art of original composition.

Our academies and high schools need also, like our colleges, thorough renovation and enlargement in their courses of study and instruction. To what a lamentable degree have they fallen into the hands of novices only, who, in their unripe manhood, have been also quite unfledged for the work that they have assumed, by any original taste or special preparation for it. For mere temporary purposes have they undertaken it ; and therefore it has lost its attractions to their dull eyes, when those objects have been gained. There is nothing more farcical, and therefore, since the interests involved are so tremendous, there is no social abuse more great, at least in our Northern States and in respectable society, than the present prevalent mode of conducting academical instruction in our country. Colleges cannot advance their requirements as fast as some of them would, because of the continued low tide of influences and results in the preparatory schools. Few of all who enter the academies of the land ever acquire while there a taste for subsequent classical study. What a proof of the fact is this : that from all the hundreds of academies that have been at different times, the supplying fountains, from all quarters, for Yale college, only some seven thousand graduates have been gleaned by that venerable institution, during one hundred and fifty-nine years past, as the contribution of educated men so called which it has been able to make to the community! And how few of those who have passed through the college-course have either entered upon it, or come out from it, true, earnest, successful scholars! Where are we to look for the right explanation of these facts? In several directions indeed; but nowhere so conclusively as to the courses of preparatory training, and the style of the men that have managed them, and of the influences that they have breathed or rather have not breathed upon them. In the plastic, formative period of preparation for the higher studies of early manhood, is the decisive spot where the horoscope of the student's future is cast. Here his aspirations acquire their full afflatus, and here his mental and moral habits their upward or downward bent. Although others may afterwards prune a tree to larger fruitfulness, or trim it into a shape of greater beauty, yet he who first sets it, and determines the soil and position in which it is to grow, and all the first beginnings of its vital energy, stamps most of all his own directive will upon its form and stature, and upon the future fulness of its flowers and fruits. In the department of educational labor, occupied by select schools, academies and high schools, is the only ground that is left open, or that should be, to the force and skill of private enterprise, which is so effective in turning all the other wheels of social progress, and which should also have scope in the field of education for its wonder-working power when fully employed, as here it does possess in sufficiency. It is certainly one of the most cheering signs of the times, that so many more than formerly have been impelled : some from one motive and some from another, but many indeed by high patriotic and Christian impulses as well as by personal tastes and the inspirations of genius : to enter upon this grand work of earnest, personal service to their age, by their own individual labors in the cause of education, as God may prosper them. And the great pecuniary success of so many, who have had the right qualifications for obtaining it, is not an insignificant item in the amount of general good realized from their lives, in adorning with the outward symbols of prosperity a profession which has long been depreciated in the public treatment of it, far below its proper level which is equal with the highest.

And the common schools, are they not indeed common enough? What immense congregations of pupils are often gathered together in them, under one roof, numbering in our large cities not merely several hundreds, as is usual, but a thousand and more, at times : a fact which several fearfully destructive school-panics from the alarm of fire would have sufficed, one would think, to have for ever abolished. But is there any end to the evils, that a spirit of parsimony will either contrive or endure ? And what should be said farther of the poor economy of placing one male teacher only in such a monstrous educational establishment as its commanding officer, with a number of subordinate young females around him, as his coadjutors ; who are themselves poorly compensated, although expected to do much work ; and many of whom have become teachers, instead of seamstresses, only because the compensation was greater, and not from any warm sense of the glory and beauty of an earnest educator's life, or with any accompanying consciousness of disciplined preparation for undertaking its duties ! The principal also himself even of such mammoth common schools is put upon a salary, on which with the utmost carefulness he can barely live ; and therefore men of collegiate education feel that they can do better, than to accept such laborious but unrewarded positions ; unrewarded either in honor or money, and so crowded with all sorts of necessary generalities of arrangement and of instruction, as to give but very unsatisfactory opportunities of real usefulness to their incumbents.

How, under such economical and superficial arrangements, does the weary pupil keep ever revolving, monotonously, in the same unbroken round, of ever learning many things and never coming to the real knowledge of any one of them. And what an utter want of any system, art or science is there, in the daily work appointed, or the general ends sought for the pupil, who is never individualized, and cannot be, in the treatment that he receives; and who therefore gets only that share of the general benefit of such a very general style of school-work, that may fall by the natural or accidental force of circumstances to him, without his looking after it or any one else looking after it for him. Mental discipline should be the aim of the common schools; and all their machinery should be so thoroughly contrived and managed in its working, that such a result should actually be gained, not only generally but also to a large degree. It is no answer to just criticism upon the insufficient arrangements or management of these or any other schools, to say that a faithful student can make great gain to himself, by a careful use of their privileges. Few faithful students are self-formed in their origin. Discipline in its very etymology means something learned from others, like the word disciple, who is such a learner. The object of schools, as of churches, is not to profit those merely who are already right, at least by approximation, but also to awaken and educate the dull and lethargic, who would otherwise pass through life unknowing and unknown.

Neither the State nor the Church nor any considerable portion of the community, at large, are at all alive to the claims of the great cause of education, whether in its special or its general forms. If the affairs of business or of government had as little watchful interest bestowed upon them, they would be in a state of general anarchy. There is indeed considerable noise made about our educational machinery at times, and in some places there is not a little clatter in its actual operations. But the product, in all high degrees, is certainly very small. There are often indeed quite wonderful exhibitions made of talent in declamation and composition, in many schools and colleges, male and female: proofs, as ambitious teachers and friends would fain have their spectators believe, of a large amount of youthful attainment, if not also of youthful genius. But what becomes afterwards of the crop of superior writers and speakers and scholars, whose promise seemed so great? Was the parade, made with such satisfaction, all a mere pitiable farce and but an elaborate and not even well-concealed system of self-glorification, for those who got it up? Or what was it? Who can tell?

The strife is everywhere, undisguisedly, for numbers in nearly all our institutions ; and to this idea every thing like an elevated standard of requirements is generally sacrificed, so that admission shall be easy ; and all vigorous closeness of drill, as of stern requisition, is afterwards relaxed, so that the student shall have no argument, from intellectual uncomfortableness in his position, for leaving it. And then, to make a good external impression all the while upon the public mind, so as to keep as many as possible pleased and interested, the plan is to prepare a grand annual demonstration, which shall have the merit of striking the senses as favorably as possible. But, alas for such contrivances ! "water will find its level ;" and "the stream will rise no higher than its fountain ;" and the outward results of our educational system do not and will not mount above the point, to which they are elevated by their own inward working merits. Let no one think that satire is our delight. We have no skill in it and no liking for it ; but the truth we do like, whether single-edged or double-edged ; and although it be "a divider asunder of the soul and the spirit, and of the joints and the marrow." We write what we write complainingly, only with sadness ; and have no such theory as that strong writing consists in sharp and bitter words. A spirit of denunciation belongs neither to a truth-loving nor to a man-loving disposition: it is our abhorrence; and God grant that it may ever be! But, while even "the truth is not to be always spoken," unless it is directly demanded, or its voluntary suppression would be a practical lie, yet, when the good of society requires its utterance, let it come, however unasked or even unwelcome, and in whatever form of gentleness or wrath that is most appropriate to the case.

Society has no interest in obtaining any thing but realities. These are its lifeblood and its power: its elements of growth and its glory. Real education is, like real religion, in all its bearings, personal and social, of priceless value. Were the prizes of life distributed into many portions, and the suitors for them parcelled into as many divisions more, the one class containing all the men of true high education would be found to possess all the prizes, except a meagre remainder too small to be worthy of much interest in their distribution. Society has, accordingly, the most vital interest in multiplying the number of its successful reapers in the harvest of life. Its true policy is, to equalize, only as it elevates, its members.

The reason of so much more wide-spread industry and success in modern times is to be found in the more general diffusion of the influences and benefits of the Higher Education. A large and true education possessed by any one man, besides the blessings directly achieved by it in his own sphere of activity, also, although indirectly, yet powerfully quickens multitudes of others to enterprise and effort.

Much has been said in all ages about the unnecessariness of high learning and education to true personal and social development; but the illustrations chosen for the exemplification of this idea have been always selected from those men of rare native genius, who, by the strong upward impulse of their natures, mount, with special helps or without them, to conspicuous heights of attainment. Genius will prove itself genius, even without external aids. It is sky-born, and will soar: it is its nature. And so dulness cannot be galvanized into splendid talent, by mere energetic determination to stimulate and improve it. But let genius and scholarly toil combine their energies and influences in one result: let genius, in other words, instead of losing a large amount of its native momentum in moving against a sea of difficulties, move with a strong tide of advantages in its favor; and what an argument for giving it all possible facilities does its high use of them when obtained present. But the cause of education, as it always has been, so always will be, abundantly underrated by mean thinkers as so many have treated in all ages the cause of vital religion in like manner, by glorifying natural goodness, in instances of large original development, at the supposed expense of practical Christianity, as manifested in the moral fruitage to be found on the cold unfriendly soil of a disposition, marked with naturally small endowments, or possessing only a mass of perverted hereditary instincts.

There is still another subject, which, for its injurious influence upon the tone of our educational and Christian principles and feelings, demands distinct discussion here: the conferment of honorary degrees by our colleges and universities. Whatever good intention there may have been in their first establishment, or whatever fancied value these literary baubles may once have had, they have come, by great over-bestowment of late, and by their being so often given for feeble and false reasons, to be ridiculous and dishonorable incumbrances to our educational system. Such was the history of crowns in ancient Greece. In the earlier and better periods of their history, the Greeks made but little use of them; for worth made the man and want of it the fellow. But, from being mere honorary wreaths of olive-leaf, as they were at the first, they came to be afterwards, in more degenerate times, crowns of solid gold; that the decrease of their outward value as marks of distinction, by the frequency of their bestowal, might be compensated by a corresponding increase in the inward value of their substance. And among the Athenians, previously to the time of Alexander, crowns of gold were profusely distributed for every trifling feat, military, naval and civil. So inevitably has the tendency of all titles and badges of honor, as of the drama hitherto in every country, and indeed of public amusements generally, as such, been downward, uniformly and rapidly downward. So nobles, who, by the original signification of their name, were, at the first, men worthy to be known, have in all nations, where the title has been a civil instead of a moral one, degenerated ere long into the mere representatives of an ancestry who acquired personal distinctions for themselves, which their ignoble posterity have not only been unable to equal, but even to keep. Honor is not a matter that can be bought and sold in the market of the world, nor can it be done up and labelled and passed around wherever it is wanted. Honor, of a true quality and enduring, is always originated in the life and character of him who possesses it : it cannot be taken from him, except by his own weakness and wickedness ; nor can it be increased a particle, by the formal parade of any idlers or flatterers in his behalf, who are quite as apt to think, in whatever noise that they make over him, of rendering themselves conspicuous, as of glorifying him.

Would that, as the progress of the age has quite destroyed the power of factitious forms, in reference to clergymen as a class, and made the social position of each one of them depend, like that of every other man, on his individual character and attainments, without benefit of clergy ; and as official uniforms are obnoxious to our American feelings ; so our colleges and universities would strike their blow, also, like the rest of the people, their last, full, effectual blow at this remnant of a disposition among us, to ape the traditionary silliness of earlier ages and of other lands. No forward movement could be more Christian, or more American, in its spirit : none more beneficent in its results. Here for once a great and good reform might be achieved by a mere negative process. Let them rigidly and forever abstain from giving any and all honorary degrees in the future ; and how soon would all those which have been so lavishly given, and accepted with such inward and even undisguised satisfaction, in the past, wither up and lose all their fragrance and their life, like the branches of a tree whose main trunk had been riven with the stroke of a thunderbolt.

Honorary degrees they are denominated, except when in course : as none but the lower ones so called are ; but they are honorary in their use only to those who do not merit them, and, in a country like ours, are so often bestowed on such recipients as to make the dividing line between them, as matters of real honor or of mere compliment, not gloriously indeed, but quite ingloriously, uncertain. When merited, the college confers honor on itself, in recognizing such merit, rather than on the individual so noticed ; and when not merited the gift may be called honorary, but it actually honors neither the receiver nor the giver. A system of titular distinctions is sufficiently pleasing to weak and ambitious minds, to be sure of finding many secret if not open admirers and advocates. But it should ever be the sentiment flying on the flagstaff of all our institutions, as a Christian people ; and the higher the institution, the larger and brighter should be the letters in which it is written : that "mind is the standard of the man," and that real, honest, earnest, manliness and godliness are the only signals of honor that any man needs, or which any one, however tricked by himself or by others, really possesses. Our plain American dress, in the presence of foreign ambassadors at home, or of foreign courts abroad, bespangled and bejewelled as they are, we are quite willing to claim as indicative of our national taste ; and let it be the symbol of that true simplicity of character, in all the relations of life, of a people whose habits and customs and institutions are, according to the just conceptions of our wisest and noblest thinkers, all formed anew, under the light and heat of gospel truth, out of all the elements of human experience and of human attainment, hitherto, as their staple. Would it not be worthy of us as a people, to ascend at once, in our secret and formal estimates of men and things, to the level to which Christianity points us, where human feelings and gauges run parallel, in their course, with the divine. It is the glory of our laws, and so far only have they any glory, that they are based upon the Law of God. We are a Christian people, and are in no danger of having our consciousness of so high a fact too intensified. Public sentiment needs earnest pressure in this direction. All the slow progress of humanity, in all ages and countries hitherto, alike in the unwritten laws ,of equity, honor, kindness and charity, prevailing in society, and in the formal statutes ordained in reference to the many complications of human rights and human actions, has been but a laborious tardy passage ; and so tardy because made with so little direct request for guidance from above ; from one step to another, towards a full realized unity in the end with the law and the will of God. On this sublime elevation of entire intellectual and moral sympathy with Him will every community at last rest, as on a pinnacle of light, in bright, permanent, happy repose. To that glorious mount of exaltation, therefore, let us as a people rejoice to lead the other nations of the earth, in all matters of business, enterprise, progress, legislation, jurisprudence, religion, literature and education.

Could a book entitled The Secret History of Honorary Degrees, be prepared, according to the actual facts of the case, it would be full of comical, not to say mortifying, revelations. Many, supposed to be quite independent in their sense of their position, would be found to be full of prurient desire for the help of such a college-bolster. What appears to the uninformed to be the product of spontaneous appreciation, would be seen to be too often the result of distant contrivance. Many are the hands that pull the wires ; and sinuous enough are the paths through which the influence comes at times : in order to secure for a friend that, which, though made of such account, is after all as near the shadow of nothing as any thing can be. Boards of College-trustees have a corporate existence, and must show the public that they are alive : they must do something that others will see ; and what can it be but spend money and give degrees. It makes no matter, of course, that they have been brought into their place in the Board, on the ground of their wealth and its prospective promise of future profit perchance to the institution, or of their general good position in society, although they have never been educated themselves ; and so are utterly destitute of all scholastic ideas and all the elements of just criticism and discrimination concerning the merits of their superiors. They are yet good tools for a few designing minds, that know well how to use them. And besides, as our colleges are each of them, openly or by implication, a denominational pet, or, if not, somehow or other, do not commonly succeed, every denomination is anxious to hold its banner as high as any other, and to rank as many conspicuous men among its representatives, as possible. And what way is there of manufacturing great men to order, like doctoring them with a title ? And then too how much good can a kind clergyman himself do sometimes, as he is very conscientious in believing : remembering well at the same time how much benefit a kindred service once realized to him : in obtaining for a fellow-clergyman, who has begun from his idleness or dulness to hold his position by a loose tenure, a doctorate which shall make his people think that they were mistaken in their estimate of him, and that the real dulness was in themselves after all, instead of being in their minister. And if there be no other reason for giving doctorates, where they would not otherwise be bestowed, what an all-constraining argument for action may it sometimes be, to an institution that wishes to drop anchors to windward for funds or students, over a given area which it would fain secure as its own, to bind to itself by such empty but influential flatteries ; and which from whatever motive given will always be rightly interpreted by the vanity of their recipients : the occupants of the leading pulpits at the more important points of action. Such are some of the sources, among others of no higher character, from which these so-called honors are annually scattered, ad nauseam, over the land. And, so far has the influence of this weak unintellectual and undignified, not to say immoral, action of many of our colleges pervaded the community, that barbers and fiddlers, hair-dyers and pill-makers everywhere announce themselves, and with as much comfortable self-consciousness as any one else, as Professors of their several trades. They see many, called Doctors of Laws and of Divinity, that are utterly incapable of teaching either the law or the gospel, and imagine that, if an empty title helps others so much, one that they deserve in their calling, as they know, will certainly help them. And if colleges and clergymen value mere names so much, surely there must be something, they think, in a name. But it should be one of our fixed American fashions, not to generate, harbor or endure any shams. We are believed, and not without reason, across the waters, to abound in them. Humbug, they say, is an American word ; and turning its edge upon us they use it to describe, in one brief term, all our character and all our institutions. Nowhere they say too are titles coveted so much, as among that famous democratic people ; nowhere do they cleave so tenaciously to those who have once received them ; and nowhere are they conferred, on such frivolous and unintelligible grounds. With such ancestral and historical antecedents as we have, we should, as a matter of self-respect as a people, abstain carefully from all pretentious, as well as all unmeaning, ceremonies, forms and decorations. Our posterity will thank us for keeping the spirit of our fathers, and much more for practically exemplifying, in all our habits and customs, the spirit of the Bible. Rome, like Greece, so long as she was simple in her tastes and honored real merit and therefore abounded in true workers, was inwardly great ; and so shall we be, who are, for the all-conquering tendency, or rather destiny, of our ideas and institutions, the Rome of the modern world, if we maintain those ingenuous, honest, earnest, habits as a people, which are the elements of all true success, both for individuals and for nations. And this all the more : since the Lord Jehovah will be with us, whom Rome knew not ; and who Himself bids us seek for that honor, which comes from God only. This, if obtained, will make one rich indeed ; while without it whatever ornaments any one may wear they are but the ornaments of a beggar : the honor which He bestows on him, who gives all diligence in getting and doing, at all times, every kind of good.

The intellectual and moral littleness of hankering after degrees has come to be one of the signs of the times among us ; as also, in the light of what has been said, of our degeneracy so far as a people. As college commencements annually recur, what numerous eyes are turned longingly towards them, for the bestowment of these tawdry honors. Letters, few of them self-moved from the source whence they appear to come, and hints and requests, buzz about the faculty and trustees of colleges, at such a time, as bees about sweet flowers in summer ; and a thinking observer comes to fear, that the Republic of letters is almost wholly demoralized, in reference to its points of honor : for such petty reasons do those, who keep the mystic keys to these desired treasures, arise, at such a time, in all haste for the deliverance of hopes long deferred.

Were this ridiculous system of manufacturing honors to order now sought to be introduced for the first time, could it possibly be started, so as to go ?

Would it encounter less derision, than the new-fangled idea of conferring degrees on literary women receives in its initiation? And is it in itself any more beautiful or respectable, when perpetuated than when initiated? Time may accustom men to abuses, and make them callous to their evils; but it only aggravates instead of diminishing the abuses themselves. How strange too the inconsistencies of even intelligent and good men! He who would smile at an European official, for exhibiting habitually upon his person, with whatever seeming unconsciousness, the decorations of his office; or, at a savage, for walking about in all gravity with a very dignified sense of the fact, that he had a large brass ring hanging from his nose; or, at a child, for peering constantly into a mirror to enjoy the sight of some ribbons that were flaunting about its head: will yet value for himself, quite as much, the tinkling of a few alphabetic symbols around about his name, when fastened upon it by way of honor: a fact which they who added them foresaw, and bestowed them therefore for the sake of pleasing him. If this does not exemplify the idea of being "pleased with a rattle and tickled with a straw," what illustration could be furnished of it? How different from such an estimation of these literary trinkets, which, like the pewter watches of children, have nothing, but their looks to recommend them, was that of the great Humboldt, recently deceased, after whose death the many badges of honor which he had received, through a long life, were found, to the surprise of every one, lying around in neglected nooks and corners, among rags and old papers; while the leaves of trees and specimens of minerals and pressed flowers were laid by in choice places, and kept with jealous care. Thanks to this great man for this undesigned, but true and manly, utterance concerning the utter insignificance of such "semilunar fardels."

It is the church that sustains this system of glittering follies. Rich churches, in large places and small alike, desire to exhibit as many signals as possible of metropolitan grandeur; and therefore relish architectural magnificence, and a large brotherhood, for the good outward show that it makes, and a preacher that carries about with him as many public recognitions as may be of his superiority to others in his neighborhood. And so long as such churches have leaders that covet these ribbons, and it is manifest that both pastor and people can be gained at one complimentary throw of good feeling toward them, in such a way, the temptation will be well-nigh irresistible to young and weak colleges, seeking for growth in popularity, to cater freely to their expectations. In the accounts of ecclesiastical meetings how careful are the clerks of record tc file off the Doctors of Divinity by themselves as if of higher rank than the rest. So universal is this custom, and so long has it been maintained, that the weaker victims of the system have really come to feel, from the special parade that is made of their names by their brethren, that they are in fact entitled to it on their own account. In the magazines, also, published by our Religious Societies, Foreign Missionary, Home Missionary and all, the same special care to place all such titled officers and members in a separate seat of honor, where their empty distinctions shall be sure to be noticed, is clearly observable. And all this in the church of God! whose corner-stone is Christ, the meek and lowly crucified one; and the voice of whose word to each one of His followers is, "except ye have the spirit of Christ ye are none of His." That spirit is the spirit of the cross: the spirit of service unto others, through any degrees of joyful self-sacrifice that their greatest good may demand. The answer to that question of strife which arose in the church in his day: "which of them should be the greatest;" and that so often arises in it now: is the same that it was then: "he who would be the greatest of all must be the servant of all." Are not those therefore, who give in the household of Jesus Christ a special place of notice to brethren, whose distinctions are as cheaply obtained, as were those gold rings, which some regarded in James' day and said to their wearers, "sit ye here in a good place:" just as truly "judges of evil thoughts" as were they? and all the more so, since, being warned by their wicked example, they have yet knowingly fallen into the same snare?

There are two specific commands of the great Head of the Church, besides many general ones, that, according to all natural principles of interpretation, are directly relevant to this subject. "Call no man your Father upon the earth;" and "Be not ye called Rabbi." Taken in connection with another passage: "My brethren, be not many" of you "masters" or teachers, "knowing that thereby" (that is, if unfaithful) "ye shall receive the greater condemnation:" their sense is plain. The Head of the Church is very jealous of having any of its members act as Heads in it unto any of His children whom He would have all look directly to Him and not to Apollos, Paul, Calvin or Edwards, who were "but ministers" or servants "by whom they believed." It is not pleasing to Christ that any who preach in His name should use any power or hold any position of factitious origin or influence over others. Power belongeth unto Him; and the weapons of their warfare are not carnal but spiritual: simply truth and love used faithfully and with full trust in Him. Any influence acquired in the church in any other way is false and pernicious.

How then can this great organized system, of annually manufactured follies, be overthrown, as it ought to be, for the good of man and the glory of God? There are not wanting favorable signs of progress in this direction. A few men, by looking steadfastly up into the sky in silence, can lead a large crowd to gather around them and look with them. A few men, by getting up an alarm in a public assembly, can soon make all the rest as alarmed as themselves. The sympathies of men are as quick as they are universal. And so, every man who keeps quiet and cheerful in a general alarm, leads others to imitate him, as every man that passes by a gaping crowd, intent upon his business, helps to disperse them. Many are now already full of the feeling concerning honorary degrees that is expressed in these pages, and regard their continuance not only as farcical, but as greatly injurious to the progress of true scholarship and of true religion. Instead also of the long array of titles with which authors, a little while ago, were careful to drape their names on title-pages, as if wishing to walk in robes of state before their readers at their very introduction to them, the growing fashion is coming to be, as we are glad to discover, to use the bare name by itself, which is certainly more beautiful alone than with any appendages. Let Authors one and all follow this new and American fashion : it deserves a full establishment. Le' secretaries also drop the custom of putting two D's after any one's name, which are no better than two Q's or Z's ; and which if any man values, let him put them on his own name for himself. Whoever thinks, except in College Catalogues, of keeping track of the LL. D's that different lawyers have received, in writing or speaking their names. If colleges will persist in giving these titles, let them be dropped from public observation in the case of clergymen, just as in Germany scholars take no note of them in publishing each other's names. And let the editors of papers and periodicals contribute their influence to make degrees preserve their own vitality, without any help whatever from them. In correspondence also much may be done, to let them drop to the ground and be forgotten as they certainly will be, without artificial help to sustain them.

Since the church makes such account of ecclesiastical titles, a similar fashion for folly has come into vogue, of late, in reference to civil offices : of calling those who have once been their incumbents, ever afterwards, Honorable. And many are the men over all the land, who, having, by political accident and even it may be in ways less honorable, obtained public promotion, are now moving about in the community, with a very satisfying persuasion of their honorableness, since everybody writes and calls them such, that are yet among the smallest or most unworthy specimens of the race.

If any one thinks that too much prominence, relatively, is given to this topic of our general subject, in this place, his convictions will change to ours, we believe, on farther thought. Its connections with the Higher Christian Education of our country are vital. So long as social distinctions can be gotten by machinery, or under sinister influences of any kind, the public tone of feeling concerning the necessary relation appointed of God between labor and its rewards, and between personal merit and public consideration and usefulness is so far assailed and lowered; and the traditions of men are practically substituted for the commandments of God. All the elevation of estimate and aim which the community at large are to acquire anew from one age to another, they are to gain from the views and feelings of our educated and Christian thinkers; and it is surely high time that they should set the example in every thing, of acting according to things as they are. The tide of public sentiment on all great things, even in Christian lands, always runs much below high-water-mark; and the currents of manly enterprise and energy are always slower and weaker in most men's hearts, than they ought to be. What an evil therefore and what a sin is it, for the leaders of society to knowingly impair, and pervert the elements of right and strong thought and of true principles in the community! We have ventured indeed over more space in this part of our subject than we should have done, did we know of any other similar discussion of this subject elsewhere.

II. The connection of the Higher Education, specifically, with all the lower forms of general education.

Where in all nature is what is high developed, only or chiefly by what is underneath it? All growths are indeed by necessity from beneath upwards. But where resides, where acts, the stimulating power? The busy springs and wheels of vegetable life are set in motion daily by the sun, with ever increasing force, as he mounts continually on his ascending pathway to high noon. Under the magic touch of his beams, the vapors rise, that, as they go up, bathe the leaves with those invisible drops of mist that suffice to meet their minute invisible wants, only to descend in copious fulness for a greater blessing on them, in the hour of their greater need. From the same upper sphere comes down the heat which, rising towards its source again, gives in its reflex benefit that warmth, by which with moisture all things grow. In the laboratory of leaves which to most eyes merely crown the otherwise unsightly shapes of trees, with beauty of form for the eye, or with fulness of shelter from the burning sun, goes on the work of deoxidation and assimilation, by which they keep ever rising and spreading, with their burden of flowers, or fruit, or shade, towards the skies. So in the head, regnant over all the members of the body, from the height of whose visual orbs flashes forth the light of thought and of purposed will, in that high secret place of power resides the full electric energy of the man. Down from above, through all the currents of life, pass the quickening impulses of the ever-wakeful mind. So, in the vital economy of God's plans and powers, He "sits above in the circle of the Heavens," not simply "to behold the children of men," and "see if there are any that seek after God," but also, much more, to communicate, with love and skill and all-pervasive watchfulness, the vital contact of His providence and grace to every creature, as he needs.

Let not this true philosophy of all acquired elevations and growths be unnoticed or forgotten. The quickening, attractive, elevating, force must always be found or placed above. And so, the higher classes raise the lower to new points of progress and enjoyment, by the force of their own example and the real superiority of their own attainments ; rather than by any formal theories or mechanical contrivances that they may apply to them. Men imitate, without consciousness of the fact, or at least reflection upon it, as if by a law of instinct, their superiors. Classes, communities and nations do it ; and so do educational and religious institutions.

Elevation, real or supposed, makes one at once, it is true, a mark for envious eyes to many in the same neighborhood, or elsewhere in the same employment, who stand upon a lower level of observation or of privileges. The world would not be depraved, if such facts did not appear in it. Human nature nowhere likes to be, or to be put, in the background. Its opposition to such a dilemma is hereditary and perpetual ; and, in the manifestation of this fact, extremes here as in other things often meet, in ways strangely humorous, connected with those at the same time which are as strangely solemn, wicked or objectionable. But other tendencies and more influential appear also, in minds of any natural nobility of constitution : a disposition to follow in the footsteps of those who are mounting upwards and onwards to new heights of achievement. And however our common nature may be overlaid with accumulations of folly and of guilt, the instinct to imitate and equal those possessing more privileges and a better position than ourselves, is ever-present and ever-active, as one of the strongest impulses of our being, in each one of us. A good example is one of the greatest earthly electrifiers known to the human heart; and the great and good reign, by their very character, with kingly power over those who gaze at them and are spell-bound, as they gaze.

Where universities and colleges are poor, there poor academies will appear; and where these abound, common schools will be also poor. They will all dwell together in a common poverty, or rise together into a common excellence. The true mode of elevating them is not, to stand beneath, and, by the lever of authorship or of public lecturing or of formal state-action, undertake to raise up, by degrees, the lower stratum of these educational appliances, with all the superincumbent mass above it; but, commencing with the highest Form of education, to raise it higher still, making its advantages as widely accessible in a right way as possible. The Form ranged next below will then itself have opportunity to expand and, by the powerful attraction of influences from above, and the pleasurable motive for undertaking to rise, since there is room for it, by its own efforts into a new atmosphere of faculties and privileges, will move upwards, as if by the force of inward instincts, and these so full perchance of conscious energy, as to make it seem difficult to keep from rising. So, in society, when its leaders fall, the stimulus to arise and occupy the places above them operates at once on minds that before were subordinate, alike in their position and in their feelings ; so that they mount from their new impulses into their new spheres and move in them, as easily as if they had always occupied them before.

One of the great practical rules of social philosophy is, that "to him who hath shall more be given." And as men delight most, in giving benefactions and endowments to institutions that have already strong foundations, and are sure to live, instead of to those whose feebleness, while it makes the strongest appeals to their beneficence, casts at the same time a cloud of doubt over their future ; so, the community at large are best pleased, when those institutions are still more enlarged and aggrandized, in whatever way, that possess already the greatest functions for occupying well the greatest sphere of activity. If in the past they have squandered their resources and abused the privileges of their position, the desire to see them glorified with greater resources will be indeed exceedingly, and perhaps fatally, diminished ; but still the fact remains, that, so long as power of any kind is rightly used, or supposed to be, the minds of men are pleased with its accumulation.

There are doubtless many ignorant persons in every enlightened community, who think that the rich are the natural enemies of the poor : forgetting that, but for the enterprises, expenditures and capital, employed or loaned, of the rich, the poor would be poor without mitigation and beyond redemption, having no change or hope of change at any time in their circumstances. Such minds will of course look askance at the idea of locking up either money or men in institutions entirely separate, as they seem to them to be, from the business and bosom of society around them. But schools and colleges are the forts and castles of the land ; and the higher their grade and the style of their working influences, as of their workmanship, the greater is their service to the Church and to the State. Let therefore the highest of them be made higher still, and let the State itself show increased zeal for their prosperity, like that which it is so fond of showing at least in name for common schools.

III. The necessity and beauty of the Higher Education being, in all its influence upon the masses, thoroughly and inspiringly Christian.

Society has a fundamental interest in the greatest possible spread of Christianity, and especially in its highest forms. Objective Christianity is one thing, and Subjective Christianity quite another.

The one, like geometry or any other absolute science, is abstract and ideal and as such perfect and unchangeable. The other is ever-varying in every age and in every individual that possesses it, and is Christianity, not as it is in itself, but as it appears when realized and vitalized in those human hearts into which it has been introduced, as the great permanent principle of life. Real subjective Christianity is therefore in an ignorant mind of far lower qualities, for joy to its possessor and for beauty to a beholder, than in a mind full of intelligent views, and of perpetually high strong thought; and such a mind has also a far different amount of momentum in it, in respect to all the elements of personal activity and of social influence. In no field therefore does intellectual cultivation, on the one hand, manifest its value more than in that of personal religion; and so also, on the other, nowhere does practical Christianity show such a height and breadth of development, in power of thought and conception and in beauty of faith and grace, as in minds of great native and acquired enlargement, that have been thoroughly sanctified from above.

Society has therefore the greatest possible interest in the universal prevalence of Christianity. On two points, particularly, is this interest most concentrated: the true, living, earnest, Christianity of those who are its actual leaders, and that likewise of its educators, who are ever busy in preparing the succession of its leaders, from one generation to another.

§ 1. The leaders of society in whatever age are its thinkers, especially those whose thoughts are transfused with energy into all their actions. The higher the style of development in the community at large, the higher will be the quality of thought required in its leaders ; and the more depth and uniformity of power in its demonstration. Society has therefore as great an interest in the right accoutrement of its thinkers for their work and their right action in it, as in the nature and degree of the great results which are to flow from their aims and efforts. As mankind will have and must have leaders, the only question is, what kind they will demand and what kind they will accept. Those only should society welcome to the van of its movements, who, by their attainments, energy and aims, intellectually and morally, are qualified and disposed to do the true work of leaders. All who are not leaders for God and to God are sure of discomfiture, sooner or later, in their plans, because He is against them, and they only lead their followers away at every step from true honor and prosperity. The wanderings of the Israelites in the wilderness on their way to Canaan, for forty years, forwards and backwards, up and down, now near and now away from the true path out of Egypt to the Promised Land : a journey, which to modern travel consists of but a few brief days : is but a type of the errant directions in which God will lead about all those in their plans, who undertake to dispense with His guidance and blessing. Is not the history of the nations hitherto sufficiently sad ? Is not their wail over their own perished hopes of greatness in all the past, which has been in every nation but a mass of broken hopes and broken hearts, long enough and deep enough to fill the most vacant ear with its weight of wo ? A true picture of the Angel of Humanity standing, and looking in mute survey over the desolations of ages, would be in every land but a mourning Rachel, weeping over her children and refusing to be comforted because they are not. And, as in ancient fable Niobe was represented as metamorphosed into a stone and yet even then shedding tears over her offspring which had been slain, so, to a true interpreter of the silent hills, as they stand in quiet majesty around the vales and cities of the old world, they seem to be ever looking down in still, stony grief, upon the wrecks of human fate and fortune that they have witnessed. That cheerful outlook upon life, which Religion bids us always take, is not to be obtained from the stand-point of human experience, human history or human character. All is mist and darkness here. Hard indeed must his heart be, who can look over the great sepulchral fields of national ruin, for six thousand years, and feel no deep pity for mankind, no wonder at their follies and no admiration at God's amazing patience towards the race! Harder than the heart of Xerxes, who, in all his gorgeous vanity, yet wept to think that of that vast multitude which stood before him, not one would be alive at the end of a hundred years, to remember him or them! Caius Marius, that man who, though of stern and iron heart, sat, himself a fugitive, with tearful eyes, amid the ruins of Carthage, meditating on all its wide waste of splendor, is no inapt image of the picture, which the Muse of History presents to every thoughtful mind, as she lays by her pen and sits down to recall to her own thoughts the lessons of sword and fire and sorrow, which she has recounted unto others.

And when will the dawn of "The good time coming," of which every one loves to hear and dream and sing, appear over all the earth? When will the voice of Universal Humanity change from a low wail, as now in every land, to outbursts of gladness everywhere? Not, until the leaders of society, in politics, business, fashion, enterprise, literature, thought and religion are men of high thought, pure purposes and holy aims. Every community is what its leaders are, as truly as is every army. And the history of the progressive advancements of society: and these are the elements of history that give it its value: is but a portrayal of the lives of its leaders, as seen in their outward effects, instead of in their inward workings. What a few leaders of the right sort can do, when they are in earnest, let the history of the Reformation, or of Plymouth Colony, or of Modern Missionary Propagandism, in their now grand and ever enlarging issues, testify.

§ 2. Society has also the greatest possible interest in the actual religious character and activity of its educators.

There are no such benefactors to any people, as its true educators. Their bestowments are not consumed as they are made, but are laid by in permanent investment for ever new use while the world stands. They do a double work of love: that, of holding up the light of their individual character and attainments unto others of their own day and that, of training the future men who are to distribute through the next generation the ideas and influences with which they inspire them. Those impossible wishes that so many utter, with so much feeling: that they would fain live their lives over again, since now they could improve them so much, and would be careful to shake off, if they could, those personal disabilities which now confine the energies that they feel ever swelling, though restrained, within them : these are all open every day to the realization of the teacher. He does daily live over his life again in his pupils, and can accomplish in them and for them what he would like to have the opportunity of doing anew for himself. In their persons, electrified by his thoughts and feelings, his plans and efforts, he becomes, and with almost if not quite a sort of double consciousness of his multiplied existence, hundred-handed for action in the world.

To the community, therefore, the question, who are to manufacture the character of the people, especially in reference to their next stage of development, and how they are to do it, is one altogether above that of tariffs and all matters of mere monetary loss and gain. To do their work rightly they must be of course in advance, in their ideas, of the generation with which they are living : men of large attainments, of high-breathing energy, of active public spirit and of all heroic manliness of character. The style of their work also should be in its own nature that which will endure the wear of time, and stand firm amid all the changes of human feeling and of human experience. But the first necessity that they or their work may be right is, that they shall both be intelligently and earnestly Christian.

The connection between general intelligence and general Christianity is such, that many social philosophers have mistaken the relation between them, and pertinaciously, if not honestly, maintained that the true mode of Christianizing any heathen people is first, to enlighten and elevate them by other appliances, and then to introduce the gospel as a divine after-growth among them. But there is no fountain of quickening, intellectual influences, like the Bible. Nothing will so stir the reason to its profoundest depths of thought, as its amazing truths : nothing so kindle the imagination as the magnificence of its revelations. It makes time grand, by connecting it in all its minutest affairs with eternity : and it sets over against our own finite consciousness and finite weakness an Infinite Object of thought and feeling, of love and of action. Christianity is the only real and the only possible elevator of man. How does the miserably imperfect and impure civilization of ancient Greece and Rome, amid all their beautiful works of material or literary art, in its echo to this truth, as declared in the better state of modern times, as Christianized, give this truth a double significance. Intellectual cultivation can indeed exist, and in a high degree, by itself and neither imply nor induce in any degree true religion ; but not so with Christianity, which is something more than a mere form of social ornamentation, and which, being in its own nature a quickener to all the higher demonstrations of the highest elements of our nature individually and collectively, cannot exist alone. Its march among the nations is everywhere with a bright train of attending benefits. Man is fundamentally a religious being and must be so treated, in order to receive any true development in any part of his nature, and much more in the whole harmonious round of all its united complications.

In the Higher Christian Education, as generally diffused as possible, lie all the means of improving or even of preserving society. It has been often asked in a reverie, whether the hosts of Barbarism, which are still as ever in the majority for numbers, may not after all come down yet upon the civilized world, and sweep away, as with a deluge of wrath, all its facts and fixtures. We answer spontaneously and emphatically, No ! And why ? Because of the sure promise of God that society shall keep ever advancing towards a perfect state, so that "righteousness shall one day cover the earth as the waters cover the depths of the sea ;" and because also of the inherent, unconquerable, vitality of Christianity itself, as the greatest of all the forces that ever have acted upon the world, or can act upon it. The barriers of high gospel-truth are indeed invisible, but all the more impregnable. Truth can no more be fought with guns and swords than can light and air. And around the ramparts of Christianity stand flaming angels, out of sight, who love the truth as we love our lives, and who stand there strong and flaming not in vain.

The highest possible degree therefore of true Christian education, both among the leaders and the masses of society, is the greatest real necessity both of the Church and of the world.

IV. Some of the chief results already accomplished by high Christian Scholarship in the world.

The apparent sources of power are seldom the real ones. There is usually a power behind the throne, as well as on it ; and the greater, in modern times, is this one of the two. In the civil organization of society, woman is not recognized at all as a citizen ; and in many communities has not the common privilege even of receiving and transferring property in her own name ; and yet who does not know that her influence is felt, with not only subduing but also inspiring and controlling power, in every part of the social fabric. So scholars, in their quiet retreats and by the silent movements of their thoughts, set in motion the great noisy machinery of the times. The thoughts are generated in their minds to-day, that are to give shock and sway to the forces of the age to-morrow. The difference between civilized and savage life is this: that in the civilized we have a vast accumulation of living influences and living results, that have been poured forth from the fountains of thought in multitudes of men in all the past; while in savage life, not more overgrown with forests, to which the word savage * itself has reference, is the face of nature, than wild and uncultivated also is every heart and every mind. Modern civilization is therefore the splendid accumulation of all the great and good thoughts of the past, preserved in material fabrics and improvements, in books, in institutions, laws and customs and in the habits of the Living Age; and the new improvements of the times have come from new tides of thought, pouring out new blessings upon the community.

The progress of the Age is therefore the progress of Thought realized, and fixed in abiding forms. Scholars are the miners, in hidden places, of the solid ores, which the busy throng around convert into the current coin of life. Some, as they see them walk in meditative moods about the world, imagine that they are misanthropes, or at least quite ascetic in their tastes, and full of all impracticable abstractions: mere shadows of what they might have been, endurable as necessary evils in the social

* French sauvage, Lat. silvaticus, belonging to a wood.

state, but without form or comeliness themselves as specimens of humanity. But hold, ye triflers, who think so lightly of them! These tranquil, modest men are revolving studiously in their hearts, all the while, some larger plans of good for you. Whatever new discoveries are to be made for the advancement of your personal comfort, or of your personal sphere of activity and prosperity, they must be originated in their thoughts.

The material workers of the world know not how materialistic are their conceptions. Happy are they, if they do not entirely exclude God Himself from the orb of their vision; even from both the centre and the circumference of His own works, in their comprehension of them. This at least is an instructive fact, that the sceptical thinkers among the masses are the most abundant among mechanics, who are perpetually at work amid the fixed laws and elements of matter and upon them. False political economists, applying the gauge of material productiveness to the men of thought, claim that, as they do not produce the means of bodily subsistence, they are no true producers at all: forgetting that, as they give higher facilities and finish and wider applications and uses to even the physical and mechanical products of the age, they add, in the direction of greater fertility of soil and greater skill in working it, greater ease and extent of manufacture, and greater range of use for both space and time, the highest of all material elements of advantage to material products; while, in elevating the inward character and power of those who use them, they make those, for whom all forms of matter as originated from God or modified by man were made, and but for whom they are utterly functionless of themselves, of a far nobler and better style of being. Others therefore enjoy under their influence the good to be obtained from things physical in higher degrees than otherwise; and their varied elements are thereby made to contribute to the sustenance, activity and enjoyment, practically, of a higher order of Humanity. Metals and products and fabrics of any large or high sort are not wanted, where the products of the mind are wanting.

Scholarship is usually thought to be inherently addicted to conservative ideas. It is indeed; but it is also full, in all its high and true forms, of an earnest spirit of progress. Both elements are essential to a true well-harmonized character in an individual, or in the community at large. Every thing good is to be carefully conserved at the same time that every evil thing is to be diligently removed. The two ordinances, to "hold fast that which is good," and to "turn men from the power of Satan unto God," agree together and must be combined in any individual or State, that would have a divine temper or do an abiding work for God. In an age and a country so full of the chances of material prosperity as ours, it is indeed true that the majority of those who have chosen a life of study have been men of quiet and even of phlegmatic temperaments: especially those who have devoted themselves to education, where, of all fields of labor, both for the style of work to be done and the style of results to be gained in it, it is absolutely requisite, that those who undertake it should be men of the most energetic manly qualities of person, intellect and action. The preponderance accordingly of conservative tendencies in the educated men of our land is to be greatly charged, to the special constitutional type of the class of minds that have thus far been influenced to choose the life of the scholar. He who enters in this country upon the profession of the ministry or of education, or becomes one of that small number entitled the literary class, must ordinarily relinquish, at the outset, all those prospects of gain which are so abundant in every other calling, in a land so full of all great resources of material wealth, and so suddenly opened, with its many secret springs of prosperity, to the range of modern enterprise, and to all the appliances of modern invention, activity and progress.

The two great speculative tendencies of men in

wrong directions are those to Scepticism and Superstition, or to doubt and credulity, which are the two opposite poles of a wrong heart. These, with the accompanying ignorance from which they spring, are the sources of all human error. There is nothing of power enough to destroy them, and nothing really antagonistic to them, but Christian Truth and Christian Scholarship. Education and religion each tend to destroy both scepticism and superstition, and consequently with double force, when combined. They meet at many, yea rather, when in their full development and activity, at all points, in harmonious action. If true religion tends to make a man modest and humble, so does true education. Each liberalizes the mind, and each tends to make the balance firm and true of all its thoughts and impulses. Each habituates it to circumspection, prudence, care, and watchful continuity of right purpose and of right action. Each is full of all strong restraints from folly and from crime: and crime is but folly in its stronger forms; and each abounds also in all quickening influences and results. From the records of crime the names of highly educated men are delightfully absent; and in communities, where there is the most education among the masses, there is to be found with those born on the soil the most general freedom from all the grosser forms of depravity.

Such an upward bearing has our Maker given to our natures, that, in all nations men look instinctively to those above them for guidance. In Heathen lands they turn, if bold, to their chieftains, to lead them on to deeds of blood; or, if submissive and desponding, under the power of despotic masters, they bend before them in craven obeisance to thank them for the privilege of breathing in their presence. In more enlightened lands the same spell of influence, although more invisible in its action, is thrown by those who are superior in power, over those beneath them. Men, accordingly, move even in the Church, composed nominally of the Lord's freemen, in denominational lines and in philosophical schools and under prescribed doctrinal banners and with the certain sound of creed-trumpets. Fashion rules in matters of opinion as imperiously over the mass, as in the minor articles of dress and manners. The elements of society are not merely compacted together as if by some fortunate action of human affinities in such a way, but are rather constructed into a great harmonious mechanism, as a wondrous piece of divine workmanship; and all the more wondrous, for its stability and elasticity and impressible qualities of every kind, because made of living hearts each endowed with full power of self-direction, and composed of members that are not the same for any considerable time, either in themselves or in their combinations. Of this grand enginery the scholars of the world are the directors, determining towards what ends it shall work, and with what amount of inward force. But for them it would be motionless, or if moving it would move only in perverted directions. All the new inventions of the day are but the new ideas of studious thinkers wrought into wood and stone and iron. Without scholars the world would be without books, without philosophy, without inventions, without opinions, without thought and without religion.

How great then are the responsibilities of educated men! Their ideas and tastes and habits and decrees are the mighty, though unwritten, laws of society. From the energy of their mental movements, comes the shock that moves all its wheels.

And how great are the duties of each generation, in this matter, to posterity! The utmost possible facilities should be furnished in every age, not only for procuring and diffusing at the time the Higher Christian Education, but also for perpetuating it for ever. As all the advanced points of Modern Civilization have been gained by earnest Christian study, thought, argument and authorship, in the same way must they be maintained and new points beyond be reached. What has been gained in the past must be both preserved, and enlarged to new degrees of extent and of excellence.

Let then the people know well their own guides and deliverers. Let them recognize their indebtedness to Christianity, for all the light of life and the glory of society. And, if they would wreathe their names with grateful memories in the hearts of their descendants, let them be careful to leave, in every permanent form, as large a legacy as possible of true sanctified thoughts and influences. The real riches of any life to mankind consist in the contribution that it makes, directly or indirectly, to the common stock of Human Intelligence, Human Comfort and Human Goodness.

INDEX.

THE END.

THE NATIONAL SERIES OF READERS.

COMPLETE IN TWO INDEPENDENT PARTS.

I.
THE NATIONAL READERS.

By PARKER & WATSON.

No. 1.—National Primer, ...	*64 pp., 16mo,*	$0 25
No. 2.—National First Reader, . . .	*128 pp., 16mo,*	38
No. 3.—National Second Reader, . .	*224 pp., 16mo,*	63
No. 4.—National Third Reader, . .	*288 pp., 12mo,*	1 00
No. 5.—National Fourth Reader, . .	*432 pp., 12mo,*	1 50
No. 6.—National Fifth Reader, . .	*600 pp., 12mo,*	1 88
National Elementary Speller, . . .	*160 pp., 16mo,*	25
National Pronouncing Speller, . . .	*188 pp., 12mo,*	50

II.
THE INDEPENDENT READERS.

By J. MADISON WATSON.

The Independent First Reader, . .	*80 pp., 16mo,*	25
The Independent Second Reader, .	*160 pp., 16mo,*	50
The Independent Third Reader, . .	*240 pp., 16mo,*	75
The Independent Fourth Reader, . .	*264 pp., 12mo,*	1 00
The Independent Fifth Reader, . .	*336 pp., 12mo,*	1 25
The Independent Sixth Reader, . .	*474 pp., 12mo,*	1 50
The Independent Child's Speller (Script),	*80 pp., 16mo,*	25
The Independent Youth's Speller (Script),		—
The Independent Spelling Book, . .	*160 pp., 16mo,*	25

***** The Readers constitute two complete and entirely distinct series, either of which is adequate to every want of the best schools. The Spellers may accompany either Series.**

PARKER & WATSON'S NATIONAL READERS.

The salient features of these works which have combined to render them so popular may be briefly recapitulated as follows:

1. THE WORD-BUILDING SYSTEM.—This famous progressive method for young children originated and was copyrighted with these books. It constitutes a process with which the beginner with *words* of one letter is gradually introduced to additional lists formed by prefixing or affixing single letters, and is thus led almost insensibly to the mastery of the more difficult constructions. This is one of the most striking modern improvements in methods of teaching.

2. TREATMENT OF PRONUNCIATION.—The wants of the youngest scholars in this department are not overlooked. It may be said that from the first lesson the student by this method need never be at a loss for a prompt and accurate rendering of every word encountered.

3. ARTICULATION AND ORTHOEPY are considered of primary importance.

4. PUNCTUATION is inculcated by a series of interesting *reading lessons*, the simple perusal of which suffices to fix its principles indelibly upon the mind.

5. ELOCUTION. Each of the higher Readers (3d, 4th and 5th) contains elaborate, scholarly, and thoroughly practical treatises on elocution. This feature alone has secured for the series many of its warmest friends.

6. THE SELECTIONS are the crowning glory of the series. Without exception it may be said that no volumes of the same size and character contain a collection so diversified, judicious, and artistic as this. It embraces the choicest gems of English literature, so arranged as to afford the reader ample exercise in every department of style. So acceptable has the taste of the authors in this department proved, not only to the educational public but to the reading community at large, that thousands of copies of the Fourth and Fifth Readers have found their way into public and private libraries throughout the country, where they are in constant use as manuals of literature, for reference as well as perusal.

7. ARRANGEMENT. The exercises are so arranged as to present constantly alternating practice in the different styles of composition, while observing a definite plan of progression or gradation throughout the whole. In the higher books the articles are placed in formal sections and classified topically, thus concentrating the interest and inculcating a principle of association likely to prove valuable in subsequent general reading.

8. NOTES AND BIOGRAPHICAL SKETCHES. These are full and adequate to every want. The biographical sketches present in pleasing style the history of every author laid under contribution.

9. ILLUSTRATIONS. These are plentiful, almost profuse, and of the highest character of art. They are found in every volume of the series as far as and including the Third Reader.

10. THE GRADATION is perfect. Each volume overlaps its companion preceding or following in the series, so that the scholar, in passing from one to another, is only conscious, by the presence of the new book, of the transition.

11. THE PRICE is reasonable. The National Readers contain more matter than any other series in the same number of volumes published. Considering their completeness and thoroughness they are much the cheapest in the market.

12. BINDING. By the use of a material and process known only to themselves, in common with all the publications of this house, the National Readers are warranted to outlast any with which they may be compared—the ratio of relative durability being in their favor as two to one.

WATSON'S INDEPENDENT READERS.

This Series is designed to meet a general demand for smaller and cheaper books than the National Series proper, and to serve as well for intermediate volumes of the National Readers in large graded schools requiring more books than one ordinary series will supply.

Beauty. The most casual observer is at once impressed with the unparalleled mechanical beauty of the Independent Readers. The Publishers believe that the æsthetic tastes of children may receive no small degree of cultivation from their very earliest school books, to say nothing of the importance of making study attractive by all such artificial aids that are legitimate. In accordance with this view, not less than $25,000 was expended in their preparation before publishing, with a result which entitles them to be considered "The Perfection of Common School Books."

Selections. They contain, of course, none but entirely new selections. These are arranged according to a strictly progressive and novel method of developing the elementary sounds in order in the lower numbers, and in all, with a view to topics and general literary style. The mind is thus led in fixed channels to proficiency in every branch of good reading, and the evil results of 'scattering' as practised by most school-book authors, avoided.

The Illustrations, as may be inferred from what has been said, are elegant beyond comparison. They are profuse in every number of the series from the lowest to the highest. This is the only series published of which this is true.

The Type is semi-phonetic, the invention of Prof. Watson. By it every letter having more than one sound is clearly distinguished in all its variations without in any way mutilating or disguising the normal form of the letter.

Elocution is taught by prefatory treatises of constantly advancing grade and completeness in each volume, which are illustrated by wood-cuts in the lower books, and by black-board diagrams in the higher. Prof. Watson is the first to introduce Practical Illustrations and Black-board Diagrams for teaching this branch.

Foot Notes on every page afford all the incidental instruction which the teacher is usually required to impart. Indices of words refer the pupil to the place of their first use and definition. The Biographies of Authors and others are in every sense excellent.

Economy. Although the number of pages in each volume is fixed at the minimum, for the purpose recited above, the utmost amount of matter available without overcrowding is obtained in the space. The pages are much wider and larger than those of any competitor and contain *twenty per cent* more matter than any other series of the same type and number of pages.

All the Great Features. Besides the above all the popular features of the National Readers are retained except the Word-Building system. The latter gives place to an entirely new method of progressive development, based upon some of the best features of the Word System, Phonetics and Object Lessons.

NATIONAL READERS.

ORIGINAL AND "INDEPENDENT" SERIES.

SPECIMEN TESTIMONIALS.

From D. H. Harris, *Supt. Public Schools, Hannibal, Mo.*

The National Series of Readers are now in use in our public schools, and I regard them *the best* that I have ever examined or used.

From Hon. J. K. Jillson, *Supt. of Education, State of South Carolina.*

I have carefully examined your new and beautiful Series of Readers known as "The Independent Readers," and do not hesitate to recommend it as the finest and most excellent ever presented to the public.

From D. N. Rook, *Sec. of School Board, Williamsport, Pa.*

I would say that Parker & Watson's Series of Readers and Spellers give the best satisfaction in our schools of any Series of Readers and Spellers that have ever been used. There is nothing published for which we would exchange them

From Prof. H. Seele, *New Braunfels Academy, Texas.*

I recommend the National Readers for four good reasons: (1.) The printing, engraving, and binding is excellent. (2.) They contain choice selections from English Literature. (3.) They inculcate good morals without any sectarian bias. (4.) They are truly *National*, because they teach pure patriotism and not sectional prejudice.

From S. Findley, *Supt. Akron Schools, Ohio.*

We use no others, and have no desire to. They give entire satisfaction. We like the freshness and excellence of the selections. We like the biographical notes and the definitions at the foot of the page. We also like the white paper and clear and beautiful type. In short, we do not know where to look for books which would be so satisfactory both to teachers and pupils.

From Pres. Robert Allyn, *McKendree College, Ill.*

Since my connection with this college, we have used in our preparatory department the Series of Readers known as the "National Readers," compiled by Parker & Watson, and published by Messrs. A. S. Barnes & Co. They are *excellent;* afford choice selections; contain the right system of elocutionary instruction, and are well printed and bound so as to be serviceable as well as interesting. I can commend them as among the excellent means used by teachers to make their pupils proficient in that noblest of school arts, Good Reading.

From W. T. Harris, *Supt. Public Schools, St. Louis, Mo.*

I have to admire these excellent selections in prose and verse, and the careful arrangement which places first what is easy of comprehension, and proceeds gradually to what is difficult. I find the lessons so arranged as to bring together different treatments of the same topic, thereby throwing much light on the pupil's path, and I doubt not adding greatly to his progress. The proper variety of subjects chosen, the concise treatise on elocution, the beautiful typography and substantial binding—all these I find still more admirable than in the former series of National Readers, which I considered *models* in these respects.

From H. T. Phillips, Esq., *of the Board of Education, Atlanta, Ga.*

The Board of Education of this city have selected for use in the public schools of Atlanta the entire series of your Independent Readers, together with Steele's Chemistry and Philosophy. As a member of the Board, and of the Committee on Text-books, the subject of Readers was referred to me for examination. I gave a pretty thorough examination to ten (10) different series of Readers, and in endeavoring to arrive at a decision upon the sole question of merit, and entirely independent of any extraneous influence, I very cordially recommended the Independent Series. This verdict was approved by the Committee and adopted by the Board.

From Report of Rev. W. T. Brantly, D.D., *late Professor of Belles Lettres, University of Georgia, on "Text-Books in Reading," before the Teachers' Convention of Georgia, May 4, 1870.*

The *National Series*, by Parker & Watson, is deserving of its high reputation. The Primary Books are suited to the weakest capacity; whilst those more advanced supply instructive illustration on all that is needed to be known in connection with the art.

WATSON'S CHILD'S SPELLER.

THE INDEPENDENT CHILD'S SPELLER.

Price 25 Cents.

This unique book, published in 1872, is the first to be consistently printed in imitation of writing; that is, it teaches orthography as we use it. It is for the smallest class of learners, who soon become familiarized with words by their forms, and learn to read writing while they spell.

EXTRACT FROM THE PREFACE.

Success in teaching English orthography is still exceptional, and it must so continue until the principles involved are recognized in practice. Form is foremost: the eye and the hand must be trained to the formation of words; and since spelling is a part of writing, the written form only should be used. The laws of mental association, also—especially those of resemblance, contrast, and contiguity in time and place—should receive such recognition in the construction of the text-book as shall insure, whether consciously or not, their appropriate use and legitimate results. Hence, the spelling-book, properly arranged, is a necessity from the first; and, though primers, readers, and dictionaries may serve as aids, it can have no competent substitute.

Consistently with these views, the words used in the Independent Child's Speller have such original classifications and arrangements in columns—in reference to location, number of letters, vowel sounds, alphabetic equivalents, and consonant terminations—as exhibit most effectively their formation and pronunciation. The vocabulary is strictly confined to the simple and significant monosyllables in common use. He who has mastered these may easily learn how to spell and pronounce words of more than one syllable.

The introduction is an illustrated alphabet in script, containing twenty-six pictures of objects, and their names, commencing both with capitals and small letters. Part First embraces the words of one, two, and three letters; Part Second, the words of four letters; and Part Third, other monosyllables. They are divided into short lists and arranged in columns, the vowels usually in line, so as to exhibit individual characteristics and similarity of formation. The division of words into paragraphs is shown by figures in the columns. Each list is immediately followed by sentences for reading and writing, in which the same words are again presented with irregularities of form and sound. Association is thus employed, memory tested, and definition most satisfactorily taught.

Among the novel and valuable features of the lessons and exercises, probably the most prominent are their adaptedness for young children and their being printed in exact imitation of writing. The author believes that hands large enough to spin a top, drive a hoop, or catch a ball, are not too small to use a crayon, or a slate and pencil; that the child's natural desire to draw and write should not be thwarted, but gratified, encouraged, and wisely directed; and that since the written form is the one actually used in connection with spelling in after-life, the eye and the hand of the child should be trained to that form from the first. He hopes that this little work, designed to precede all other spelling-books and conflict with none, may satisfy the need so universally recognized of a fit introduction to orthography, penmanship, and English composition.

The National Readers and Spellers.

THEIR RECORD.

These books have been adopted by the School Boards, or official authority, of the following important States, cities, and towns—in most cases for exclusive use.

The State of Minnesota.
The State of Texas.
The State of Missouri.
The State of Alabama.
The State of North Carolina.
The State of Louisiana.

New York.
New York City.
Brooklyn.
Buffalo.
Albany.
Rochester.
Troy.
Syracuse.
Elmira.
&c., &c.

Pennsylvania.
Reading.
Lancaster.
Erie.
Scranton.
Carlisle.
Carbondale.
Westchester.
Schuylkill Haven.
Williamsport.
Norristown.
Bellefonte.
Wilkesbárre.
&c., &c.

New Jersey.
Newark.
Jersey City.
Paterson.
Trenton.
Camden.
Elizabeth.
New Brunswick.
Phillipsburg.
Orange.
&c., &c.

Delaware.
Wilmington.

D. C.
Washington.

Illinois.
Chicago.
Peoria.
Alton.
Springfield.
Aurora.
Galesburg.
Rockford.
Rock Island.
&c., &c.

Wisconsin.
Milwaukee.
Fond du Lac.
Oshkosh.
Janesville.
Racine.
Watertown.
Sheboygan.
La Crosse.
Waukesha.
Kenosha.
&c., &c.

Michigan.
Grand Rapids.
Kalamazoo.
Adrian.
Jackson.
Monroe.
Lansing.
&c., &c.

Ohio.
Toledo.
Sandusky.
Conneaut.
Chardon.
Hudson.
Canton.
Salem.
&c., &c.

Indiana.
New Albany.
Fort Wayne.
Lafayette.
Madison.
Logansport.
Indianapolis.

Iowa.
Davenport.
Burlington.
Muscatine.
Mount Pleasant.
&c.

Nebraska.
Brownsville.
Lincoln.
&c.

Oregon.
Portland.
Salem.
&c.

Virginia.
Richmond.
Norfolk.
Petersburg.
Lynchburg.
&c.

South Carolina.
Columbia.
Charleston.

Georgia.
Savannah.

Louisiana.
New Orleans.

Tennessee.
Memphis

The *Educational Bulletin* records periodically all new points gained.

SCHOOL-ROOM CARDS.

Baade's Reading Case, ...*$10 00

A frame containing movable cards, with arrangement for showing one sentence at a time, capable of 28,000 transpositions.

Eureka Alphabet Tablet *1 50

Presents the alphabet upon the Word Method System, by which the child will learn the alphabet in nine days, and make no small progress in reading and spelling in the same time.

National School Tablets, 10 Nos. *8 00

Embrace reading and conversational exercises, object and moral lessons, form, color, &c. A complete set of these large and elegantly illustrated Cards will embellish the school-room more than any other article of furniture.

READING.

Fowle's Bible Reader $1 00

The narrative portions of the Bible, chronologically and topically arranged, judiciously combined with selections from the Psalms, Proverbs, and other portions which inculcate important moral lessons or the great truths of Christianity. The embarrassment and difficulty of reading the Bible itself, by course, as a class exercise, are obviated, and its use made feasible, by this means.

North Carolina First Reader 40

North Carolina Second Reader 65

North Carolina Third Reader 1 00

Prepared expressly for the schools of this State, by C. H. Wiley, Superintendent of Common Schools, and F. M. Hubbard, Professor of Literature in the State University.

Parker's Rhetorical Reader 1 00

Designed to familiarize Readers with the pauses and other marks in general use, and lead them to the practice of modulation and inflection of the voice.

Introductory Lessons in Reading and Elocution 75

Of similar character to the foregoing, for less advanced classes.

High School Literature 1 50

Admirable selections from a long list of the world's best writers, for exercise in reading, oratory, and composition. Speeches, dialogues, and model letters represent the latter department.

ORTHOGRAPHY.

SMITH'S SERIES

Supplies a speller for every class in graded schools, and comprises the most complete and excellent treatise on English Orthography and its companion branches extant.

1. Smith's Little Speller . . . . $ 20

First Round in the Ladder of Learning.

2. Smith's Juvenile Definer 45

Lessons composed of familiar words grouped with reference to similar signification or use, and correctly spelled, accented, and defined.

3. Smith's Grammar-School Speller 50

Familiar words, grouped with reference to the sameness of sound of syllables differently spelled. Also definitions, complete rules for spelling and formation of derivatives, and exercises in false orthography.

4. Smith's Speller and Definer's Manual . 90

A complete *School Dictionary* containing 14,000 words, with various other useful matter in the way of Rules and Exercises.

5. Smith's Etymology—Small, 75; Complete . 1 25

The first and only Etymology to recognize the *Anglo-Saxon* our *mother tongue;* containing also full lists of derivatives from the Latin, Greek, Gaelic, Swedish, Norman, &c., &c ; being, in fact, a complete etymology of the language for schools.

Sherwood's Writing Speller 15

Sherwood's Speller and Definer 15

Sherwood's Speller and Pronouncer . . . 15

The Writing Speller consists of properly ruled and numbered blanks to receive the words dictated by the teacher, with space for remarks and corrections. The other volumes may be used for the dictation or ordinary class exercises.

Price's English Speller *15

A complete spelling-book for all grades, containing more matter than "Webster," manufactured in superior style, and sold at a lower price—consequently the cheapest speller extant.

Northend's Dictation Exercises 63

Embracing valuable information on a thousand topics, communicated in such a manner as at once to relieve the exercise of spelling of its usual tedium, and combine it with instruction of a general character calculated to profit and amuse.

Wright's Analytical Orthography 25

This standard work is popular, because it teaches the elementary sounds in a plain and philosophical manner, and presents orthography and orthoepy in an easy, uniform system of analysis or parsing.

Fowle's False Orthography 45

Exercises for correction.

Page's Normal Chart *3 75

The elementary sounds of the language for the school-room walls.

ORTHOGRAPHY—Continued.

Barber's Critical Writing Speller. . . . . .. 20 cts.

"The Student's Own Hand-Book of Orthography, Definitions, and Sentences, consisting of Written Exercises in the Proper Spelling, Meaning, and Use of Words." (Published 1873.) This differs from Sherwood's and other Writing Spellers in its more comprehensive character. Its blanks are adapted to writing whole sentences instead of detached words, with the proper divisions for numbering, corrections, etc. Such aids as this, like Watson's Child's Speller and Sherwood's Writing Speller, find their *raison d'être* in the postulate that the art of correct spelling is dependent upon written, and not upon spoken language, for its utility, if not for its very existence. Hence the indirectness of purely oral instruction.

ETYMOLOGY.

Smith's Complete Etymology, ... $1 25
Smith's Condensed Etymology, ... 75

Containing the Anglo-Saxon, French, Dutch, German, Welsh, Danish, Gothic, Swedish, Gaelic, Italian, Latin, and Greek Roots, and the English words derived therefrom accurately spelled, accented, and defined.

From HON. JNO. G. MCMYNN, *late State Superintendent of Wisconsin.*

I wish every teacher in the country had a copy of this work.

From PRIN. WM. F. PHELPS, *Minn. State Normal.*

The book is superb—just what is needed in the department of etymology and spelling.

From PROF. C. H. VERRILL, *Pa. State Normal School.*

The Etymology (Smith's) which we procured of you we like much. It is the best work for the class-room we have seen.

From HON. EDWARD BALLARD, *Supt. of Common Schools, State of Maine.*

Many a teacher who has turned his attention to the derivation of words has rejoiced in the helps furnished by dictionaries and smaller "hand-books," where his taste could be gratified, and the labors of patient students have been available to his own improvement. A treatise on this subject, called "A Complete Etymology of the English Language," contains very much information in a small space. The author, W. W. Smith, is evidently a lover of this branch of study, and has furnished a manual of singular utility for its purpose.

DICTIONARY.

The Topical Lexicon, ... 1 75

This work is a School Dictionary, an Etymology, a compilation of synonyms, and a manual of general information. It differs from the ordinary lexicon in being arranged by topics instead of the letters of the alphabet, thus realizing the apparent paradox of a "Readable Dictionary." An unusually valuable school-book.

ENGLISH GRAMMAR.

CLARK'S DIAGRAM SYSTEM.

Clark's Beginner's Grammar, ... $0 60

(Published 1872.) The Beginner's Grammar contains illustrated object-lessons of the most attractive character, and is couched in language freed as much as possible from the dry technicalities of the science. Part I is adapted to youngest scholars, and the whole forms a complete "brief course" in one volume.

This work is designed to take the place of the same author's well-known "First Lessons," with all the improvements which sixteen years of additional experience and the criticisms of our best teachers have suggested. It is fuller, while more simple, than its predecessor, more space being given to examples and exercises. The whole subject is also more broadly treated.

Clark's Normal Grammar, ... 1 00

Published 1870, and designed to take the place of Prof. Clark's veteran "Practical" Grammar, though the latter is still furnished upon order. The Normal is an entirely new treatise. It is a full exposition of the system as described below, with all the most recent improvements. Some of its peculiarities are—A happy blending of SYNTHESES with ANALYSES; thorough Criticisms of common errors in the use of our Language; and important improvements in the Syntax of Sentences and of Phrases.

Clark's Key to the Diagrams, ... 1 00

Clark's Analysis of the English Language, . 60

Clark's Grammatical Chart, ... *3 75

The theory and practice of teaching grammar in American schools is meeting with a thorough revolution from the use of this system. While the old methods offer proficiency to the pupil only after much weary plodding and dull memorizing, this affords from the inception the advantage of *practical Object Teaching*, addressing the eye by means of illustrative figures; furnishes association to the memory, its most powerful aid, and diverts the pupil by taxing his ingenuity. Teachers who are using Clark's Grammar uniformly testify that they and their pupils find it the most interesting study of the school course.

Like all great and radical improvements, the system naturally met at first with much unreasonable opposition. It has not only outlived the greater part of this opposition, but finds many of its warmest admirers among those who could not at first tolerate so radical an innovation. All it wants is an impartial trial to convince the most skeptical of its merit. No one who has fairly and intelligently tested it in the school-room has ever been known to go back to the old method. A great success is already established, and it is easy to prophecy that the day is not far distant when it will be the *only system of teaching English Grammar*. As the SYSTEM is copyrighted, no other text-books can appropriate this obvious and great improvement.

Welch's Analysis of the English Sentence, . 1 25

Remarkable for its new and simple classification, its method of treating connectives, its explanations of the idioms and constructive laws of the language, etc.

Clark's Diagram English Grammar.

TESTIMONIALS.

From J. A. T. Durnin, *Principal Dubuque R. C. Academy, Iowa.*

In my opinion, it is well calculated by its system of analysis to develop those rational faculties which in the old systems were rather left to develop themselves, while the memory was overtaxed, and the pupils discouraged.

From B. A. Cox, *School Commissioner, Warren County, Illinois.*

I have examined 150 teachers in the last year, and those having studied or taught Clark's System have universally stood fifty per cent. better examinations than those having studied other authors.

From M. H. B. Burket, *Principal Masonic Institute, Georgetown, Tennessee.*

I traveled two years amusing myself in instructing (exclusively) Grammar classes with Clark's system. The first class I instructed fifty days, but found that this was more time than was required to impart a theoretical knowledge of the science. During the two years thereafter I instructed classes only *thirty* days each. I invariably I proposed that unless I prepared my classes for a more thorough, minute, and accurate knowledge of English Grammar than that obtained from the ordinary books and in the ordinary way in from one to two years, I would make no charge. I never failed in a solitary case to far exceed the hopes of my classes, and made money and character rapidly as an instructor.

From A. B. Douglass, *School Commissioner, Delaware County, New York.*

I have never known a class pursue the study of it under a *live* teacher, that has not succeeded; I have never known it to have an opponent in an educated teacher who had *thoroughly* investigated it; I have never known an *ignorant* teacher to examine it; I have never known a teacher who has used it, to try any other.

From J. A. Dodge, *Teacher and Lecturer on English Grammar, Kentucky.*

We are tempted to assert that it foretells the dawn of a brighter age to our mother-tongue. Both pupil and teacher can fare sumptuously upon its contents, however highly they may have prized the manuals into which they may have been initiated, and by which their expressions have been moulded.

From W. T. Chapman, *Superintendent Public Schools, Wellington, Ohio.*

I regard Clark's System of Grammar the best published. For teaching the analysis of the English Language, it surpasses any I ever used.

From F. S. Lyon, *Principal South Norwalk Union School, Connecticut.*

During ten years' experience in teaching, I have used six different authors on the subject of English Grammar. I am fully convinced that Clark's Grammar is better calculated to make thorough grammarians than any other that I have seen.

From Catalogue of Rohrer's Commercial College, *St. Louis, Missouri.*

We do not hesitate to assert, without fear of successful contradiction, that a better knowledge of the English language can be obtained by this system in six weeks than by the old methods in as many months.

From A. Pickett, *President of the State Teachers' Association, Wisconsin.*

A thorough experiment in the use of many approved authors upon the subject of English Grammar has convinced me of the superiority of Clark. When the pupil has completed the course, he is left upon a foundation of *principle*, and not upon the *dictum* of the author.

From Geo. F. McFarland, *Prin. McAllisterville Academy, Juniata Co., Penn.*

At the first examination of public-school teachers by the county superintendent, when one of our student teachers commenced analyzing a sentence according to Clark, the superintendent listened in mute astonishment until he had finished, then asked what that meant, and finally, with a very knowing look, said such work wouldn't do here, and asked the applicant to parse the sentence right, and gave the lowest certificates to all who barely mentioned Clark. Afterwards, I presented him with a copy, and the next fall he permitted it to be partially used, while the third of last fall, he openly commended the system, and appointed three of my best teachers to explain it at the two Institutes and one County Convention held since September.

☞ For further testimony of equal force, see the Publishers' Special Circular, or current numbers of the Educational Bulletin.

GEOGRAPHY.

NATIONAL GEOGRAPHICAL SYSTEM.

THE SERIES.

I.	**Monteith's First Lessons in Geography,** . . .	$ 35
II.	**Monteith's New Manual of Geography,** . . .	1 10
III.	**McNally's System of Geography,**	2 00

INTERMEDIATE OR ALTERNATE VOLUMES.

I*.	**Monteith's Introduction to Geography,**	63
2*.	**Monteith's Physical and Political Geography,** . . .	1 88

ACCESSORIES.

Monteith's Wall Maps (per set)	*20 00
Monteith's Manual of Map-Drawing (Allen's System) .	25
Monteith's Map-Drawing and Object-Lessons, . .	75
Monteith's Map-Drawing Scale, ...	*25

1. PRACTICAL OBJECT TEACHING. The infant scholar is first introduced to *a picture* whence he may derive notions of the shape of the earth, the phenomena of day and night, the distribution of land and water, and the great natural divisions, which mere words would fail entirely to convey to the untutored mind. Other pictures follow on the same plan, and the child's mind is called upon to grasp no idea without the aid of a pictorial illustration. Carried on to the higher books, this system culminates in Physical Geography, where such matters as climates, ocean currents, the winds, peculiarities of the earth's crust, clouds and rain, are pictorially explained and rendered apparent to the most obtuse. The illustrations used for this purpose belong to the highest grade of art.

2. CLEAR, BEAUTIFUL, AND CORRECT MAPS. In the lower numbers the maps avoid unnecessary detail, while respectively progressive, and affording the pupil new matter for acquisition each time he approaches in the constantly enlarging circle the point of coincidence with previous lessons in the more elementary books. In the Physical and Political Geography the maps embrace many new and striking features. One of the most effective of these is the new plan for displaying on each map the relative sizes of countries not represented, thus obviating much confusion which has arisen from the necessity of presenting maps in the same atlas drawn on different scales. The maps of "McNally" have long been celebrated for their superior beauty and completeness. This is the only school-book in which the attempt to make a *complete* atlas *also clear and distinct*, has been successful. The map *coloring* throughout the series is also noticeable. Delicate and subdued tints take the place of the startling glare of inharmonious colors which too frequently in such treatises dazzle the eyes, distract the attention, and serve to overwhelm the names of towns and the natural features of the landscape.

GEOGRAPHY—Continued.

3. **THE VARIETY OF MAP EXERCISE.** Starting each time from a different basis, the pupil in many instances approaches the same fact no less than *six times*, thus indelibly impressing it upon his memory. At the same time this system is not allowed to become wearisome—the extent of exercise on each subject being graduated by its relative importance or difficulty of acquisition.

4. **THE CHARACTER AND ARRANGEMENT OF THE DESCRIPTIVE TEXT.** The cream of the science has been carefully culled, unimportant matter rejected, elaboration avoided, and a brief and concise manner of presentation cultivated. The orderly consideration of topics has contributed greatly to simplicity. Due attention is paid to the facts in history and astronomy which are inseparably connected with, and important to the proper understanding of geography—and *such only* are admitted on any terms. In a word, the National System teaches geography as a science, pure, simple, and exhaustive.

5. **ALWAYS UP TO THE TIMES.** The authors of these books, editorially speaking, never sleep. No change occurs in the boundaries of countries, or of counties, no new discovery is made, or railroad built, that is not at once noted and recorded, and the next edition of each volume carries to every school-room the new order of things.

6. **SUPERIOR GRADATION.** This is the only series which furnishes an available volume for every possible class in graded schools. It is not contemplated that a pupil must necessarily go through every volume in succession to attain proficiency. On the contrary, *two* will suffice, but *three* are advised; and if the course will admit, the whole series should be pursued. At all events, the books are at hand for selection, and every teacher, of every grade, can find among them one *exactly suited* to his class. The best combination for those who wish to abridge the course consists of Nos. 1, 2, and 3, or where children are somewhat advanced in other studies when they commence geography, Nos. 1*, 2, and 3. Where but *two* books are admissible, Nos. 1* and 2*, or Nos. 2 and 3, are recommended.

7. **FORM OF THE VOLUMES AND MECHANICAL EXECUTION.** The maps and text are no longer unnaturally divorced in accordance with the time-honored practice of making text-books on this subject as inconvenient and expensive as possible. On the contrary, all map questions are to be found on the page opposite the map itself, and each book is complete in one volume. The mechanical execution is unrivalled. Paper and printing are everything that could be desired, and the binding is—A. S. Barnes and Company's.

8. **MAP-DRAWING.** In 1869 the system of Map-Drawing devised by Professor Jerome Allen was secured *exclusively* for this series. It derives its claim to originality and usefulness from the introduction of a *fixed unit of measurement* applicable to every Map. The principles being so few, simple and comprehensive, the subject of Map-Drawing is relieved of all practical difficulty. (In Nos. 2, 2*, and 3, and published separately.)

8. **ANALOGOUS OUTLINES.** At the same time with Map-Drawing was also introduced (in No. 2), a new and ingenious variety of Object Lessons, consisting of a comparison of the outlines of countries with familiar objects pictorially represented.

GEOGRAPHY—Continued.

MONTEITH'S COMPREHENSIVE GEOGRAPHY.

Price $1.60.

This book (published 1872) is the fruit and condensation of all the author's experience. It is not an old book revamped—not an addition to any series, but a ***book by itself;*** complete, independent, comprehensive, yet simple, brief, cheap, an popular. A "series" in one volume, adequate to the entire common-school course It presents the following features, skillfully interwoven—the student learning all about one country at a time.

LOCAL GEOGRAPHY, or the Use of Maps, of which the work contains ninety-eight distinct ones. Important features of the Maps are the coloring of States as objects, and the care taken not to overcrowd them with names of secondary importance.

PHYSICAL GEOGRAPHY, or the Natural Features of the Earth, illustrated by the original and striking ***Relief Maps,*** being bird's-eye views or photographic pictures of the Earth's surface.

DESCRIPTIVE GEOGRAPHY, including the Physical; with some account of Governments, and Races, Animals, etc.

HISTORICAL GEOGRAPHY, or a brief summary of the salient points of history, explaining the present distribution of nations, origin of geographical names, etc.

MATHEMATICAL GEOGRAPHY, including ASTRONOMICAL, which describes the Earth's position and character among planets; also the Zones, Parallels, etc.

COMPARATIVE GEOGRAPHY, or a system of analogy, connecting new lessons with the previous ones. Comparative sizes and latitudes are shown on the margin of each Map, and all countries are measured in the "*frame of Kansas.*"

TOPICAL GEOGRAPHY, consisting of questions for review, and testing the student's general and specific knowledge of the subject, with suggestions for *Geographical Compositions.*

ANCIENT GEOGRAPHY. A section devoted to this subject, with Maps, will be appreciated by teachers. It is seldom taught in our common schools, because it has heretofore required the purchase of a separate book.

GRAPHIC GEOGRAPHY, or MAP-DRAWING by Allen's "Unit of Measurement" system (now almost universally recognized as without a rival), is introduced throughout the lessons, and not as an appendix.

CONSTRUCTIVE GEOGRAPHY, or GLOBE-MAKING. With each book a set of Map Segments is furnished, with which each student may make his own Globe by following the directions given.

RAILROAD GEOGRAPHY, with a grand Map illustrating routes of travel in the United States.

The National System of Geography,

BY MONTEITH & MCNALLY.

ITS RECORD.

These popular text-books have been adopted, by official authority, for the schools of the following States, cities, and associations—in most cases for exclusive and uniform use.

STATES.

CALIFORNIA.	VERMONT.	FLORIDA.
MISSOURI.	IOWA.	MINNESOTA.
ALABAMA.	LOUISIANA.	NORTH CAROLINA.
TENNESSEE.		KANSAS.
TEXAS.		MISSISSIPPI.

CITIES.

New York City.	Louisville.	Nashville.	Portland.
Brooklyn.	Newark.	Utica.	Savannah.
New Orleans.	Milwaukee.	Wilmington.	Indianapolis.
Buffalo.	Charleston.	Trenton.	Springfield.
Richmond.	Rochester.	Norfolk.	Wheeling.
Jersey City.	Mobile.	Norwich.	Toledo.
Hartford.	Syracuse.	Lockport.	Bridgeport.
Worcester.	Memphis.	Dubuque.	St. Paul.

ASSOCIATIONS.

The Society of the CHRISTIAN BROTHERS, representing 40,000 pupils.
The FRANCISCAN BROTHERS, 8,000 pupils.
AMERICAN MISSIONARY SOCIETY, 60,000 pupils.

Monteith's Physical and Political Geography.

This is the most recently published of the Geographical Series, and as might have been anticipated, was very warmly received.

TESTIMONIALS IN BRIEF.

The more I examine the better I am pleased.—J. T. GOODNOW, *late St. Supt. Kan.*
Has no superior as a text-book.—E. J. THOMPSON, *Supt. Fillmore Co., Minn.*
Brief, clear, suggestive, and admirably adapted.—E. CONANT, *Prin. Vt. Normal.*
It is a gem of a book.—E. A. STRONG, *Supt. Public Schools, Grand Rapids, Mich.*
The best adapted we have seen.—O. FAVILLE, *late State Supt., Iowa.*
A book that has long been needed.—A. J. KINGMAN, *Supt. McHenry Co., Ill.*
Prepared with labor, care, and well adapted.—C. B. HALSTEAD, *Supt. Newburg, N. Y.*
The best Geography ever published.—J. HUTCHISON, *Prin. Boys' Sch. Jefferson, La.*
I like it very much.—A. J. CRAIG, *late State Supt., Wisconsin.*
Cannot fail to awaken a new interest.—*Vermont School Journal.*
A new field cultivated with great success.—T. C. JOHNSON, *Pres. Randolph Macon. Coll., Va.*
Contains more common sense than any other.—J. ANGEAR, *Prin. Madison Ac. Iowa.*

Monteith & McNally's National Geographies.

CRITICAL OPINIONS.

From R. A. ADAMS, *Member of Board of Education, New York.*

I have found, by examination of the Book of Supply of our Board, that considerably the largest number of any series now used in our public schools is the National, by Monteith and McNally.

From BRO. PATRICK, *Chief Provincial of the Vast Educational Society of the* CHRISTIAN BROTHERS *in the United States.*

Having been convinced for some time past that the series of Geographies in use in our schools were not giving satisfaction, and came far short of meeting our most reasonable expectations, I have felt it my imperative duty to examine into this matter, and see if a remedy could not be found.

Copies of the different Geographies published in this country have been placed at our command for examination. On account of other pressing duties we have not been able to give as much time to the investigation of all these different series as we could have desired; yet we have found enough to convince us that there are many others better than those we are now using; but we cheerfully give our most decided preference, above all others, to the National Series, by Monteith & McNally.

Their easy gradation, their thoroughly practical and independent character, their comprehensive completeness as a full and accurate system, the wise discrimination shown in the selection of the subject matter, the beautiful and copious illustrations, the neat cut type, the general execution of the works, and *other excellencies*, will commend them to the friends of education everywhere.

From the "HOME MONTHLY," *Nashville, Tenn.*

MONTEITH'S AND MCNALLY'S GEOGRAPHIES.—Geography is so closely connected with Astronomy, History, Ethnology, and Geology, that it is difficult to define its limits in the construction of a text-book. If the author confines himself strictly to a description of the earth's surface, his book will be dry, meager, and unintelligible to a child. If, on the other hand, he attempts to give information on the cognate sciences, he enters a boundless field, and may wander too far. It seems to us that the authors of the series before us have hit on the happy medium between too much and too little. *The First Lessons*, by applying the system of object-teaching, renders the subject so attractive that a child, just able to read, may become deeply interested in it. The second book of the course enlarges the view, but still keeps to the maps and simple descriptions. Then, in the third book, we have Geography combined with History and Astronomy. A general view of the solar system is presented, so that the pupil may understand the earth's position on the map of the heavens. The first part of the fourth book treats of Physical Geography, and contains a vast amount of knowledge compressed into a small space. It is made bright and attractive by beautiful pictures and suggestive illustrations, on the principle of object-teaching. The maps in the second part of this volume are remarkably clear, and the map exercises are copious and judicious. In the fifth and last volume of the series, the whole subject is reviewed and systematized. This is strictly a Geography. Its maps are beautifully engraved and clearly printed. The map exercises are full and comprehensive. In all these books the maps, questions and descriptions are given in the same volume. In most geographies there are too many details and minute descriptions—more than any child out of purgatory ought to be required to learn. The power of memory is overstrained; there is confusion—no clearly defined idea is formed in the child's mind. But in these books, in brief, pointed descriptions, and constant use of bright, accurate maps, the whole subject is photographed on the mind.

MATHEMATICS.

DAVIES' NATIONAL COURSE.

ARITHMETIC.

			SLATED.
1. Davies'	Primary Arithmetic,	$ 25	$ 32
2. Davies'	Intellectual Arithmetic,	40	48
3. Davies'	Elements of Written Arithmetic,	50	60
4. Davies'	Practical Arithmetic,	90	1 00
	Key to Practical Arithmetic,	90	
5. Davies'	University Arithmetic,	1 40	1 50
	Key to University Arithmetic,	*1 40	

ALGEBRA.

1. Davies'	New Elementary Algebra,	*1 25	1 35
	Key to Elementary Algebra,	*1 25	
2. Davies'	University Algebra,	1 50	1 60
	Key to University Algebra,	*1 50	
3. Davies'	New Bourdon's Algebra,	2 25	2 38
	Key to Bourdon's Algebra,	*2 25	

GEOMETRY.

1. Davies'	Elementary Geometry and Trigonometry,	1 40	1 50
2. Davies'	Legendre's Geometry,	2 25	2 38
3. Davies'	Analytical Geometry and Calculus,	2 50	2 63
4. Davies'	Descriptive Geometry,	2 75	2 88
5. Davies'	New Calculus,	2 00	

MENSURATION.

1. Davies'	Practical Mathematics and Mensuration,	1 50	1 60
2. Davies'	Elements of Surveying,	2 50	2 63
3. Davies'	Shades, Shadows, and Perspective,	3 75	3 88

MATHEMATICAL SCIENCE.

Davies' Grammar of Arithmetic,	* 50
Davies' Outlines of Mathematical Science,	*1 00
Davies' Nature and Utility of Mathematics, 8vo, *2 00, 12mo,	*1 50
Davies' Metric System,	*1 50
Davies & Peck's Dictionary of Mathematics,	*5 00
Davies' Foundations Mathematical Science,	* 25

DAVIES' NATIONAL COURSE of MATHEMATICS.

ITS RECORD.

In claiming for this series the first place among American text-books, of what ever class, the Publishers appeal to the magnificent record which its volumes have earned during the *thirty-five years* of Dr. Charles Davies' mathematical labors. The unremitting exertions of a life-time have placed *the modern series* on the same proud eminence among competitors that each of its predecessors has successively enjoyed in a course of constantly improved editions, now rounded to their perfect fruition—for it seems almost that this science is susceptible of no further demonstration.

During the period alluded to, many authors and editors in this department have started into public notice, and by borrowing ideas and processes original with Dr. Davies, have enjoyed a brief popularity, but are now almost unknown. Many of the series of to-day, built upon a similar basis, and described as "modern books," are destined to a similar fate; while the most far-seeing eye will find it difficult to fix the time, on the basis of any data afforded by their past history, when these books will cease to increase and prosper, and fix a still firmer hold on the affection of every educated American.

One cause of this unparalleled popularity is found in the fact that the enterprise of the author did not cease with the original completion of his books. Always a practical teacher, he has incorporated in his text-books from time to time the advantages of every improvement in methods of teaching, and every advance in science. During all the years in which he has been laboring, he constantly submitted his own theories and those of others to the practical test of the class-room—approving, rejecting, or modifying them as the experience thus obtained might suggest. In this way he has been able to produce an almost perfect series of class-books, in which every department of mathematics has received minute and exhaustive attention.

Nor has he yet retired from the field. Still in the prime of life, and enjoying a ripe experience which no other living mathematician or teacher can emulate, his pen is ever ready to carry on the good work, as the progress of science may demand. Witness his recent exposition of the "Metric System," which received the official endorsement of Congress, by its Committee on Uniform Weights and Measures.

DAVIES' SYSTEM IS THE ACKNOWLEDGED NATIONAL STANDARD FOR THE UNITED STATES, for the following reasons:—

1st. It is the basis of instruction in the great national schools at West Point and Annapolis.

2d. It has received the *quasi* endorsement of the National Congress.

3d. It is exclusively used in the public schools of the National Capital.

4th. The officials of the Government use it as authority in all cases involving mathematical questions.

5th. Our great soldiers and sailors commanding the national armies and navies were educated in this system. So have been a majority of eminent scientists in this country. All these refer to "Davies" as authority.

6th. A larger number of American citizens have received their education from this than from any other series.

7th. The series has a larger circulation throughout the whole country than any other, being *extensively used in every State in the Union.*

Davies' National Course of Mathematics.

TESTIMONIALS.

From L. VAN BOKKELEN, *State Superintendent Public Instruction, Maryland.*

The series of Arithmetics edited by Prof. Davies, and published by your firm, have been used for many years in the schools of several counties, and the city of Baltimore, and have been approved by teachers and commissioners.

Under the law of 1865, establishing a uniform system of Free Public Schools, these Arithmetics were unanimously adopted by the State Board of Education, after a careful examination, and are now used in all the Public Schools of Maryland.

These facts evidence the high opinion entertained by the School Authorities of the value of the series theoretically and practically.

From HORACE WEBSTER, *President of the College of New York.*

The undersigned has examined, with care and thought, several volumes of Davies' Mathematics, and is of the opinion that, as a whole, it is the most complete and best course for Academic and Collegiate instruction, with which he is acquainted.

From DAVID N. CAMP, *State Superintendent of Common Schools, Connecticut.*

I have examined Davies' Series of Arithmetics with some care. The language is clear and precise; each principle is thoroughly analyzed, and the whole so arranged as to facilitate the work of instruction. Having observed the satisfaction and success with which the different books have been used by eminent teachers, it gives me pleasure to commend them to others.

From J. O. WILSON, *Chairman Committee on Text-Books, Washington, D. C.*

I consider Davies' Arithmetics decidedly superior to any other series, and in this opinion I am sustained, I believe, by the entire Board of Education and Corps of Teachers in this city, where they have been used for several years past.

From JOHN L. CAMPBELL, *Professor of Mathematics, Wabash College, Indiana.*

A proper combination of abstract reasoning and practical illustration is the chief excellence in Prof. Davies' Mathematical works. I prefer his Arithmetics, Algebras, Geometry and Trigonometry to all others now in use, and cordially recommend them to all who desire the advancement of sound learning.

From MAJOR J. H. WHITTLESEY, *Government Inspector of Military Schools.*

Be assured, I regard the works of Prof. Davies, with which I am acquainted, as by far the best text-books in print on the subjects which they treat. I shall certainly encourage their adoption wherever a word from me may be of any avail.

From T. McC. BALLANTINE, *Prof. Mathematics Cumberland College, Kentucky.*

I have long taught Prof. Davies' Course of Mathematics, and I continue to like their working.

From JOHN McLEAN BELL, B. A., *Prin. of Lower Canada College.*

I have used Davies' Arithmetical and Mathematical Series as text-books in the schools under my charge for the last six years. These I have found of great efficacy in exciting, invigorating, and concentrating the intellectual faculties of the young.

Each treatise serves as an introduction to the next higher, by the similarity of its reasonings and methods; and the student is carried forward, by easy and gradual steps, over the whole field of mathematical inquiry, and that, too, in a *shorter* time than is usually occupied in mastering a single department. I sincerely and heartily recommend them to the attention of my fellow-teachers in Canada.

From D. W. STEELE, *Prin. Philekoian Academy, Cold Springs, Texas.*

I have used Davies' Arithmetics till I know them nearly by heart. A better series of school-books never were published. I have recommended them until they are now used in all this region of country.

A large mass of similar "Opinions" may be obtained by addressing the publishers for special circular for Davies' Mathematics. New recommendations are published in current numbers of the *Educational Bulletin.*

MATHEMATICS—Continued.

ARITHMETICAL EXAMPLES.

Reuck's Examples in Denominate Numbers $ 50

Reuck's Examples in Arithmetic 1 00

These volumes diffei from the ordinary arithmetic in their peculiarly *practical* character. They are composed mainly of examples, and afford the most severe and thorough discipline for the mind. While a book which should contain a complete treatise of theory and practice would be too cumbersome for every-day use, the insufficiency of *practical* examples has been a source of complaint.

HIGHER MATHEMATICS.

Church's Elements of Calculus 2 50

Church's Analytical Geometry 2 50

Church's Descriptive Geometry, with Shades, Shadows, and Perspective 4 00

These volumes constitute the "West Point Course" in their several departments.

Courtenay's Elements of Calculus 3 00

A work especially popular at the South.

Hackley's Trigonometry 2 50

With applications to navigation and surveying, nautical and practical geometry and geodesy.

Peck's Analytical Geometry 1 75

Peck's Practical Calculus 1 75

APPLIED MATHEMATICS.

Peck's Ganot's Popular Physics 1 75

Peck's Elements of Mechanics 2 00

Peck's Practical Calculus 1 75

Prof. W G. Peck, of Columbia College, has designed the first of these works for the ordinary wants of schools in the department of Natural Philosophy. The work enjoys a high reputation.

The Mechanics and Calculus are the briefest treatises on those subjects now published. Their methods are purely practical, and unembarrassed by the details which rather confuse than simplify science.

SLATED ARITHMETICS.

This consists of the application of an artificially slated surface to the inner cover of a book, with flap of the same opening outward, so that students may refer to the book and use the slate at one and the same time, and as though the slate were detached. When folded up, the slate preserves examples and memoranda til' needed. The material used is as durable as the stone slate. The additional cost of books thus improved is trifling.

HISTORY.

Monteith's Youth's History, ... $ 75

A History of the United States for beginners. It is arranged upon the catechetical plan, with illustrative maps and engravings, review questions, dates in parentheses (that their study may be optional with the younger class of learners), and interesting biographical Sketches of all persons who have been prominently identified with the history of our country.

Willard's United States, School edition, . . . 1 40
Do. do. University edition, . 2 25

The plan of this standard work is chronologically exhibited in front of the title-page; the Maps and Sketches are found useful assistants to the memory, and dates, usually so difficult to remember, are so systematically arranged as in a great degree to obviate the difficulty. Candor, impartiality, and accuracy, are the distinguishing features of the narrative portion.

Willard's Universal History, ... 2 25

The most valuable features of the "United States" are reproduced in this. The peculiarities of the work are its great conciseness and the prominence given to the chronological order of events. The margin marks each successive era with great distinctness, so that the pupil retains not only the event but its time, and thus fixes the order of history firmly and usefully in his mind. Mrs. Willard's books are constantly revised, and at all times written up to embrace important historical events of recent date.

Berard's History of England, ... 1 75

By an authoress well known for the success of her History of the United States. The social life of the English people is felicitously interwoven, as in fact, with the civil and military transactions of the realm.

Ricord's History of Rome, ... 1 75

Possesses the charm of an attractive romance. The Fables with which this history abounds are introduced in such a way as not to deceive the inexperienced, while adding materially to the value of the work as a reliable index to the character and institutions, as well as the history of the Roman people.

Hanna's Bible History, ... 1 25

The only compendium of Bible narrative which affords a connected and chronological view of the important events there recorded, divested of all superfluous detail.

Summary of History, Complete 60
American History, $0 40. French and Eng. Hist. 35

A well proportioned outline of leading events, condensing the substance of the more extensive text-book in common use into a series of statements so brief, that every word may be committed to memory, and yet so comprehensive that it presents an accurate though general view of the whole continuous life of nations.

Marsh's Ecclesiastical History, ... 2 00
Questions to ditto, ... 75

Affording the History of the Church in all ages, with accounts of the pagan world during Biblical periods, and the character, rise, and progress of all Religions, as well as the various sects of the worshipers of Christ. The work is entirely non-sectarian, though strictly catholic.

Mill's History of the Jews, ... 1 75

HISTORY—Continued.

BARNES' ONE-TERM HISTORY.

A Brief History of the United States, . . . $1 50

This is probably the MOST ORIGINAL SCHOOL-BOOK published for many years, in any department. A few of its claims are the following:

1. Brevity.—The text is complete for Grammar School or intermediate classes, in 290 12mo pages, large type. It may readily be completed, if desired, in one term of study.

2. Comprehensiveness.—Though so brief, this book contains the pith of all the wearying contents of the larger manuals, and a great deal more than the memory usually retains from the latter.

3. Interest has been a prime consideration. Small books have heretofore been bare, full of dry statistics, unattractive. This one is charmingly written, replete with anecdote, and brilliant with illustration.

4. Proportion of Events.—It is remarkable for the discrimination with which the different portions of our history are presented according to their importance. Thus the older works being already large books when the civil war took place, give it less space than that accorded to the Revolution.

5. Arrangement.—In six epochs, entitled respectively, Discovery and Settlement. the Colonies, the Revolution, Growth of States, the Civil War, and Current Events.

6. Catch Words.—Each paragraph is preceded by its leading thought in prominent type, standing in the student's mind for the whole paragraph.

7. Key Notes.—Analogous with this is the idea of grouping battles, etc., about some central event, which relieves the sameness so common in such descriptions, and renders each distinct by some striking peculiarity of its own.

8. Foot Notes.—These are crowded with interesting matter that is not strictly a part of history proper. They may be learned or not, at pleasure. They are certain in any event to be read.

9. Biographies of all the leading characters are given in full in foot-notes.

10. Maps.—Elegant and distinct Maps from engravings on copper-plate, and beautifully colored, precede each epoch, and contain all the places named.

11. Questions are at the back of the book, to compel a more independent use of the text. Both text and questions are so worded that the pupil must give intelligent answers IN HIS OWN WORDS. "Yes" and "No" will not do.

12. Historical Recreations.—These are additional questions to test the student's knowledge, in review, as: "What trees are celebrated in our history?" "When did a fog save our army?" "What Presidents died in office?" "When was the Mississippi our western boundary?" "Who said, 'I would rather be right than President?'" etc.

13. The Illustrations, about seventy in number, are the work of our best artists and engravers, produced at great expense. They are vivid and interesting, and mostly upon subjects never before illustrated in a school-book.

14. Dates.—Only the leading dates are given in the text, and these are so associated as to assist the memory, but at the head of each page is the date of the event first mentioned, and at the close of each epoch a summary of events and dates.

15. The Philosophy of History is studiously exhibited—the causes and effects of events being distinctly traced and their interconnection shown.

16. Impartiality. — All sectional, partisan, or denominational views are avoided. Facts are stated after a careful comparison of all authorities without the least prejudice or favor.

17. Index.—A verbal index at the close of the book perfects it as a work of reference.

It will be observed that the above are all particulars in which School Histories have been signally defective, or altogether wanting. Many other claims to favor it shares in common with its predecessors.

BARNES' BRIEF UNITED STATES HISTORY.

Already prescribed under authority of law for exclusive and uniform use in the public schools of TWO STATES—Texas and Arkansas. Also adopted for HUNDREDS of important CITIES and TOWNS—among which we name Brooklyn, N.Y.; Jersey City, N.J.; Scranton, Pa.; Wilmington, Del.; Portland, Me.; Springfield, Mass.; Louisville, Ky.; Vicksburg, Miss.; Madison, Wis.; Rochester, Minn.; Macon, Mo.; Springfield, Ill., etc.

SOME TESTIMONIALS.

From HON. J. M. MCKENZIE, *Supt. Pub. Inst., Nebraska.*

I have examined your "Brief History of the United States," and like it *real well;* and were I teaching a graded school, I think I should use it as a text-book.

From HON. H. B. WILSON, *Supt. Pub. Inst., Minnesota.*

I have read with much interest the "One-Term History of the United States" I am much pleased with it. In my judgment, it contains all of the United States history that the majority of pupils in our common schools can spare time to study.

From PRES. EDWARD BROOKS, *Millersville State Normal School, Pa.*

It is a work that will be a favorite with teachers and pupils. Its scope and style especially adapt it for use in our public schools. I cordially commend it to teachers desiring to introduce an interesting and practical text-book upon this subject.

From PRES. BARKER, *Buffalo State Normal School, N.Y.*

In the copy of your "Brief History," before me, the important items to be learned in history seem most ingeniously brought out and kept in the foreground. These items are *time, persons, places,* and *events.* It has the appearance of an exceedingly fresh and systematic work. I think I shall put it into my classes

From PROF. WM. F. ALLEN, *State Univ. of Wisconsin.*

I think the author of the new "Brief History of the United States" has been very successful in combining brevity with sufficient fullness and interest. *Particularly,* he has avoided the excessive number of names and dates that most histories contain. Two features that I like *very much* are the *anecdotes* at the foot of the page and the "*Historical Recreations*" in the Appendix. The latter, I think, is quite a *new* feature, and the other is *very* well executed.

From S. G. WRIGHT, *Assist.-Supt. Pub. Inst., Kansas.*

It is with extreme pleasure we submit our recommendation of the "Brief History of the United States." It meets the needs of young and older children, combining concision with perspicuity, and if "brevity is the soul of wit," this "Brief History" contains not only that well-chosen ingredient, but wisdom sufficient to enlighten those students who are wearily longing for a "new departure" from certain old and uninteresting presentations of fossilized writers. We congratulate a progressive public upon a progressive book.

From HON. NEWTON BATEMAN, *Supt. Pub. Inst., Illinois.*

Barnes' One-Term History of the United States is an exceedingly attractive and spirited little book. Its claim to several new and valuable features seems well founded. Under the form of six well-defined Epochs, the History of the United States is traced tersely, yet pithily, from the earliest times to the present day. A good map precedes each epoch, whereby the history and geography of the period may be studied together, *as they always should be.* The syllabus of each paragraph is made to stand in such bold relief, by the use of large, heavy type, as to be of much *mnemonic* value to the student. The book is written in a sprightly and piquant style, the interest never flagging from beginning to end—a rare and difficult achievement in works of this kind.

From the "Chicago Schoolmaster" (Editorial).

A thorough examination of Barnes' Brief History of the United States brings the examiner to the conclusion that it is a superior book in almost every respect. The book is neat in form, and of good material. The type is clear, large, and distinct. The facts and dates are correct. The arrangement of topics is just the thing needed in a history text-book. By this arrangement the pupil can see at once what he is expected to do. The topics are well selected, embracing the leading ideas or principal events of American history. . . . The book as a whole is much superior to any I have examined. So much do I think this, that I have ordered it for my class, and shall use it in my school. (Signed) B. W. BAKER.

Baker's Brief History of Texas, ... $1 25

PENMANSHIP.

Beers' System of Progressive Penmanship.

Per dozen $1 68

This "round hand" system of Penmanship in twelve numbers, commends itself by its simplicity and thoroughness. The first four numbers are primary books. Nos. 5 to 7, advanced books for boys. Nos. 8 to 10, advanced books for girls. Nos. 11 and 12, ornamental penmanship. These books are printed from steel plates (engraved by McLees), and are unexcelled in mechanical execution. Large quantities are annually sold.

Beers' Slated Copy Slips, per set *50

All beginners should practice, for a few weeks, slate exercises, familiarizing them with the form of the letters, the motions of the hand and arm, &c., &c. These copy slips, 32 in number, supply all the copies found in a complete series of writing-books, at a trifling cost.

Payson, Dunton & Scribner's Copy-B'ks. P. doz., *1 80

The National System of Penmanship, in three distinct series—(1) Common School Series, comprising the first six numbers; (2) Business Series, Nos. 8, 11, and 12; (3) Ladies' Series, Nos. 7, 9, and 10.

Fulton & Eastman's Chirographic Charts, *3 75

To embellish the school room walls, and furnish class exercise in the elements of Penmanship.

Payson's Copy-Book Cover, per hundred . *4 00

Protects every page except the one in use, and furnishes "lines" with proper slope for the penman, under. Patented.

National Steel Pens, Card with all kinds . . . *15

Pronounced by competent judges the perfection of American-made pens, and superior to any foreign article.

SCHOOL SERIES.	
School Pen, per gross, . .	$ 60
Academic Pen, do . .	63
Fine Pointed Pen, per gross	70
POPULAR SERIES.	
Capitol Pen, per gross, . .	1 00
do do pr. box of 2 doz.	25
Bullion Pen (imit. gold) pr. gr.	75
Ladies' Pen do	63
Index Pen, per gross . . .	75
BUSINESS SERIES.	
Albata Pen, per gross, . .	40
Bank Pen, do . .	70
Empire Pen, do . .	70
Commercial Pen, per gross .	60
Express Pen, do .	75
Falcon Pen, do .	70
Elastic Pen, do .	75

Stimpson's Scientific Steel Pen, per gross . *2 00

One forward and two backward arches, ensuring great strength, well-balanced elasticity, evenness of point, and smoothness of execution. One gross in twelve contains a Scientific Gold Pen.

Stimpson's Ink-Retaining Holder, per doz. . *2 00

A simple apparatus, which does not get out of order, withholds at a single dip as much ink as the pen would otherwise realize from a dozen trips to the inkstand, which it supplies with moderate and easy flow.

Stimpson's Gold Pen, $3 00; with Ink Retainer *4 50

Stimpson's Penman's Card, ... * 50

One dozen Steel Pens (assorted points) and Patent Ink-retaining Pen holder.

BOOK-KEEPING.

Folsom's Logical Book-keeping, ... $2 00
Folsom's Blanks to Book-keeping, ... 4 50

This treatise embraces the interesting and important discoveries of Prof. Folsom (of the Albany "Bryant & Stratton College"), the partial enunciation of which in lectures and otherwise has attracted so much attention in circles interested in commercial education.

After studying business phenomena for many years, he has arrived at the positive laws and principles that underlie the whole subject of Accounts; finds that the science is based in *Value* as a generic term; that value divides into *two classes* with varied species; that all the exchanges of values are reducible to nine equations; and that all the results of all these exchanges are limited to *thirteen* in number.

As accounts have been universally taught hitherto, without setting out from a radical analysis or definition of values, the science has been kept in great obscurity, and been made as difficult to impart as to acquire. On the new theory, however, these obstacles are chiefly removed. In reading over the first part of it, in which the governing laws and principles are discussed, a person with ordinary intelligence will obtain a fair conception of the *double entry* process of accounts. But when he comes to study thoroughly these laws and principles as there enunciated, and works out the examples and memoranda which elucidate the *thirteen results* of business, the student will neither fail in readily acquiring the science as it is, nor in becoming able intelligently to apply it in the interpretation of business.

Smith & Martin's Book-keeping, ... 1 25
Smith & Martin's Blanks, ... *60

This work is by a practical teacher and a practical book-keeper. It is of a thoroughly popular class, and will be welcomed by every one who loves to see theory and practice combined in an easy, concise, and methodical form.

The Single Entry portion is well adapted to supply a want felt in nearly all other treatises, which seem to be prepared mainly for the use of wholesale merchants, leaving retailers, mechanics, farmers, etc., who transact the greater portion of the business of the country, without a guide. The work is also commended, on this account, for general use in Young Ladies' Seminaries, where a thorough grounding in the simpler form of accounts will be invaluable to the future housekeepers of the nation.

The treatise on Double Entry Book-keeping combines all the advantages of the most recent methods, with the utmost simplicity of application, thus affording the pupil all the advantages of actual experience in the counting-house, and giving a clear comprehension of the entire subject through a judicious course of mercantile transactions.

The shape of the book is such that the transactions can be presented as in actual practice; and the simplified form of Blanks—three in number—adds greatly to the ease experienced in acquiring the science.

DRAWING.

Chapman's American Drawing Book, . . . *$6 00

The standard American text-book and authority in all branches of art. A compilation of art principles. A manual for the amateur, and basis of study for the professional artist. Adapted for schools and private instruction.

CONTENTS.—"Any one who can Learn to Write can Learn to Draw."—Primary Instruction in Drawing.—Rudiments of Drawing the Human Head.—Rudiments in Drawing the Human Figure.—Rudiments of Drawing.—The Elements of Geometry.—Perspective.—Of Studying and Sketching from Nature.—Of Painting.—Etching and Engraving.—Of Modeling.—Of Composition —Advice to the American Art-Student. The work is of course magnificently illustrated with all the original designs.

Chapman's Elementary Drawing Book, . . 1 50

A Progressive Course of Practical Exercises, or a text-book for the training of the eye and hand. It contains the elements from the larger work, and a copy should be in the hands of every pupil; while a copy of the "American Drawing Book," named above, should be at hand for reference by the class.

The Little Artist's Portfolio, ... *50

25 Drawing Cards (progressive patterns), 25 Blanks, and a fine Artist's Pencil, all in one neat envelope.

Clark's Elements of Drawing, ... *1 00

A complete course in this graceful art, from the first rudiments of outline to the finished sketches of landscape and scenery.

Fowle's Linear and Perspective Drawing, . *60

For the cultivation of the eye and hand, with copious illustrations and directions for the guidance of the unskilled teacher.

Monk's Drawing Books—Six Numbers, per set, *2 25

Each book contains *eleven* large patterns, with opposing blanks. No. 1. Elementary Studies. No. 2. Studies of Foliage. No. 3. Landscapes. No. 4. Animals, I. No. 5. Animals, II. No. 6. Marine Views, etc.

Allen's Map-Drawing, . . . 25 cts.; Scale, 25

This method introduces a new era in Map-Drawing, for the following reasons:—1. It is a system. This is its greatest merit.—2. It is easily understood and taught.—3. The eye is trained to exact measurement by the use of a scale.—4. By no special effort of the memory, distance and comparative size are fixed in the mind.—5. It discards useless construction of lines.—6. It can be taught by any teacher, even though there may have been no previous practice in Map-Drawing.—7. Any pupil old enough to study Geography can learn by this System, in a short time, to draw accurate maps.—8. The System is not the result of theory, but comes directly from the school-room. It has been thoroughly and successfully tested there, with all grades of pupils.—9. It is economical, as it requires no mapping plates. It gives the pupil the ability of rapidly drawing accurate maps.

Ripley's Map-Drawing, ... 1 25

Based on the Circle. One of the most efficient aids to the acquirement of a knowledge of Geography is the practice of map-drawing. It is useful for the same reason that the best exercise in orthography is the *writing* of difficult words. Sight comes to the aid of hearing, and a double impression is produced upon the memory. Knowledge becomes less mechanical and more intuitive. The student who has sketched the outlines of a country, and dotted the important places, is little likely to forget either. The impression produced may be compared to that of a traveller who has been over the ground, while more comprehensive and accurate in detail.

MUSIC.

Jepson's Music Readers. 3 vols. . . . Each, 75 cts.

These are not books from which children simply learn songs, parrot-like, but teach the subject progressively—the scholar learning to read music by methods similar to those employed in teaching him to read printed language. Any teacher, however ignorant of music, provided he can, upon trial, simply sound the scale, may teach it without assistance, and will end by being a good singer himself. The "Elementary Music Reader," or first volume, heretofore issued by another publisher, has attained results in the State of Connecticut, where only it has been known, entirely unprecedented in the history of teaching music. The two companion volumes carry the same method into the higher grades.

Nash & Bristow's Cantara. No. 1, $1.15; No. 2, $1.40

The first volume is a complete musical text-book for schools of every grade. No. 2 is a choice selection of Solos and Part Songs. The authors are Directors of Music in the public schools of New York City, in which these books are the standard of instruction.

Curtis' Little Singer, ... $0 60

Curtis' School Vocalist, ... 1 00

Kingsley's School-Room Choir, ... 60

Kingsley's Young Ladies' Harp, ... 1 00

Hager's Echo, ... 75

Perkins' Sabbath Carols, ... 35

For Sunday-schools.

DEVOTION.

Brooks' School Manual of Devotion, . . . $0 75

This volume contains daily devotional exercises, consisting of a hymn, selections of Scripture for alternate reading by teacher and pupils, and a prayer. Its value for opening and closing school is apparent.

Brooks' School Harmonist, ... *75

Contains appropriate *tunes* for each hymn in the "Manual of Devotion" described above.

NATURAL SCIENCE.

FAMILIAR SCIENCE.

Norton & Porter's First Book of Science, . $1 75

By eminent Professors of Yale College. Contains the principles of Natural Philosophy, Astronomy, Chemistry, Physiology, and Geology. Arranged on the Catechetical plan for primary classes and beginners.

Chambers' Treasury of Knowledge, ... 1 25

Progressive lessons upon—*first*, common things which lie most immediately around us, and first attract the attention of the young mind; *second*, common objects from the Mineral, Animal, and Vegetable kingdoms, manufactured articles, and miscellaneous substances; *third*, a systematic view of Nature under the various sciences. May be used as a Reader or Text-book.

NATURAL PHILOSOPHY.

Norton's First Book in Natural Philosophy, 1 00

By Prof. NORTON, of Yale College. Designed for beginners. Profusely illustrated, and arranged on the Catechetical plan.

Peck's Ganot's Course of Nat. Philosophy, . 1 75

The standard text-book of France, Americanized and popularized by Prof. PECK, of Columbia College. The most magnificent system of illustration ever adopted in an American school-book is here found. For intermediate classes.

Peck's Elements of Mechanics, ... 2 00

A suitable introduction to Bartlett's higher treatises on Mechanical Philosophy, and adequate in itself for a complete academical course.

Bartlett's SYNTHETIC AND ANALYTIC **Mechanics,** . each 5 00

Bartlett's Acoustics and Optics, ... 3 50

A system of Collegiate Philosophy, by Prof. BARTLETT, of West Point Military Academy.

Steele's 14 Weeks Course in Philos. (see p. 34) 1 50

Steele's Philosophical Apparatus, ... *125 00

Adequate to performing the experiments in the ordinary text-books. The articles will be sold separately, if desired. See special circular for details.

GEOLOGY.

Page's Elements of Geology, ... 1 25

A volume of Chambers' Educational Course. Practical, simple, and eminently calculated to make the study interesting.

Emmons' Manual of Geology, ... 1 25

The first Geologist of the country has here produced a work worthy of his reputation.

Steele's 14 Weeks Course (see p. 34) 1 50

Steele's Geological Cabinet, ... *40 00

Containing 125 carefully selected specimens. In four parts. Sold separately, if desired. See circular for details.

Peck's Ganot's Popular Physics.

TESTIMONIALS.

From PROF. ALONZO COLLIN, *Cornell College, Iowa.*

I am pleased with it. I have decided to introduce it as a text-book.

From H. F. JOHNSON, *President Madison College, Sharon, Miss.*

I am pleased with Peck's Ganot, and think it a magnificent book.

From PROF. EDWARD BROOKS, *Pennsylvania State Normal School.*

So eminent are its merits, that it will be introduced as the text-book upon elementary physics in this institution.

From H. H. LOCKWOOD, *Professor Natural Philosophy U. S. Naval Academy.*

I am so pleased with it that I will probably add it to a course of lectures given to the midshipmen of this school on physics.

From GEO. S. MACKIE, *Professor Natural History University of Nashville, Tenn.*

I have decided on the introduction of Peck's Ganot's Philosophy, as I am satisfied that it is the best book for the purposes of my pupils that I have seen, combining simplicity of explanation with elegance of illustration.

From W. S. MCRAE, *Superintendent Vevay Public Schools, Indiana.*

Having carefully examined a number of text-books on natural philosophy, I do not hesitate to express my decided opinion in favor of Peck's Ganot. The matter, style, and illustration eminently adapt the work to the popular wants.

From REV. SAMUEL MCKINNEY, D.D., *Pres't Austin College, Huntsville, Texas.*

It gives me pleasure to commend it to teachers. I have taught some classes with it as our text, and must say, for simplicity of style and clearness of illustration, I have found nothing as yet published of equal value to the teacher and pupil.

From C. V. SPEAR, *Principal Maplewood Institute, Pittsfield, Mass.*

I am much pleased with its ample illustrations by plates, and its clearness and simplicity of statement. It covers the ground usually gone over by our higher classes, and contains many fresh illustrations from life or daily occurrences, and new applications of scientific principles to such.

From J. A. BANFIELD, *Superintendent Marshall Public Schools, Michigan.*

I have used Peck's Ganot since 1863, and with increasing pleasure and satisfaction each term. I consider it superior to any other work on physics in its adaptation to our high schools and academies. Its illustrations are superb—better than three times their number of pages of fine print.

From A. SCHUYLER, *Prof. of Mathematics in Baldwin University, Berea, Ohio.*

After a careful examination of Peck's Ganot's Natural Philosophy, and an actual test of its merits as a text-book, I can heartily recommend it as admirably adapted to meet the wants of the grade of students for which it is intended. Its diagrams and illustrations are *unrivaled*. We use it in the Baldwin University.

From D. C. VAN NORMAN, *Principal Van Norman Institute, New York.*

The Natural Philosophy of M. Ganot, edited by Prof. Peck, is, in my opinion, the best work of its kind, for the use intended, ever published in this country. Whether regarded in relation to the natural order of the topics, the precision and clearness of its definitions, or the fullness and beauty of its illustrations, it is certainly, I think, an advance.

☞ For many similar testimonials, see current numbers of the Illustrated Educational Bulletin.

CHEMISTRY.

Porter's First Book of Chemistry, ... $1 00

Porter's Principles of Chemistry, ... 2 00

The above are widely known as the productions of one of the most eminent scientific men of America. The extreme simplicity in the method of presenting the science, while exhaustively treated, has excited universal commendation.

Darby's Text-Book of Chemistry, ... 1 75

Purely a Chemistry, divesting the subject of matters comparatively foreign to it (such as heat, light, electricity, etc.), but usually allowed to engross too much attention in ordinary school-books.

Gregory's Organic Chemistry, ... 2 50

Gregory's Inorganic Chemistry, ... 2 50

The science exhaustively treated. For colleges and medical students.

Steele's Fourteen Weeks Course, ... 1 50

A successful effort to reduce the study to the limits of a *single term*, thereby making feasible its general introduction in institutions of every character. The author's felicity of style and success in making the science pre-eminently *interesting* are peculiarly noticeable features. (See page 34.)

Steele's Chemical Apparatus, ...*20 00

Adequate to the performance of all the important experiments in the ordinary text-book.

Steele's New Chemistry, (see p. 34) 1 50

Contains the new nomenclature.

BOTANY.

Thinker's First Lessons in Botany, ... 40

For children. The technical terms are largely dispensed with in favor of an easy and familiar style adapted to the smallest learner.

Wood's Object-Lessons in Botany, ... 1 50

Wood's American Botanist and Florist, . . 2 50

Wood's New Class-Book of Botany, ... 3 50

The standard text-books of the United States in this department. In style they are simple, popular, and lively; in arrangement, easy and natural; in description, graphic and strictly exact. The Tables for Analysis are reduced to a perfect system. More are annually sold than of all others combined.

Wood's Plant Record, ... *75

A simple form of Blanks for recording observations in the field.

Wood's Botanical Apparatus, ... *8 00

A portable Trunk, containing Drying Press, Knife, Trowel, Microscope, and Tweezers, and a copy of Wood's Plant Record—composing a complete outfit for the collector.

Young's Familiar Lessons, ... 2 00

Darby's Southern Botany, ... 2 00

Embracing general Structural and Physiological Botany, with vegetable products, and descriptions of Southern plants, and a complete Flora of the Southern States.

WOOD'S BOTANIES.

TESTIMONIALS.

From Pres. R. B. Burleson, *Waco University, Texas.*
Wood's Botanies—books that meet every want in their line.

From Prin. J. G. Ralston, *Norristown Seminary, Pa.*
We find the "Class-Book" entirely satisfactory.

From Pres. D. F. Bittle, *Roanoke College, Va.*
Your text-books on Botany are the best for students.

From Prof. W. C. Pierce, *Baldwin University, Ohio.*
I think his Flora the best we have. His method of analysis is excellent.

From Prof. Blakeslee, *State Normal School, Potsdam, N. Y.*
It is admirably concise, yet it does not seem to be deficient or obscure. In paper, print, and binding, the book leaves little to be desired.

From Pres. J. M. Gregory, *State Agricultural College, Ill.*
I find myself greatly pleased with the perspicuity, compactness, and completeness of the book (Wood's Botanist and Florist). I shall recommend it freely to my friends.

From Prof. A. Winchell, *University of Michigan.*
I am free to say that I had been deeply impressed, I may say almost astonished, at the evidences which the work bears of skillful and experienced authorship in this field, and nice and constant adaptation to the wants and conveniences of students of Botany. I pronounce it emphatically an admirable text-book.

From Prof. Richard Owen, *University of Indiana.*
I am well pleased with the evidence of philosophical method exhibited in the general arrangement, as well as with the clearness of the explanations, the ready intelligibility of the analytical tables, and the illustrative aid furnished by the numerous and excellent wood-cuts. I design using the work as a text-book with my next class.

From Prin. B. R. Anderson, *Columbus Union School, Wisconsin.*
I have examined several works with a view to recommending some good text-book on Botany, but I lay them all aside for "Wood's Botanist and Florist." The arrangement of the book is in my opinion excellent, its style fascinating and attractive, its treatment of the various departments of the science is thorough, and last, but far from unimportant, I like the topical form of the questions to each chapter. It seems to embrace the entire science. In fact, I consider it a complete, attractive, and exhaustive work.

From M. A. Marshall, *New Haven High School, Conn.*
It has all the excellencies of the well-known Class-Book of Botany by the same author in a smaller book. By a judicious system of condensation, the size of the Flora is reduced one-half, while no species are omitted, and many new ones are added. The descriptions of species are very brief, yet sufficient to identify the plant, and, when taken in connection with the generic description, form a complete description of the plant. The book as a whole will suit the wants of classes better than anything I have yet seen. The adoption of the Botanist and Florist would not require the exclusion of the Class-Book of Botany, as they are so arranged that both might be used by the same class.

From Prof. G. H. Perkins, *University of Vermont and State Agricultural College.*
I can truly say that the more I examine Wood's Class-Book, the better pleased I am with it. In its illustrations, especially of particulars not easily observed by the student, and the clearness and compactness of its statements, as well as in the territory its flora embraces, it appears to me to surpass any other work I know of. The whole science, so far as it can be taught in a college course, is well presented, and rendered unusually easy of comprehension. The mode of analysis is excellent, avoiding as it does to a great extent those microscopic characters which puzzle the beginner, and using those that are obvious as far as possible. I regard the work as a most admirable one, and shall adopt it as a text-book another year.

PHYSIOLOGY.

Jarvis' Elements of Physiology, ...$ 75

Jarvis' Physiology and Laws of Health, . 1 65

The only books extant which approach this subject with a proper view of the true object of teaching Physiology in schools, viz., that scholars may know how to take care of their own health. In bold contrast with the abstract *Anatomies*, which children learn as they would Greek or Latin (and forget as soon), to *discipline the mind*, are these text-books, using the *science* as a secondary consideration, and only so far as is necessary for the comprehension of the *laws of health.*

Hamilton's Vegetable & Animal Physiology, 1 25

The two branches of the science combined in one volume lead the student to a proper comprehension of the Analogies of Nature.

Dana's Physiology, Ethics, and Ethnology, 1 25

Steele's Fourteen Weeks in Phy., (see p. 34) 1 50

ASTRONOMY.

Steele's Fourteen Weeks' Course, ... 1 50

Reduced to a single term, and better adapted to school use than any work heretofore published. Not written for the information of scientific men, but for the inspiration of youth, the pages are not burdened with a multitude of figures which no memory could possibly retain. The whole subject is presented in a clear and concise form. (See p. 34.)

Willard's School Astronomy, ... 1 00

By means of clear and attractive illustrations, addressing the eye in many cases by analogies, careful definitions of all necessary technical terms, a careful avoidance of verbiage and unimportant matter, particular attention to analysis, and a general adoption of the simplest methods, Mrs. Willard has made the best and most attractive *elementary* Astronomy extant.

McIntyre's Astronomy and the Globes, . . 1 50

A complete treatise for intermediate classes. Highly approved.

Bartlett's Spherical Astronomy, ... 5 00

The West Point course, for advanced classes, with applications to the current wants of Navigation, Geography, and Chronology.

NATURAL HISTORY.

Carl's Child's Book of Natural History, . . 0 50

Illustrating the Animal, Vegetable, and Mineral Kingdoms, with application to the Arts. For beginners. Beautifully and copiously illustrated.

ZOOLOGY.

Chambers' Elements of Zoology, ... 1 50

A complete and comprehensive system of Zoology, adapted for academic instruction, presenting a systematic view of the Animal Kingdom as a portion of external Nature.

Jarvis' Physiology and Laws of Health.

TESTIMONIALS.

From SAMUEL B. MCLANE, *Superintendent Public Schools, Keokuk, Iowa.*

I am glad to see a really good text-book on this much neglected branch. This is clear, concise, accurate, and eminently adapted to the *class-room.*

From WILLIAM F. WYERS, *Principal of Academy, West Chester, Pennsylvania*

A thorough examination has satisfied me of its superior claims as a text-book to the attention of teacher and taught. I shall introduce it at once.

From H. R. SANFORD, *Principal of East Genesee Conference Seminary, N. Y.*

"Jarvis' Physiology" is received, and fully met our expectations. We immediately adopted it.

From ISAAC T. GOODNOW, *State Superintendent of Kansas—published in connection with the "School Law."*

"Jarvis' Physiology," a common-sense, practical work, with just enough of anatomy to understand the physiological portions. The last six pages, on Man's Responsibility for his own health, are worth the price of the book.

From D. W. STEVENS, *Superintendent Public Schools, Fall River, Mass.*

I have examined Jarvis' "Physiology and Laws of Health," which you had the kindness to send to me a short time ago. In my judgment it is far the best work of the kind within my knowledge. It has been adopted as a text-book in our public schools.

From HENRY G. DENNY, *Chairman Book Committee, Boston, Mass.*

The very excellent "Physiology" of D. Jarvis I had introduced into our High School, where the study had been temporarily dropped, believing it to be by far the best work of the kind that had come under my observation; indeed, the reintroduction of the study was delayed for some months, because Dr. Jarvis' book could not be had, and we were unwilling to take any other.

From PROF. A. P. PEABODY, D.D., LL.D., *Harvard University.*

* * I have been in the habit of examining school-books with great care, and I hesitate not to say that of all the text-books on Physiology which have been given to the public, Dr. Jarvis' deserves the first place on the score of accuracy, thoroughness, method, simplicity of statement, and constant reference to topics of practical interest and utility.

From JAMES N. TOWNSEND, *Superintendent Public Schools, Hudson, N. Y.*

Every human being is appointed to take charge of his own body; and of all books written upon this subject, I know of none which will so well prepare one to do this as "Jarvis' Physiology"—that is, in so small a compass of matter. It considers the pure, simple *laws of health* paramount to science; and though the work is thoroughly scientific, it is divested of all cumbrous technicalities, and presents the subject of physical life in a manner and style really charming. It is unquestionably the best text-book on physiology I have ever seen. It is giving great satisfaction in the schools of this city, where it has been adopted as the standard.

From L. J. SANFORD, M.D., *Prof. Anatomy and Physiology in Yale College*

Books on human physiology, designed for the use of schools, are more generally a failure perhaps than are school-books on most other subjects.

The great want in this department is met, we think, in the well-written treatise of Dr. Jarvis, entitled "Physiology and Laws of Health." * * The work is not too detailed nor too expansive in any department, and is clear and concise in all. It is not burdened with an excess of anatomical description, nor rendered discursive by many zoological references. Anatomical statements are made to the extent of qualifying the student to attend, understandingly, to an exposition of those functional processes which, collectively, make up health; thus the laws of health are enunciated, and many suggestions are given which, if heeded, will tend to its preservation.

☞ For further testimony of similar character, see current numbers of the Illustrated Educational Bulletin.

NATURAL SCIENCE.

"FOURTEEN WEEKS" IN EACH BRANCH.

By J. DORMAN STEELE, A. M.

Steele's 14 Weeks Course in Chemistry NEW ED., $1 50

Steele's 14 Weeks Course in Astronomy . 1 50

Steele's 14 Weeks Course in Philosophy . 1 50

Steele's 14 Weeks Course in Geology. . 1 50

Steele's 14 Weeks Course in Physiology . 1 50

Our Text-Books in these studies are, as a general thing, dull and uninteresting. They contain from 400 to 600 pages of dry facts and unconnected details. They abound in that which the student cannot learn, much less remember. The pupil commences the study, is confused by the fine print and coarse print, and neither knowing exactly what to learn nor what to hasten over, is crowded through the single term generally assigned to each branch, and frequently comes to the close without a definite and exact idea of a single scientific principle.

Steele's Fourteen Weeks Courses contain only that which every well-informed person should know, while all that which concerns only the professional scientist is omitted. The language is clear, simple, and interesting, and the illustrations bring the subject within the range of home life and daily experience. They give such of the general principles and the prominent facts as a pupil can make familiar as household words within a single term. The type is large and open; there is no fine print to annoy; the cuts are copies of genuine experiments or natural phenomena, and are of fine execution.

In fine, by a system of condensation peculiarly his own, the author reduces each branch to the limits of a single term of study, while sacrificing nothing that is essential, and nothing that is usually retained from the study of the larger manuals in common use. Thus the student has rare opportunity to *economize his time*, or rather to employ that which he has to the best advantage.

A notable feature is the author's charming "style," fortified by an enthusiasm over his subject in which the student will not fail to partake. Believing that Natural Science is full of fascination, he has moulded it into a form that attracts the attention and kindles the enthusiasm of the pupil.

The recent editions contain the author's "Practical Questions" on a plan never before attempted in scientific text-books. These are questions as to the nature and cause of common phenomena, and are not directly answered in the text, the design being to test and promote an intelligent use of the student's knowledge of the foregoing principles.

Steele's General Key to his Works *1 50

This work is mainly composed of Answers to the Practical Questions and Solutions of the Problems in the author's celebrated "Fourteen Weeks Courses" in the several sciences, with many hints to teachers, minor Tables, &c. Should be on every teacher's desk.

Steele's 14 Weeks in each Science.

TESTIMONIALS.

From L. A. BIKLE, *President N. C. College.*

I have not been disappointed. Shall take pleasure in introducing this series.

From J. F. COX, *Prest. Southern Female College, Ga.*

I am much pleased with these books, and expect to introduce them.

From J. R. BRANHAM, *Prin. Brownsville Female College, Tenn.*

They are capital little books, and are now in use in our institution.

From W. H. GOODALE, *Professor Readville Seminary, La.*

We are using your 14 Weeks Course, and are much pleased with them.

From W. A. BOLES, *Supt. Shelbyville Graded School, Ind.*

They are as entertaining as a story book, and much more improving to the mind.

From S. A. SNOW, *Principal of High School, Uxbridge, Mass.*

Steele's 14 Weeks Courses in the Sciences are a perfect success.

From JOHN W. DOUGHTY, *Newburg Free Academy, N. Y.*

I was prepared to find Prof. Steele's Course both attractive and instructive. My highest expectations have been fully realized.

From J. S. BLACKWELL, *Prest. Ghent College, Ky.*

Prof. Steele's unexampled success in providing for the wants of academic classes, has led me to look forward with high anticipations to his forthcoming issue.

From J. F. COOK, *Prest. La Grange College, Mo.*

I am pleased with the neatness of these books and the delightful diction. I have been teaching for years, and have never seen a lovelier little volume than the Astronomy.

From M. W. SMITH, *Prin. of High School, Morrison, Ill.*

They seem to me to be admirably adapted to the wants of a public school, containing, as they do, a sufficiently comprehensive arrangement of elementary principles to excite a healthy thirst for a more thorough knowledge of those sciences.

From J. D. BARTLEY, *Prin. of High School, Concord, N. H.*

They are just such books as I have looked for, viz., those of interesting style, not cumbersome and filled up with things to be omitted by the pupil, and yet sufficiently full of facts for the purpose of most scholars in these sciences in our high schools; there is nothing but what a pupil of average ability can thoroughly master.

From ALONZO NORTON LEWIS, *Principal of Parker Academy, Conn.*

I consider Steele's Fourteen Weeks Courses in Philosophy, Chemistry, &c., the *best* school-books that have been issued in this country.

As an introduction to the various branches of which they treat, and especially for that numerous class of pupils who have not the time for a more extended course, I consider them *invaluable.*

From EDWARD BROOKS, *Prin. State Normal School, Millersville, Pa.*

At the meeting of Normal School Principals, I presented the following resolution, which was unanimously adopted: "*Resolved,* That Steele's 14 Weeks Courses in Natural Philosophy and Astronomy, or an amount equivalent to what is contained in them, be adopted for use in the State Normal Schools of Pennsylvania." The works themselves will be adopted by at least three of the schools, and, I presume, by them all.

LITERATURE.

Cleveland's Compendiums . . . . each, $*2 50

ENGLISH LITERATURE. AMERICAN LITERATURE.
ENGLISH LITERATURE OF THE XIXTH CENTURY.

In these volumes are gathered the cream of the literature of the English speaking people for the school-room and the general reader. Their reputation is national. More than 125,000 copies have been sold.

Boyd's English Classics . . . . . each, *1 25

MILTON'S PARADISE LOST. THOMSON'S SEASONS.
YOUNG'S NIGHT THOUGHTS. POLLOK'S COURSE OF TIME.
COWPER'S TASK, TABLE TALK, &C. LORD BACON'S ESSAYS.

This series of annotated editions of great English writers, in prose and poetry, is designed for critical reading and parsing in schools. Prof. J. R. Boyd proves himself an editor of high capacity, and the works themselves need no encomium. As auxiliary to the study of Belles Lettres, etc., these works have no equal.

Pope's Essay on Man *20

Pope's Homer's Iliad *80

The metrical translation of the great poet of antiquity, and the matchless "Essay on the Nature and State of Man," by ALEXANDER POPE, afford superior exercise in literature and parsing.

Steele's Brief History of Literature, . . . 1 50

AESTHETICS.

Huntington's Manual of the Fine Arts . .*1 75

A view of the rise and progress of Art in different countries, a brief account of the most eminent masters of Art, and an analysis of the principles of Art. It is complete in itself, or may precede to advantage the critical work of Lord Kames.

Boyd's Kames' Elements of Criticism . .*1 75

The best edition of this standard work; without the study of which none may be considered proficient in the science of the Perceptions. No other study can be pursued with so marked an effect upon the taste and refinement of the pupil.

POLITICAL ECONOMY.

Champlin's Lessons on Political Economy 1 25

An improvement on previous treatises, being shorter, yet containing every thing essential, with a view of recent questions in finance, etc., which is not elsewhere found.

CLEVELAND'S COMPENDIUMS.

TESTIMONIALS.

From the New Englander.

This is the very best book of the kind we have ever examined.

From GEORGE B. EMERSON, Esq., *Boston.*

The Biographical Sketches are just and discriminating; the selections are admirable, and I have adopted the work as a text-book for my first class.

From PROF. MOSES COIT TYLER, *of the Michigan University.*

I have given your book a thorough examination, and am greatly delighted with it; and shall have great pleasure in directing the attention of my classes to a work which affords so admirable a bird's-eye view of recent "English Literature."

From the Saturday Review.

It acquaints the reader with the characteristic method, tone, and quality of all the chief notabilities of the period, and will give the careful student a better idea of the recent history of English Literature than nine educated Englishmen in ten possess.

From the Methodist Quarterly Review, New York.

This work is a transcript of the best American mind; a vehicle of the noblest American spirit. No parent who would introduce his child to a knowledge of our country's literature, and at the same time indoctrinate his heart in the purest principles, need fear to put this manual in the youthful hand.

From REV. C. PEIRCE, *Principal, West Newton, Mass.*

I do not believe the work is to be found from which, within the same limits, so much interesting and valuable information in regard to English writers and English literature of every age, can be obtained; and it deserves to find a place in all our high schools and academies, as well as in every private library.

From the Independent.

The work of selection and compilation—requiring a perfect familiarity with the whole range of English literature, a judgment clear and impartial, a taste at once delicate and severe, and a most sensitive regard to purity of thought or feeling—has been better accomplished in this than in any kindred volume with which we are acquainted.

From the Christian Examiner.

To form such a Compendium, good taste, fine scholarship, familiar acquaintance with English literature, unwearied industry, tact acquired by practice, an interest in the culture of the young, a regard for truth, purity, philanthropy, religion, as the highest attainment and the highest beauty,—all these were needed, and they are united in Mr. Cleveland.

CHAMPLIN'S POLITICAL ECONOMY.

From J. L. BOTHWELL, *Prin. Public School No. 14, Albany, N. Y.*

I have examined Champlin's Political Economy with much pleasure, and shall be pleased to put it into the hands of my pupils. In quantity and quality I think it superior to anything that I have examined.

From PRES. N. E. COBLEIGH, *East Tennessee Wesleyan University.*

An examination of Champlin's Political Economy has satisfied me that it is the book I want. For brevity and compactness, division of the subject, and clear statement, and for appropriateness of treatment, I consider it a better text-book than any other in the market.

From the Evening Mail, New York.

A new interest has been imparted to the science of political economy since we have been necessitated to raise such vast sums of money for the support of the government. The time, therefore, is favorable for the introduction of works like the above. This little volume of two hundred pages is intended for beginners, for the common school and academy. It is intended as a basis upon which to rear a more elaborate superstructure. There is nothing in the principles of political economy above the comprehension of average scholars, when they are clearly set forth. This seems to have been done by President Champlin in an easy and graceful manner.

ELOCUTION.

Watson's Practical Elocution $0 25

A brief, clear, and most satisfactory treatise—same as in "Independent Fifth Reader." The subject fully illustrated by diagrams.

Zachos' Analytic Elocution 1 50

All departments of elocution—such as the analysis of the voice and the sentence. phonology, rhythm, expression, gesture, &c.—are here arranged for instruction in classes, illustrated by copious examples.

Sherwood's Self Culture 1 00

Self-culture in reading, speaking, and conversation—a very valuable treatise to those who would perfect themselves in these accomplishments.

SPEAKERS.

Northend's Little Orator, *60—Child's Speaker*60

Two little works of the same grade but different selections, containing simple and attractive pieces for children under twelve years of age.

Northend's Young Declaimer *75

Northend's National Orator *1 25

Two volumes of Prose, Poetry, and Dialogue, adapted to intermediate and grammar classes respectively.

Northend's Entertaining Dialogues *1 25

Extracts eminently adapted to cultivate the dramatic faculties, as well as entertain an audience.

Swett's Common School Speaker *1 25

Selections from recent literature.

Raymond's Patriotic Speaker *2 00

A superb compilation of modern eloquence and poetry, with original dramatic exercises. Nearly every eminent *living* orator is represented, without distinction of place or party.

COMPOSITION, &c.

Brookfield's First Book in Composition . 50

Making the cultivation of this important art feasible for the smallest child. By a new method, to induce and stimulate thought.

Boyd's Composition and Rhetoric 1 50

This work furnishes all the aid that is needful or can be desired in the various departments and styles of composition, both in prose and verse.

Day's Art of Rhetoric 1 25

Noted for exactness of definition, clear limitation, and philosophical development of subject; the large share of attention given to **Invention,** as a branch of Rhetoric, and the unequalled analysis of style

MENTAL PHILOSOPHY.

Mahan's Intellectual Philosophy $1 75

The subject exhaustively considered. The author has evinced learning, candor, and independent thinking.

Mahan's Science of Logic 2 00

A profound analysis of the laws of thought. The system possesses the merit of being intelligible and self consistent. In addition to the author's carefully elaborated views, it embraces results attained by the ablest minds of Great Britain, Germany, and France, in this department.

Boyd's Elements of Logic 1 25

A systematic and philosophic condensation of the subject, fortified with additions from Watts, Abercrombie, Whately, &c.

Watts on the Mind 50

The Improvement of the Mind, by Isaac Watts, is designed as a guide for the attainment of useful knowledge. As a text-book it is unparalleled; and the discipline it affords cannot be too highly esteemed by the educator.

MORALS.

Peabody's Moral Philosophy, ... 1 25

For Colleges and High Schools.

Willard's Morals for the Young *75

Lessons in conversational tyle to inculcate the elements of moral philosophy. The study is made attractive by narratives and engravings.

GOVERNMENT.

Howe's Young Citizen's Catechism 75

Explaining the duties of District, Town, City, County, State, and United States Officers, with rules for parliamentary and commercial business—that which every future "sovereign" ought to know, and so few are taught.

Young's Lessons in Civil Government . . 1 25

A comprehensive view of Government, and abstract of the laws showing the rights, duties, and responsibilities of citizens.

Mansfield's Political Manual 1 25

This is a complete view of the theory and practice of the General and State Governments of the United States, designed as a text-book. The author is an esteemed and able professor of constitutional law, widely known for his sagacious utterances in matters of statecraft through the public press. Recent events teach with emphasis the vital necessity that the rising generation should comprehend the noble polity of the American government, that they may act intelligently when endowed with a voice in it.

MODERN LANGUAGE.

French and English Primer, ...$ 10
German and English Primer, ... 10
Spanish and English Primer, ... 10

The names of common objects properly illustrated and arranged in easy lessons.

Ledru's French Fables, ... 75
Ledru's French Grammar, ...1 00
Ledru's French Reader, ...1 00

The author's long experience has enabled him to present the most thoroughly practical text-books extant, in this branch. The system of pronunciation (by phonetic illustration) is original with this author, and will commend itself to all American teachers, as it enables their pupils to secure an absolutely correct pronunciation without the assistance of a native master. This feature is peculiarly valuable also to "self-taught" students. The directions for ascertaining the gender of French nouns—also a great stumbling-block—are peculiar to this work, and will be found remarkably competent to the end proposed. The criticism of teachers and the test of the school-room is invited to this excellent series, with confidence.

Worman's French Echo, ...1 25

To teach conversational French by actual practice, on an entirely new plan, which recognizes the importance of the student learning *to think* in the language which he speaks. It furnishes an extensive vocabulary of words and expressions in common use, and suffices to free the learner from the embarrassments which the peculiarities of his own tongue are likely to be to him, and to make him thoroughly familiar with the use of proper idioms.

Worman's German Echo, ... 1 25

On the same plan. See Worman's German Series, page 29.

Pujol's Complete French Class-Book, . . . 2 25

Offers, in one volume, methodically arranged, a complete French course—usually embraced in series of from five to twelve books, including the bulky and expensive Lexicon. Here are Grammar, Conversation, and choice Literature—selected from the best French authors. Each branch is thoroughly handled; and the student, having diligently completed the course as prescribed, may consider himself, without further application, *au fait* in the most polite and elegant language of modern times.

Maurice-Poitevin's Grammaire Francaise, . 1 00

American schools are at last supplied with an American edition of this famous text-book. Many of our best institutions have for years been procuring it from abroad rather than forego the advantages it offers. The policy of putting students who have acquired some proficiency from the ordinary text-books, into a Grammar written in the vernacular, can not be too highly commended. It affords an opportunity for finish and review at once; while embodying abundant practice of its own rules.

Joynes' French Pronunciation, ... 30

Willard's Historia de los Estados Unidos, . 2 00

The History of the United States, translated by Professors TOLON and DE TORNOS, will be found a valuable, instructive, and entertaining reading-book for Spanish classes.

Pujol's Complete French Class-Book.

TESTIMONIALS.

From PROF. ELIAS PEISSNER, *Union College.*

I take great pleasure in recommending Pujol and Van Norman's French Class-Book, as there is no French grammar or class-book which can be compared with it in completeness, system, clearness, and general utility.

From EDWARD NORTH, *President of Hamilton College.*

I have carefully examined Pujol and Van Norman's French Class-Book, and am satisfied of its superiority, for college purposes, over any other heretofore used. We shall not fail to use it with our next class in French.

From A. CURTIS, *Pres't of Cincinnati Literary and Scientific Institute.*

I am confident that it may be made an instrument in conveying to the student, in from six months to a year, the art of speaking and writing the French with almost native fluency and propriety.

From HIRAM ORCUTT, A. M., *Prin. Glenwood and Tilden Ladies' Seminaries.*

I have used Pujol's French Grammar in my two seminaries, exclusively, for more than a year, and have no hesitation in saying that I regard it the best text-book in this department extant. And my opinion is confirmed by the testimony of Prof. F. De Launay and Mademoiselle Marindin. They assure me that the book is eminently accurate and practical, as tested in the school-room.

From PROF. THEO. F. DE FUMAT, *Hebrew Educational Institute, Memphis, Tenn.*

M. Pujol's French Grammar is one of the best and most practical works. The French language is chosen and elegant in style—modern and easy. It is far superior to the other French class-books in this country. The selection of the conversational part is very good, and will interest pupils; and being all completed in only one volume, it is especially desirable to have it introduced in our schools.

From PROF. JAMES H. WORMAN, *Bordentown Female College, N. J.*

The work is upon the same plan as the text-books for the study of French and English published in Berlin, for the study of those who have not the aid of a teacher, and these books are considered, by the first authorities, the best books. In most of our institutions, Americans teach the modern languages, and heretofore the trouble has been to give them a text-book that would dispose of the difficulties of the French pronunciation. This difficulty is successfully removed by P. and Van N., and I have every reason to believe it will soon make its way into most of our best schools.

From PROF. CHARLES S. DOD, *Ann Smith Academy, Lexington, Va.*

I cannot do better than to recommend "Pujol and Van Norman." For comprehensive and systematic arrangement, progressive and thorough development of all grammatical principles and idioms, with a due admixture of theoretical knowledge and practical exercise, I regard it as superior to any (other) book of the kind.

From A. A. FORSTER, *Prin. Pinehurst School, Toronto, C. W.*

I have great satisfaction in bearing testimony to M. Pujol's System of French Instruction, as given in his complete class-book. For clearness and comprehensiveness, adapted for all classes of pupils, I have found it superior to any other work of the kind, and have now used it for some years in my establishment with great success.

From PROF. OTTO FEDDER, *Maplewood Institute, Pittsfield, Mass.*

The conversational exercises will prove an immense saving of the hardest kind of labor to teachers. There is scarcely any thing more trying in the way of teaching language, than to rack your brain for short and easily intelligible bits of conversation, and to repeat them time and again with no better result than extorting at long intervals a doubting "oui," or a hesitating "non, monsieur"

☞ For further testimony of a similar character, see special circular, and current numbers of the Educational Bulletin.

GERMAN.

A COMPLETE COURSE IN THE GERMAN.

By JAMES H. WORMAN, A. M.

Worman's Elementary German Grammar . $1 50
Worman's Complete German Grammar . 2 00

These volumes are designed for intermediate and advanced classes respectively. The bitterness with which they have been attacked, and their extraordinary success in the face of an unprincipled opposition, are facts which have stamped them as possessing unparalleled merit.

Though following the same general method with "Otto" (that of 'Gaspey'), our author differs essentially in its application. He is more practical, more systematic, more accurate, and besides introduces a number of invaluable features which have never before been combined in a German grammar.

Among other things, it may be claimed for Prof. Worman that he has been *the first* to introduce in an American text-book for learning German, a system of analogy and comparison with other languages. Our best teachers are also enthusiastic about his methods of inculcating the art of speaking, of understanding the spoken language, of correct pronunciation; the sensible and convenient original classification of nouns (in four declensions), and of irregular verbs, also deserves much praise. We also note the use of heavy type to indicate etymological changes in the paradigms, and, in the exercises, the parts which specially illustrate preceding rules.

Worman's Elementary German Reader, . 1 50
Worman's German Reader 1 75

The finest compilation of classical and standard German Literature ever offered to American students. It embraces, progressively arranged, selections from the masterpieces of Goethe, Schiller, Korner, Seume, Uhland, Freiligrath, Heine, Schlegel, Holty, Lenau, Wieland, Herder, Lessing, Kant, Fichte, Schelling, Winkelmann, Humboldt, Ranke, Raumer, Menzel, Gervinus, &c., and contains complete Goethe's "Iphigenie," Schiller's "Jungfrau;" also, for instruction in modern conversational German, Benedix's "Eigensinn."

There are besides, Biographical Sketches of each author contributing, Notes, explanatory and philological (after the text), Grammatical References to all leading grammars, as well as the editor's own, and an adequate Vocabulary.

Worman's German Echo 1 25

Consists of exercises in colloquial style entirely in the German, with an adequate vocabulary, not only of words but of idioms. The object of the system developed in this work (and its companion volume in the French) is to break up the laborious and tedious habit of *translating the thoughts*, which is the student's most effectual bar to fluent conversation, and to lead him to *think in the language in which he speaks*. As the exercises illustrate scenes in actual life, a considerable knowledge of the manners and customs of the German people is also acquired from the use of this manual.

Worman's German Grammars.

TESTIMONIALS.

From Prof. R. W. JONES, *Petersburg Female College, Va.*

From what I have seen of the work it is almost certain *I shall introduce it* into this institution.

From Prof. G. CAMPBELL, *University of Minnesota.*

A valuable addition to our school-books, and will find many friends, and do great good.

From Prof. O. H P. CORPREW, *Mary Military Inst*, *Md.*

I am better pleased with them than any I have ever taught. I have already ordered through our booksellers.

From Prof. R. S. KENDALL, *Vernon Academy, Conn.*

I at once put the Elementary Grammar into the hands of a class of beginners, and have used it *with great satisfaction.*

From Prof. D. E. HOLMES, *Berlin Academy, Wis.*

Worman's German works are *superior.* I shall use them hereafter in my German classes.

From Prof. MAGNUS BUCHHOLTZ, *Hiram College, Ohio.*

I have examined the Complete Grammar, and find it *excellent.* You may rely that it will be used here.

From Prin. THOS. W. TOBEY, *Paducah Female Seminary, Ky.*

The Complete German Grammar is worthy of an extensive circulation. It is *admirably adapted* to the class-room. I shall use it.

From Prof. ALEX. ROSENSPITZ, *Houston Academy, Texas.*

Bearer will take and pay for 3 dozen copies. Mr. Worman deserves the approbation and esteem of the teacher and the thanks of the student.

From Prof. G. MALMENE, *Augusta Seminary, Maine.*

The Complete Grammar cannot fail to *give great satisfaction* by the simplicity of its arrangement, and by its completeness.

From Prin. OVAL PIRKEY, *Christian University, Mo.*

Just such a series as is positively necessary. I do hope the author will succeed as well in the French, &c., as he has in the German.

From Prof. S. D. HILLMAN, *Dickinson College, Pa.*

The class have lately commenced, and my examination thus far warrants me in saying that I regard it as *the best* grammar for instruction in the German.

From Prin. SILAS LIVERMORE, *Bloomfield Seminary, Mo.*

I have found a classically and scientifically educated Prussian gentleman whom I propose to make German instructer. I have shown him both your German grammars. He has expressed *his approbation* of them generally.

From Prof. Z. TEST, *Howland School for Young Ladies, N. Y.*

I shall introduce the books. From a cursory examination I have no hesitation in pronouncing the Complete Grammar *a decided improvement* on the text-books at present in use in this country.

From Prof. LEWIS KISTLER, *Northwestern University, Ill.*

Having looked through the Complete Grammar with some care I must say that you have produced *a good book;* you may be rewarded with this gratification—that your grammar promotes the facility of learning the German language, and of becoming acquainted with its rich literature.

From Pres. J. P. ROUS, *Stockwell Collegiate Inst., Ind.*

I supplied a class with the Elementary Grammar, and it gives *complete satisfaction.* The conversational and reading exercises are well calculated to illustrate the principles, and lead the student on an easy yet thorough course. I think the Complete Grammar equally attractive.

THE CLASSICS.

LATIN.

Silber's Latin Course, ... $1 25

The book contains an Epitome of Latin Grammar, followed by Reading Exercises, with explanatory Notes and copious References to the leading Latin Grammars, and also to the Epitome which precedes the work. Then follow a Latin-English Vocabulary and Exercises in Latin Prose Composition, being thus complete in itself, and a very suitable work to put in the hands of one about to study the language.

Searing's Virgil's Æneid, ... 2 25

It contains only the first six books of the Æneid. 2. A very carefully constructed Dictionary. 3. Sufficiently copious Notes. 4. Grammatical references to four leading Grammars. 5. Numerous Illustrations of the highest order. 6. A superb Map of the Mediterranean and adjacent countries. 7. Dr. S. H. Taylor's "Questions on the Æneid." 8. A Metrical Index, and an Essay on the Poetical Style. 9. A photographic *fac simile* of an early Latin M.S. 10. The text according to Jahn, but paragraphed according to Ladewig. 11. Superior mechanical execution.

Blair's Latin Pronunciation, ... 1 00

Hanson's Latin Prose Book, ... 3 00
Hanson's Latin Poetry, ... 3 00

Andrews & Stoddard's Latin Grammar, *1 50
Andrews' Questions on the Grammar, . *0 15
Andrews' Latin Exercises, ... *1 25
Andrews' Viri Romæ, ... *1 25
Andrews' Sallust's Jugurthine War, &c. *1 50
Andrews' Eclogues & Georgics of Virgil, *1 50
Andrews' Cæsar's Commentaries, ... *1 50
Andrews' Ovid's Metamorphoses, . . . *1 25

GREEK.

Crosby's Greek Grammar, ... 2 00
Crosby's Xenophon's Anabasis, ... 1 25

Searing's Homer's Iliad, ... ——

MYTHOLOGY.

Dwight's Grecian and Roman Mythology.

School edition, $1 25; University edition, *3 00

A knowledge of the fables of antiquity, thus presented in a systematic form, is as indispensable to the student of general literature as to him who would peruse intelligently the classical authors. The mythological allusions so frequent in literature are readily understood with such a Key as this.

SEARING'S VIRGIL.

SPECIMEN FRAGMENTS OF LETTERS.

"I adopt it gladly."—PRIN. V. DABNEY, *Loudoun School, Va.*

"I like Searing's Virgil."—PROF. BRISTOL, *Ripon College, Wis.*

"Meets my desires very thoroughly."—PROF. CLARK, *Berea College, Ohio.*

"Superior to any other edition of Virgil."—PRES. HALL, *Macon College, Mo.*

"Shall adopt it at once."—PRIN. B. P. BAKER, *Searcy Female Institute, Ark.*

"Your Virgil is a *beauty*."—PROF. W. H. DE MOTTE, *Illinois Female College.*

"After use, I regard it the best."—PRIN. G. H. BARTON, *Rome Academy, N. Y.*

"We like it better every day."—PRIN. R. K. BUEHRLE, *Allentown Academy, Pa.*

"I am delighted with your Virgil."—PRIN. W. T. LEONARD, *Pierce Academy, Mass.*

"Stands well the test of class-room."—PRIN. F. A. CHASE, *Lyons Col. Inst., Iowa.*

"I do not see how it can be improved."—PRIN. N. F. D. BROWNE, *Charl. Hall, Md.*

"The most complete that I have seen."—PRIN. A. BROWN, *Columbus High School, Ohio.*

"Our Professor of Language very highly approves."—SUPT. J. G. JAMES, *Texas Military Institute.*

"It responds to a want long felt by teachers. It is beautiful and complete."—PROF. BROOKS, *University of Minnesota.*

"The ideal edition. We want a few more classics of the same sort."—PRIN. C. F. P. BANCROFT, *Lookout Mountain Institute, Tenn.*

"I certainly have never seen an edition so complete with important requisites for a student, nor with such fine text and general mechanical execution."—PRES. J. R. PARK, *University of Deseret, Utah.*

"It is charming both in its design and execution. And, on the whole, I think it is the best thing of the kind that I have seen."—PROF. J. DE F. RICHARDS, *Pres. pro tem. of University of Alabama.*

"In beauty of execution, in judicious notes, and in an adequate vocabulary, it merits all praise. I shall recommend its introduction."—PRES. J. K. PATTERSON, *Kentucky Agricultural and Mechanical College.*

"Containing a good vocabulary and judicious notes, it will enable the industrious student to acquire an accurate knowledge of the most interesting part of Virgil's works."—PROF. J. T. DUNKLIN, *East Alabama College.*

"It wants no element of completeness. It is by far the best classical text-book with which I am acquainted. The notes are just right. They help the student when he most needs help."—PRIN. C. A. BUNKER, *Caledonia Grammar School, Vt.*

"I have examined Searing's Virgil with interest, and find that it more nearly meets the wants of students than that of any other edition with which I am acquainted. I am able to introduce it to some extent at once."—PRIN. J. EASTER, *East Genesee Conference Seminary.*

"I have been wishing to get a sight of it, and it exceeds my expectations. It is a beautiful book in every respect, and bears evidence of careful and critical study. The engravings add instruction as well as interest to the work. I shall recommend it to my classes."—PRIN. CHAS. H. CHANDLER, *Glenwood Ladies' Seminary.*

"A. S. Barnes & Co. have published an edition of the first six books of Virgil's Æneid, which is superior to its predecessors in several respects. The publishers have done a good service to the cause of classical education, and the book deserves a large circulation."—PROF. GEORGE W. COLLORD, *Brooklyn Polytechnic, N. Y.*

"My attention was called to Searing's Virgil by the fact of its containing a vocabulary which would obviate the necessity of procuring a lexicon. But use in the class-room has impressed me most favorably with the accuracy and just proportion of its notes, and the general excellence of its grammatical suggestions. The general character of the book in its paper, its typography, and its engravings is highly commendable, and the fac-simile manuscript is a valuable feature. I take great pleasure in commending the book to all who do not wish a complete edition of Virgil. It suits our short school courses admirably."—HENRY L. BOLTWOOD, *Master of Princeton High School, Ill.*

RECORDS.

Tracy's School Record, ...*$0 75

Tracy's Pocket Record, ... *65

For keeping a simple but exact record of Attendance, Deportment, and Scholarship; containing also a Calendar, an extensive list of Topics for Compositions and Colloquies, Themes for Short Lectures, Suggestions to Young Teachers, etc.

The pocket edition is of smaller size, with blanks on the same plan, for convenience of handling, etc.

Brooks' Teacher's Register, ... *1 00

Presents at one view a record of Attendance, Recitations, and Deportment for the whole term.

Carter's Record and Roll-Book, ... *1 50

This is the most complete and convenient Record offered to the public. Besides the usual spaces for General Scholarship, Deportment, Attendance, etc., for each name and day, there is a space in red lines enclosing six minor spaces in blue for recording Recitations.

National School Diary, ... Per dozen, *1 00

A little book of blank forms for weekly report of the standing of each scholar, from teacher to parent. A great convenience.

REWARDS.

National School Currency, ... Per set,*$1 50

A little box containing certificates in the form of Money. The most entertaining and stimulating system of school rewards. The scholar is paid for his merits and fined for his shortcomings. Of course the most faithful are the most successful in business. In this way the use and value of money and the method of keeping accounts are also taught. One box of Currency will supply a school of fifty pupils.

TACTICS.

The Boy Soldier, ... 75

Complete Infantry Tactics for Schools, with illustrations, for the use of those who would introduce this pleasing relaxation from the confining duties of the desk.

CHARTS.

McKenzie's School Reading Chart, ... $——

Baade's Reading Case, ... *10 00

This remarkable piece of school-room furniture is a receptacle containing a number of primary cards. By an arrangement of slides on the front, one sentence at a time is shown to the class. Twenty-eight thousand transpositions may be made, affording a variety of progressive exercises which no other piece of apparatus offers. One of its best features is, that it is so exceedingly simple as not to get out of order, while it may be operated with one finger.

Marcy's Eureka Tablet, ... *1 50

A new system for the Alphabet, by which it may be taught without fail in nine lessons.

Scofield's School Tablets, ... *8 00

On Five Cards, exhibiting Ten Surfaces. These Tablets teach Orthography, Reading, Object-Lessons, Color, Form, etc.

Watson's Phonetic Tablets, ... *8 00

Four Cards, and Eight Surfaces; teaching Pronunciation and Elocution phonetically—for class exercises.

Page's Normal Chart, ... *3 75

The whole science of Elementary Sounds tabulated. By the author of Page's Theory and Practice of Teaching.

Clark's Grammatical Chart, ... *3 75

Exhibits the whole Science of Language in one comprehensive diagram.

Davies' Mathematical Chart, ... *75

Mathematics made simple to the eye.

Monteith's Reference Maps, ... *20 00

Eight Numbers. Mounted on Rollers. Names all laid down in small type, so that to the pupil at a short distance they are Outline Maps, while they serve as *their own key* to the teacher.

Willard's Chronographers, ... Each, *2 00

Historical. Four Numbers. Ancient Chronographer; English Chronographer; American Chronographer; Temple of Time (general). Dates and Events represented to the eye.

APPARATUS.

Harrington's Geometrical Blocks, ... *$10 00

These patented blocks are *hinged*, so that each form can be dissected,

Steele's Chemical Apparatus, (see p.) . . *20 00

Steele's Philosophical Apparatus, (see p.) *125 00

Steele's Geological Cabinet, (see p.) . . . *40 00

Wood's Botanical Apparatus, (see p.) . . *8 00

Bock's Physiological Apparatus, ... 175 00

THE

TEACHERS' LIBRARY.

Object Lessons—Welch *$1 00

This is a complete exposition of the popular modern system of "object-teaching," for teachers of primary classes.

Theory and Practice of Teaching—Page . . *1 50

This volume has, without doubt, been read by two hundred thousand teachers, and its popularity remains undiminished—large editions being exhausted yearly. It was the pioneer, as it is now the patriarch of professional works for teachers.

The Graded School—Wells *1 25

The proper way to organize graded schools is here illustrated. The author has availed himself of the best elements of the several systems prevalent in Boston, New York, Philadelphia, Cincinnati, St. Louis, and other cities.

The Normal—Holbrook *1 50

Carries a working school on its visit to teachers, showing the most approved methods of teaching all the common branches, including the technicalities, explanations, demonstrations, and definitions introductory and peculiar to each branch.

The Teachers' Institute—Fowle *1 25

This is a volume of suggestions inspired by the author's experience at institutes, in the instruction of young teachers. A thousand points of interest to this class are most satisfactorily dealt with.

Schools and Schoolmasters—Dickens . . . *1 25

Appropriate selections from the writings of the great novelist.

The Metric System—Davies *1 50

Considered with reference to its general introduction, and embracing the views of John Quincy Adams and Sir John Herschel.

The Student; The Educator—Phelps . each,*1 50

The Discipline of Life—Phelps *1 75

The authoress of these works is one of the most distinguished writers on education; and they cannot fail to prove a valuable addition to the School and Teachers' Libraries, being in a high degree both interesting and instructive.

A Scientific Basis of Education—Hecker . . *2 50

Adaptation of study and classification by temperaments.

Orton's Liberal Education of Women, . . *1 50

The Teacher and the Parent—Northend . $*1 50

A treatise upon common-school education, designed to lead teachers to view their calling in its true light, and to stimulate them to fidelity.

The Teachers' Assistant—Northend . . .*1 50

A natural continuation of the author's previous work, more directly calculated for daily use in the administration of school discipline and instruction.

School Government—Jewell *1 50

Full of advanced ideas on the subject which its title indicates. The criticisms upon current theories of punishment and schemes of administration have excited general attention and comment.

Grammatical Diagrams—Jewell *1 00

The diagram system of teaching grammar explained, defended, and improved. The curious in literature, the searcher for truth, those interested in new inventions, as well as the disciples of Prof. Clark, who would see their favorite theory fairly treated, all want this book. There are many who would like to be made familiar with this system before risking its use in a class. The opportunity is here afforded.

The Complete Examiner—Stone *1 25

Consists of a series of questions on every English branch of school and academic instruction, with reference to a given page or article of leading text-books where the answer may be found in full. Prepared to aid teachers in securing certificates, pupils in preparing for promotion, and teachers in selecting review questions.

School Amusements—Root *1 50

To assist teachers in making the school interesting, with hints upon the management of the school-room. Rules for military and gymnastic exercises are included. Illustrated by diagrams.

Institute Lectures on Mental and Moral Culture—Bates *1 50

These lectures, originally delivered before institutes, are based upon various topics of interest to the teacher. The volume is calculated to prepare the will, awaken the inquiry, and stimulate the thought of the zealous teacher.

Method of Teachers' Institutes—Bates . . .* 75

Sets forth the best method of conducting institutes, with a detailed account of the object, organization, plan of instruction, and true theory of education on which such instruction should be based.

History and Progress of Education . .*1 50

The systems of education prevailing in all nations and ages, the gradual advance to the present time, and the bearing of the past upon the present in this regard, are worthy of the careful investigation of all concerned in

Northrop's Education Abroad, ... —

American Education—Mansfield $1 50

A treatise on the principles and elements of education, as practiced in this country, with ideas towards distinctive republican and Christian education.

American Institutions—De Tocqueville . .*1 50

A valuable index to the genius of our Government.

Universal Education—Mayhew *1 75

The subject is approached with the clear, keen perception of one who has observed its necessity, and realized its feasibility and expediency alike. The redeeming and elevating power of improved common schools constitutes the inspiration of the volume.

Higher Christian Education—Dwight . . .*1 50

A treatise on the principles and spirit, the modes, directions, and results of all true teaching; showing that right education should appeal to every element of enthusiasm in the teacher's nature.

Oral Training Lessons—Barnard *1 00

The object of this very useful work is to furnish material for instructors to impart orally to their classes, in branches not usually taught in common schools, embracing all departments of Natural Science and much general knowledge.

Lectures on Natural History—Chadbourne * 75

Affording many themes for oral instruction in this interesting science—especially in schools where it is not pursued as a class exercise.

Outlines of Mathematical Science—Davies *1 00

A manual suggesting the best methods of presenting mathematical instruction on the part of the teacher, with that comprehensive view of the whole which is necessary to the intelligent treatment of a part, in science.

Nature & Utility of Mathematics—Davies . .*1 50

An elaborate and lucid exposition of the principles which lie at the foundation of pure mathematics, with a highly ingenious application of their results to the development of the essential idea of the different branches of the science.

Mathematical Dictionary—Davies & Peck .*5 00

This cyclopædia of mathematical science defines with completeness, precision, and accuracy, every technical term, thus constituting a popular treatise on each branch, and a general view of the whole subject.

School Architecture—Barnard *2 25

Attention is here called to the vital connection between a good school-house and a good school, with plans and specifications for securing the former in the most economical and satisfactory manner.

THE SCHOOL LIBRARY.

LIBRARY OF LITERATURE.

Milton's Paradise Lost Boyd's Illustrated Ed., $1 60

Young's Night Thoughts . . . do. . . . 1 60

Cowper's Task, Table Talk, &c. do. . . . 1 60

Thomson's Seasons . . . . do. . . . 1 60

Pollok's Course of Time, . . . do. . . . 1 60

The books are beautifully illustrated, and notes explain all doubtful meanings.

Lord Bacon's Essays (Boyd's Edition) 1 60

Another grand English classic, affording the highest example of purity in language and style.

The Iliad of Homer. Translated by Pope. . . 80

Those who are unable to read this greatest of ancient writers in the original, should not fail to avail themselves of this metrical version.

The Poets of Connecticut—Everest 1 75

With the biographical sketches, this volume forms a complete history of the poetical literature of the State.

The Son of a Genius—Hofland 75

A juvenile classic which never wears out, and finds many interested readers in every generation of youth.

Lady Willoughby 1 00

The diary of a wife and mother. An historical romance of the seventeenth century. At once beautiful and pathetic, entertaining and instructive.

The Rhyming Dictionary—Walker 1 25

A complete index of allowable rhymes.

True Success in Life—Palmer 1 25

Mouth of Gold—Johnson 1 00

Berard's Poems of Consolation . . . . . —

Sunny Hours of Childhood 75

LITERATURE—Continued.

Compendium of Eng. Literature—Cleveland, $2 50

English Literature of XIX Century . . do . . 2 50

Compendium of American Literature do . . 2 50

Compendium of Classical Literature . do . . 2 50

Nearly one hundred and fifty thousand volumes of Prof. CLEVELAND'S inimitable compendiums have been sold. Taken together they present a complete view of literature "from Homer to Holmes—from the first Greek to the latest American author." To the man who can afford but a few books these will supply the place of an extensive library. From commendations of the very highest authorities the following extracts will give some idea of the enthusiasm with which the works are regarded by scholars:

With the Bible and your volumes one might leave libraries without very painful regret.—The work cannot be found from which in the same limits so much interesting and valuable information may be obtained.—Good taste, fine scholarship, familiar acquaintance with literature, unwearied industry, tact acquired by practice, an interest in the culture of the young, and regard for truth, purity, philanthropy and religion are united in Mr. Cleveland.—A judgment clear and impartial, a taste at once delicate and severe.—The biographies are just and discriminating.—An admirable bird's eye view.—Acquaints the reader with the characteristic method, tone, and quality of each writer.—Succinct, carefully written, and wonderfully comprehensive in detail, etc., etc.

Milton's Poetical Works—Cleveland . . . 2 50

This is the very best edition of the great Poet. It includes a life of the author, notes, dissertations on each poem, a faultless text, and is *the only* edition of Milton with a complete verbal Index.

LIBRARY OF REFERENCE.

Home Cyclopædia of Chronology 3 00

An index to the sources of knowledge—a dictionary of dates.

Home Cyclopædia of Geography 3 00

A complete gazetteer of the world.

Home Cyclopædia of Useful Arts 3 00

Covering the principles and practice of modern scientific enterprise, with a record of important inventions in agriculture, architecture, domestic economy, engineering, machinery, manufactures, mining, photogenic and telegraphic art, &c., &c.

Home Cyclopædia of Literature & Fine Arts 3 00

A complete index to all terms employed in belles lettres, philosophy, theology, law, mythology, painting, music, sculpture, architecture, and all kindred arts.

LIBRARY OF TRAVEL.

Life in the Sandwich Islands—Cheever . .$1 50

The "heart of the Pacific, as it was and is," shows most vividly the contrast between the depth of degradation and barbarism, and the light and liberty of civilization, so rapidly realized in these islands under the humanizing influence of the Christian religion. Illustrated.

The Republic of Liberia—Stockwell, . . . 1 25

This volume treats of the geography, climate, soil, and productions of this interesting country on the coast of Africa, with a History of its early settlement. Our colored citizens especially, from whom the founders of the new State went forth, should read Mr. Stockwell's account of it. It is so arranged as to be available for a School Reader, and in colored schools is peculiarly appropriate as an instrument of education for the young. Liberia is likely to bear an important part in the future of their race.

Ancient Monasteries of the East—Curzon . 1 50

The exploration of these ancient seats of learning has thrown much light upon the researches of the historian, the philologist, and the theologian, as well as the general student of antiquity. Illustrated.

Discoveries in Babylon & Nineveh—Layard 1 75

Valuable alike for the information imparted with regard to these most interesting ruins, and the pleasant adventures and observations of the author in regions that to most men seem like Fairyland. Illustrated.

A Run Through Europe—Benedict, ... 2 00

A work replete with instruction and interest.

St. Petersburgh—Jermann 1 00

Americans are less familiar with the history and social customs of the Russian people than those of any other modern civilized nation. Opportunities such as this book affords are not, therefore, to be neglected.

The Polar Regions—Osborn 1 25

A thrilling and intensely interesting narrative of one of the famous expeditions in search of Sir John Franklin—unsuccessful in its main object, but adding many facts to the repertoire of science.

Thirteen Months in the Confederate Army 75

The author, a northern man conscripted into the Confederate service, and rising from the ranks by soldierly conduct to positions of responsibility, had remarkable opportunities for the acquisition of facts respecting the conduct of the Southern armies, and the policy and deeds of their leaders. He participated in many engagements, and his book is one of the most exciting narratives of adventure ever published. Mr. Stevenson takes no ground as a partizan, but views the whole subject as with the eye of a neutral—only interested in subserving the ends of history by the contribution of impartial facts. Illustrated.

LIBRARY OF HISTORY.

History of Europe—Alison $2 50

A reliable and standard work, which covers with clear, connected, and complete narrative, the eventful occurrences transpiring from A. D. 1789 to 1815, being mainly a history of the career of Napoleon Bonaparte.

History of England—Berard 1 75

Combining a history of the social life of the English people with that of the civil and military transactions of the realm.

History of Rome—Ricord 1 60

Possesses all the charm of an attractive romance. The fables with which this history abounds are introduced in such a way as not to deceive the inexperienced reader, while adding vastly to the interest of the work and affording a pleasing index to the genius of the Roman people. Illustrated.

The Republic of America—Willard . . . 2 25

Universal History in Perspective—Willard 2 27

From these two comparatively brief treatises the intelligent mind may obtain a comprehensive knowledge of the history of the world in both hemispheres. Mrs. Willard's reputation as an historian is wide as the land. Illustrated.

Ecclesiastical History—Marsh 2 00

A history of the Church in all ages, with a comprehensive review of all forms of religion from the creation of the world. No other source affords, in the same compass, the information here conveyed.

History of the Ancient Hebrews—Mills . . 1 75

The record of "God's people" from the call of Abraham to the destruction of Jerusalem; gathered from sources sacred and profane.

The Mexican War—Mansfield 1 50

A history of its origin, and a detailed account of its victories; with official dispatches, the treaty of peace, and valuable tables. Illustrated.

Early History of Michigan—Sheldon . . . 1 75

A work of value and deep interest to the people of the West. Compiled under the supervision of Hon. Lewis Cass. Embellished with portraits.

LIBRARY OF BIOGRAPHY.

Life of Dr. Sam. Johnson—Boswell . . . $2 25

This work has been before the public for seventy years, with increasing approbation. Boswell is known as "the prince of biographers."

Henry Clay's Life and Speeches—Mallory
2 vols. 4 50

This great American statesman commands the admiration, and his character and deeds solicit the study of every patriot.

Life & Services of General Scott—Mansfield 1 75

The hero of the Mexican war, who was for many years the most prominent figure in American military circles, should not be forgotten in the whirl of more recent events than those by which he signalized himself. Illustrated.

Garibaldi's Autobiography 1 50

The Italian patriot's record of his own life, translated and edited by his friend and admirer. A thrilling narrative of a romantic career. With portrait.

Lives of the Signers—Dwight 1 50

The memory of the noble men who declared our country free at the peril of their own "lives, fortunes, and sacred honor," should be embalmed in every American's heart.

Life of Sir Joshua Reynolds—Cunningham 1 50

A candid, truthful, and appreciative memoir of the great painter, with a compilation of his discourses. The volume is a text-book for artists, as well as those who would acquire the rudiments of art. With a portrait.

Prison Life 75

Interesting biographies of celebrated prisoners and martyrs, designed especially for the instruction and cultivation of youth.

LIBRARY OF NATURAL SCIENCE.

The Treasury of Knowledge $1 25

A cyclopædia of ten thousand common things, embracing the widest range of subject-matter. Illustrated.

Ganot's Popular Physics 1 75

The elements of natural philosophy for both student and the general reader. The original work is celebrated for the magnificent character of its illustrations, all of which are literally reproduced here.

Principles of Chemistry—Porter 2 00

A work which commends itself to the amateur in science by its extreme simplicity, and careful avoidance of unnecessary detail. Illustrated.

Class-Book of Botany—Wood 3 50

Indispensable as a work of reference. Illustrated.

The Laws of Health—Jarvis 1 65

This is not an abstract *anatomy*, but all its teachings are directed to the best methods of preserving health, as inculcated by an intelligent knowledge of the structure and needs of the human body. Illustrated.

Vegetable & Animal Physiology—Hamilton 1 25

An exhaustive analysis of the conditions of life in all animate nature. Illustrated.

Elements of Zoology—Chambers 1 50

A complete view of the animal kingdom as a portion of external nature. Illustrated.

Astronography—Willard 1 00

The elements of astronomy in a compact and readable form. Illustrated.

Elements of Geology—Page 1 25

The subject presented in its two aspects of interesting and important. Illustrated.

Lectures on Natural History—Chadbourne 75

The subject is here considered in its relations to intellect, taste, health, and religion.

VALUABLE LIBRARY BOOKS.

The Political Manual—Mansfield $1 25

Every American youth should be familiar with the principles of the government under which he lives, especially as the policy of this country will one day call upon him to participate in it, at least to the extent of his ballot.

American Institutions—De Tocqueville . . 1 50

Democracy in America—De Tocqueville . . 2 25

The views of this distinguished foreigner on the genius of our political institutions are of unquestionable value, as proceeding from a standpoint whence we seldom have an opportunity to hear.

Constitutions of the United States . . . 2 25

Contains the Constitution of the General Government, and of the several State Governments, the Declaration of Independence, and other important documents relating to American history. Indispensable as a work of reference.

Public Economy of the United States . . . 2 25

A full discussion of the relations of the United States with other nations, especially the feasibility of a free-trade policy.

Grecian and Roman Mythology—Dwight . 3 00

The presentation, in a systematic form, of the Fables of Antiquity, affords most entertaining reading, and is valuable to all as an index to the mythological allusions so frequent in literature, as well as to students of the classics who would peruse intelligently the classical authors. Illustrated.

Modern Philology—Dwight 1 75

The science of language is here placed, in the limits of a moderate volume, within the reach of all.

General View of the Fine Arts—Huntington 1 75

The preparation of this work was suggested by the interested inquiries of a group of young people, concerning the productions and styles of the great masters of art, whose names only were familiar. This statement is sufficient index of its character.

Morals for the Young—Willard 75

A series of moral stories, by one of the most experienced of American educators. Illustrated.

Improvement of the Mind—Isaac Watts . . 50

A classical standard. No young person should grow up without having perused it.

CHURCH MUSIC

Post-paid Prices.

Songs for the Sanctuary, ... $2 00

By Rev. C. S. Robinson. 1344 Hymns, with Tunes. The most successful modern hymn and tune book for congregational singing. More than 200,000 copies have been sold. Separate editions for Presbyterian, Congregational, and Baptist Churches. Editions without Tunes, $1.50; in large type, $2.00. Abridged edition ("Songs for Christian Worship"), 859 Hymns, with Tunes, $1.35. Chapel edition, 607 Hymns, with Tunes, $1.25.

Songs of Praise, ... ——

(Undenominational.) By Rev. Drs. R. D. Hitchcock, Philip Schaff, and Z. Eddy.——Hymns, with Tunes. An elegant and scholarly compilation—the fruit of ripe learning, rare taste, and real labor. Edition without Tunes, $——.

Baptist Praise Book, ... 2 50

By Rev. Drs. Fuller, Levy, Phelps, Fish, Armitage, Winkler, Evarts, Lorimer and Manly, and J. P. Holbrook, Esq. 1311 Hymns, with Tunes. Edition without Tunes, $1.75. Chapel edition, 550 Hymns, with Tunes, $1.25.

Plymouth Collection, ... 2 50

(Congregational.) By Rev. Henry Ward Beecher. 1374 Hymns, with Tunes. Separate edition for Baptist Churches. Editions without Tunes, $1.25 and $1.75.

Hymns of the Church, ... 2 50

(Undenominational.) By Rev. Drs. Thompson, Vermilye, and Eddy. 1007 Hymns, with Tunes. The use of this book is required in all congregations of the Reformed Church in America. Edition without Tunes, $1.75. Chapel edition ("Hymns of Prayer and Praise"), 320 Hymns, with Tunes, 75 cts.

Episcopal Common Praise, ... 2 50

The Service set to appropriate Music, with Tunes for all the Hymns in the Book of Common Prayer.

Hymnal, with Tunes, ... 1 25

(Episcopal.) By Hall & Whiteley. The new Hymnal, set to Music. Edition with Chants, $1.50. Edition of Hymns only ("Companion" Hymnal), 50 cts.

Quartet and Chorus Choir, ... 3 00

By J. P. Holbrook. Containing Music for the Unadapted Hymns in Songs for the Sanctuary.

Christian Melodies. By Geo. B. Cheever. Hymns and Tunes. 1 00

Mount Zion Collection. By T. E. Perkins. For the Choir. 1 25

Selah. By Thos. Hastings. For the Choir. 1 25

WORSHIP.

The Union Prayer Book, ... $2 50

A Manual for Public and Private Worship. With those features which are objectionable to other denominations of Christians than Episcopal eliminated or modified. Contains a Service for Sunday Schools and Family Prayers.

Budington's Sermon on Resp. Worship, . 60

The Psalter, ... 16mo, 60¢. 8vo, 90

As used by Drs. Storrs and Budington.

Remember Me, or Holy Communion, . . . 1 25

For new communicants.

FURNITURE.

(SUPPLIED BY THE NATIONAL SCHOOL FURNITURE CO.)

PEARD'S PATENT FOLDING DESK AND SETTEE.

This great improvement for the school-room has come already into such astonishing demand as to tax the utmost resources of the company's two factories to supply it. By a simple movement the desk-lid is folded away over the back of the settee attached in front, making a false back, and at once converting the school-room into a lecture or assembly-room. When the seat also is folded, the whole occupies *only ten inches of space*, leaving room for gymnastic exercises, marching, etc., or for the janitor to clean the room effectively.

NATIONAL STUDY DESK AND SETTEE.

When not in use for writing, the desk-lid slides back vertically into a chamber, leaving in front an "easel," with clamps, upon which the student places his book and studies in an erect posture. As a folding-desk this offers many of the same advantages as the "Peard."

THE GEM DESK AND SETTEE.

Fixed top, and folding seat. This is the *neatest* pattern of the Standard School Desk, and the *strongest* in use.

THE ECONOMIC DESK AND SETTEE.

This is the *cheapest* good desk, with stationary lid and folding seat.

All descriptions of

HIGH SCHOOL DESKS,
TEACHERS' DESKS,
BLACKBOARDS,
CHAIRS,
SCHOOL SETTEES,
CHURCH SETTEES,
PEW ENDS,
LECTERNS, Etc.

Also,

TAYLOR'S PATENT CLASS AND LECTURE CHAIR.

The difficulty of reconciling furniture appropriate for the Lecture-room or Church with that convenient for the Sunday-school is an old one. This article effectually remedies it. It consists simply of a plan by which chairs of a somewhat peculiar shape are connected with a coupling. The rows of chairs thus adjusted may at pleasure and with ease be spread out straight in one line, forming pews or benches; or they may be bent in an instant into a semi-circular form to accommodate classes of any size to receive instruction from teachers seated in their midst.

For further particulars, consult catalogues of the National School Furniture Co. and the Taylor Patent Chair Co., which may be obtained of A. S. Barnes & Co.

GENERAL INDEX TO

A. S. BARNES & CO.'S DESCRIPTIVE CATALOGUE.

www.ingramcontent.com/pod-product-compliance
Lightning Source LLC
LaVergne TN
LVHW021149110826
845150LV00005B/1169

* 9 7 8 1 4 2 5 5 4 7 1 6 5 *